Perspectives in
Law &
Psychology

Volume 1
The Criminal
Justice System

Perspectives in

Law &

Psychology

Volume 1

The Criminal Justice System

Edited by

Bruce Dennis Sales

University of Nebraska, Lincoln

PLENUM PRESS · NEW YORK AND LONDON

Library of Congress Cataloging in Publication Data

Main entry under title:

The Criminal justice system.

(Perspectives in law and psychology; v. 1)
Includes bibliographies and index.
1. Criminal justice, Administration of — United States — Addresses,
essays, lectures, I. Sales, Bruce Dennis. II. Series.
HV8138.C695   364'.973   77-7369
ISBN 0-306-33561-1

© 1977 Plenum Press, New York
A Division of Plenum Publishing Corporation
227 West 17th Street, New York, N.Y. 10011

Printed in the United States of America

To my Parents

Contributors

James J. Alfini, Director of Research, American Judicature Society, Chicago, Illinois.

John S. Carroll, Assistant Professor of Psychology, Carnegie-Mellon University, Pittsburgh, Pennsylvania.

Amiram Elwork, University of Nebraska–Lincoln, Lincoln, Nebraska.

Michael J. Goldstein, Professor of Clinical Psychology, University of California, Los Angeles, California.

John Monahan, Assistant Professor in the Program in Social Ecology, University of California at Irvine, Irvine, California.

Norval Morris, Dean, University of Chicago Law School, Chicago, Illinois.

John W. Payne, Assistant Professor of Behavioral Sciences, Graduate School of Business, University of Chicago, Chicago, Illinois.

Bruce Dennis Sales, Associate Professor of Psychology and Law, University of Nebraska–Lincoln, Lincoln, Nebraska.

R. Kirkland Schwitzgebel, Department of Psychiatry, California Lutheran College, Thousand Oaks, California.

Saleem A. Shah, Chief, Center for Studies of Crime and Delinquency, National Institute of Mental Health, Rockville, Maryland.

Hans Toch, Professor of Social Psychology, School of Criminal Justice, State University of New York at Albany, Albany, New York.

David B. Wexler, Professor of Law, University of Arizona, Tucson, Arizona.

Preface

Although psychologists have related, scientifically and professionally, to the law for over 50 years now, the two fields have not been systematically integrated. Happily, that situation is changing today. Psychologists and lawyers are becoming increasingly aware that laws are based upon assumptions about human behavior, "assumptions about how people act and how their actions can be controlled" (Special Commission on the Social Sciences of the National Science Board, *Knowledge into Action: Improving the Nation's Use of the Social Sciences*. Washington, D.C.: National Science Foundation, 1969, p. 35), and that both fields must be concerned with carefully investigating these assumptions and communicating the findings to the legal community, in particular, and to society, in general. This joining of efforts will ensure that our legal system is not only more effective but also more just. *Perspectives in Law and Psychology* is a regular series of volumes dedicated to this goal.

The work presented in this first volume was supported in part by the National Institute of Mental Health, Center for Studies of Crime and Delinquency, through their grant (MH 13814) to the Law-Psychology Graduate Training Program at the University of Nebraska-Lincoln. Funds from that grant were used to invite six of the contributors to this volume to participate in the first Law-Psychology Research Conference (Michael Goldstein, John Monahan, Norval Morris, R. Kirkland Schwitzgebel, Hans Toch, and David Wexler). The University of Nebraska Research Council supported the participation of a seventh participant, Saleem Shah, to also attend and present his work at this conference. The presentations were subsequently revised and expanded to become chapters in this book. In addition, several of the chapters were supported by federal research grants to the authors. Each of these grants is acknowledged within the appropriate chapter.

In organizing a volume such as this, it is often the case that the editor owes a sincere debt of gratitude to one or more people who shared their thoughts about the inception and development of her or his work. I was no less fortunate. I would like to especially thank Saleem Shah, Kirk Schwitzgebel, and Norval Morris for their insightful, supportive, yet critical comments. I have also been fortunate enough to work with a publishing house whose executive editor has the patience of Job and whose unflagging support of this project has made the transference of thought into printed word a substantially easier task than would normally be the case.

Finally, I wish to thank my secretary, Rose Duarte, who regularly acts as not only my right hand but also my left. She has been a constant help in the preparation of this work.

BRUCE DENNIS SALES

Contents

Chapter 1   A Behavioral Scientist Looks at Obscenity   1
             Michael J. Goldstein

Chapter 2   Improving Comprehension for Jury Instructions   23
             Bruce Dennis Sales, Amiram Elwork,
             and James J. Alfini

Chapter 3   Dangerousness: Some Definitional, Conceptual,
             and Public Policy Issues   91
             Saleem A. Shah

Chapter 4   Criminal Commitment Contingency Structures   121
             David B. Wexler

Chapter 5   Professional Accountability in the Treatment
             and Release of Dangerous Persons   139
             R. Kirkland Schwitzgebel

Chapter 6   Who Should Go to Prison   151
             Norval Morris

Chapter 7   Prison Environments and Psychological Survival   161
             Hans Toch

Chapter 8   Judgments about Crime and the Criminal: A Model
             and a Method for Investigating Parole Decisions   191
             John S. Carroll and John W. Payne

Chapter 9   Social Accountability: Preface to an Integrated
Theory of Criminal and Mental Health Sanctions   241
John Monahan

Biographical Sketches of the Contributors   257

Index   263

1

A Behavioral Scientist Looks at Obscenity

MICHAEL J. GOLDSTEIN

Throughout history, in pictures and in words, man has recorded his preoccupation with the sexual side of his nature. From carvings in the ancient Hindu temples of Kahjurah to the murals uncovered in the ruins of Pompeii, from bawdy Boccaccio to the erotic violence in de Sade, man's sexuality asserts itself. Confronted with this vivid evidence of irrepressible sexual energy, virtually every age and every culture has chosen to impose its own limits regulating human sexual behavior and its visual or written portrayal through ritual and religion, and most recently by law.

In the United States, by virtue of its puritan heritage, the restrictions on both the overt expressions of nudity and sexuality and their symbolic representations have been severe. We were, until recently, a country where a combination of religious and legal mechanisms operated quite successfully to limit expressions of sexuality, both real and symbolic. It is always fascinating to examine the interplay of forces that permits the breakdown of long-held social taboos, but clearly many factors in the post-World War II period operated concurrently. The war itself contributed to wide dispersions of the population, and the subsequent contact with the cultures of Western Europe and the Near East obviously played a major role in challenging our value systems, particularly those related to sexual behavior.

MICHAEL J. GOLDSTEIN ● University of California, Los Angeles. This paper was presented at the Law-Psychology Conference, October 16–17, 1975, in Lincoln, Nebraska.

However, other factors, often overlooked, accelerated the process. The first of these was the Kinsey report on the American male (Kinsey, Pomeroy, & Martin, 1948) followed 4 years later by the report on the female (Kinsey, Pomeroy, Martin, & Gebhard, 1953). This report was significant at a number of levels; it challenged myths concerning our actual patterns of sexual behavior, and as we know from social psychology, such gross instances of cognitive dissonance often produce marked attitude change. The evidence regarding premarital and extramarital sex, masturbation, and homosexuality were so at variance with current values that either the values or the behavior had to be changed. Clearly, it has been the former which has been altered.

It is interesting to speculate on the lack of resistance to the findings of the Kinsey report. Was it the overwhelming size of the sample, the careful and comprehensive sampling, the sheer respectability of the biologist Kinsey? It is hard to say, but obviously all contributed. It is also possible that a latent cultural readiness to hear the Kinsey findings was already present in our society and that these rational factors were of little import. Unfortunately, despite the fascination of questions such as these regarding the sociology and psychology of cultural change, we are often at a loss for definitive answers.

But, one thing is clear and that is that the Kinsey report served to stimulate serious doubts about America's sexual mores, and since it appeared many changes have occurred in our willingness to make sexuality a topic of open discussion and acceptability. Recent studies of comparable populations using Kinsey-type interviews have raised questions of whether the changes in overt sexual behavior have been as great as the change in verbal behavior. It may be that the greatest changes have occurred in how we feel and talk about what we do sexually, how others in society evaluate our sexual behavior—not in what we actually do in bed with others.

If the norms governing overt sexual behavior can be challenged, then it is natural to question the strictures inhibiting the symbolic representation of sex. We cannot view what has happened in the area of pornography, or to use another term, *erotica*, without considering the broader context of changing sexual values. The increased availability of books, magazines, and films depicting overt nudity and sexuality is not a social phenomenon in isolation but part of a larger picture of cultural change. If we look at cultural institutions functionally, in the Mertonian sense, then strict regulation of sexual behavior and strict regulation of stimuli, arousing sexual desires, are compatible social systems. However, a change in the first social system, as has occurred, alters the functional significance of the set of regulations designed to reduce access to sexual stimuli. It is very likely that any attempts to severely restrict access to erotic materials within the social context of more relaxed sexual norms is doomed to failure.

While sanctions regulating overt sexual behavior and those regulating access to sexual stimuli form part of a comprehensive social pattern, they are separate in the way they are embedded in the legal system. Laws suppressing certain patterns of overt sexual behavior generally did not raise serious constitutional issues. But, as we all know, since books, magazines, and films are considered technically as speech, suppression of symbolic erotica does raise serious constitutional questions, particularly in regard to the First Amendment, protection of freedom of speech.

By and large, for 181 years, we dealt with this constitutional embarrassment by recognizing that certain classes of speech did not warrant First Amendment protection, and that one of these classes was termed *obscene speech*. For that 181 years (subtracting 1776 from 1957, the date of the major Roth decision), it was decided, in congruence with the cultural values of the times, that any visual or verbal display of nudity or sexual behavior was obscene and justified the waiving of the First Amendment guarantees. In the 1957 Roth decision, the court attempted to finesse the issue by trying to draw a line between works of serious intent (e.g., artistic, scientific), which contained some overt nudity or sexuality, and those works designed solely to arouse some form of sexual desire. The court did not in its decision deal with the issue of why the arousal of sexual desire, prurient or otherwise, constituted grounds for waiving constitutional protection, when material which aroused other unsavory emotions (greed, aggression, envy) did not. But, considering where the country was in 1957, one could not expect a more wide-sweeping opinion from even the most liberal jurists.

As mentioned earlier, there were two factors that were significant in fostering cultural change regarding sexual behavior. The second was the breakup of monopoly control by the great movie studios over the sources of film distribution. During the pre-World War II era, overt expressions of sexuality in films, the greatest mass medium then known, were controlled by the Hollywood producers through the code system. A film which did not receive the "Seal of Approval" would not be distributed. This could be effectively enforced because these same studios had ironclad control over the theaters that displayed the films. It should be noted that this system supported a dichotomy of films in this country such that "serious" films made for the mass market contained no sexuality, and sexual films were not made seriously—a condition which supported the legal positions of the time that sex and seriousness of purpose could not coexist in a single work. After this control was weakened by a series of antitrust decisions and film exhibitors were freer to show what they wished, a large number of foreign films were imported into this country, predominantly from France and Italy, which did blend eroticism in films of serious intent. These films were banned by local communities and ultimately were the subject of a favorable decision by the Supreme Court, resulting in the attempt, via the Roth decision, to make a relative rather than the previous absolute definition of obscenity.

Despite the efforts of the 1957 Court to draw a distinction between artful and artless sex, such a distinction has proved difficult to define in court. The results since 1957 have been obvious. The portrayal of sex in all media has increased exponentially. Books that had to be smuggled into the country 10 years before can now be borrowed from most public libraries, and films that formerly were seen only at stag shows now play at local neighborhood theaters. Many parents, educators, and clergymen became alarmed and demanded action from their legislators; they feared that this increasing exposure to erotic material would twist young minds, leading to depravity and possibly sex crimes. The response of legislators was to create a national commission in 1967 to examine the dangers inherent in free access to erotic materials. This commission and the researchers associated with it attempted to translate these understandable fears and apprehensions into empirical issues and to generate relevant data. In some cases the issue did not lend itself to a research strategy, and in other cases, the strategy was practically or ethically impossible. This chapter will try to articulate some of the issues and attempt to indicate whether each issue might be translated into a researchable question.

Issue 1. Increased access to erotica is a symptom of decline of fundamental core values of our society. Unless checked, the decline will progress further toward decay.

Interestingly, if one talks to community groups about the subject of pornography, this is one of the most frequent issues raised. Do we have here a social cancer, which, unless excised, will spread unchecked destroying the very roots of our society? If we examine this fear analytically, there are a number of complex issues raised.

First, do all societies necessarily decline and fall in the Gibbonian sense or do they continuously evolve, as we now believe the solar system does? There is a fascinating question here, but it is beyond the ken of the social scientist at this time. Assuming, however, that societies must constantly fight against a state of social entropy or face dissolution through conquest or simple fragmentation, do we have any indicators of trends which anticipate social decay at this macro-system level? It would seem that we do not. So, it becomes almost impossible to evaluate the long-term significance of a short-run social movement such as we are now encountering with regard to sexuality. The number of social institutions which are changing concurrently (e.g., sex roles, job and work functions, marriage) clearly indicates that we are in a period of major social evolution. Whether erotica, freely available, can be isolated separately from these social forces or given a special pathognomonic significance is doubtful at best. Thus, it appears that there is little the social scientist can offer the concerned citizen on this broad issue.

Issue 2. Exposure to erotica during early formative years will have a deleterious effect upon personality and sexual adjustment.

This concern is a fundamental one since it raises issues of public health policy. If erotic material, as with certain medication, produces severe side effects, then it should be withdrawn from the market. Fortunately, this issue does lend itself to a series of substantive research questions upon which some evidence exists.

First, let's consider the preadolescent period when attitudes toward sexual identity are being formed, but little overt sexual activity is feasible or likely. During this period, we are not so much concerned with what young people might do as whether erotic material induces a latent learning of values and covert behaviors detrimental to a positive sexual identity. It is helpful to consider two separate issues: (1) the effects of early exposure to books, pictures, or films that depict "normal sexuality" such as foreplay and heterosexual intercourse, and (2) the effects of material portraying atypical sexual relationships such as homosexuality, sadism, and masochism. In the case of the former, the models of behavior presented are those of "socially sanctioned" adult sexual patterns and we fear that premature exposure to such images might be disturbing to a young child. It is not that we don't want our children to learn of these things, but rather that we are concerned with the proper timing of its introduction. Now, the key word here is *premature*, as there are wide variations among families in the degree and explicitness of sexual information provided children; what is premature for one child is "old hat" to another. But somehow, unlike the case of farm animals copulating, we assume that a prepubertal child will be disturbed by depictions of human copulation.

Evidence on this issue is not easy to come by since the type of data that would be most compelling, based on longitudinal studies of groups systematically exposed and not exposed to such materials, will never be available to us because of ethical and practical considerations. A compromise strategy is to use data from a retrospective interview study in which distinctive target groups are used. In research carried out by our research group (Goldstein, Kant, & Hartman, 1973), we contrasted groups of male sexual offenders and sexually atypical males (homosexuals and transsexuals) with control males to determine whether their histories of preadolescent exposure to erotica differed. The logic of such a study is that if a correlation existed between sexual deviancy and reports of the frequency or type of preadolescent exposure, then a presumptive case could be made that such exposure played some role on the development of this deviant personality.

Interviews regarding preadolescent exposure to erotic materials revealed few differences between the sex offenders and controls. Almost all had seen pictures of full nudity and few, in fact, had seen graphic depictions of heterosexual intercourse. While there were no differences between sex offenders and controls on most data, there was one sharp difference between one of the sex offender groups—the rapists—and controls in that 30% of the former and only 7% of the latter had seen books or pictures depicting heterosexual intercourse. This is the only evidence in our study of the possible negative effects of such early exposure and must be interpreted with some caution.

Most contacts with erotic materials occur in a context which is significant for the meaning of the event to the individual. In the case of the rapists, their family backgrounds were consistently reported to be highly repressive and punitive regarding sexual curiosity, so that these early experiences were associated with parental disapproval. Such a pattern of exposure coupled with strong parental disapproval may be more significant than the exposure itself. Generally, this view has been confirmed in clinical work with parents who consulted us because their young child had encountered some unsavory erotica. Generally, where it was made clear that the child was fully accepted for his sexual curiosity, but his parents indicated their disapproval of the material, the experience was not disturbing to child or family. If, on the other hand, the child was punished *because* of his sexual curiosity and some association was made between this curiosity and the specific content of the erotica, then we could see signs of emotional difficulties in the child. Both research and clinical experience suggest little, if any, deleterious effects from exposure to heterosexual erotica if the experience is handled sensitively by the parents. In many instances such exposure in the course of some familial program of sex education is likely to be beneficial to both parents and children.

But what of preadolescent experiences with erotica which portray deviant or atypical sexuality? There are some definitional problems here regarding what, indeed, is deviant sexuality. Are oral-genital heterosexual relations something too extreme for the pre-teenager to see or know about? What about portrayals of homosexual relations? It is here that we find the most confusion and conflict in people regarding the effects of early exposure. The models of sexual behavior portrayed are no longer clearly identified as desirable stimuli for imitation by children of this age. Our data provide little guidance on this issue as most subjects in our study did not encounter materials of this sort during their formative years. Clearly, they are much more readily available now through newsstand vending racks with no control over access. But to be honest, there are no research data available derived from the current era which give us any hard facts on the consequences of exposure to erotica portraying atypical sexual behavior. In the true tradition of the social sciences, lacking data, I shall relate a recent anecdote describing a natural experiment with such materials which involved two of my children.

Last summer we spent considerable time in Denmark, spending a week on the charming island of Bornholm. One day, my two children, 13 and 9, wandered into a local store with some Danish friends of theirs to buy some ice cream. Evidently they sold more than ice cream at this store because the children found some pornographic magazines on the open magazine rack. The older children looked at one and then, as kids are wont to do, showed it to my 9-year-old daughter. It showed homosexual relations in which one man was performing fellatio on another. The children came back to report delightedly on what they found. The older ones were amused by the experience but were turned off by what they saw. The 9-year-old was obviously proud that they had included her in their "naughty experience" but was disgusted by what she saw. It was, she said, "yucky." We listened to her description of the experience, laughed at it, and chided my 13-year-old son for including her in the experience. Over the next few days, I looked for any signs of emotional disturbance, sleep difficulties, withdrawal, preoccupations, and other evidence, but could see little but some passing jocular references to the magazine among all of the children. I was also interested in whether any of the children returned to the store to see more of the erotic materials. They did not. Thus, I could see little immediate negative impact on my 9-year-old daughter. But, it should be mentioned that we are a very open family, who talk freely of sexual matters and did not react with disturbance, anger, or criticism to their report of the experience. Other outcomes might be expected in family environments which took a less casual view of the event. I reinterviewed both my son and daughter about the experience approximately 2 months after the encounter. My daughter still remembered that the pictures were "disgusting" but she claimed that she had never thought of the matter again until I asked about it. My son was generally amused about the whole thing. Interestingly, when I asked each of them whether they thought that such magazines should be banned from newsstands, they answered with an unequivocal no. Clearly, however, this was not a pleasant experience for our daughter, despite the overtones of being one of the "big guys" among the older kids, and I was left with a feeling that the solution of limited access to erotica based upon age, used in our country, was a reasonable compromise. However, even if we did opt for the Danish solution of unlimited access to erotic magazines, it is doubtful that the average pre-teenager or teenager, for that matter, would be greatly upset by such experiences or seek them out repeatedly thereafter. The research approach needed at present would use the public health approach of searching for cases of psychiatric casualties associated with exposure to erotica. Such research must be conducted with great care to see that the sample is not biased by irate parents and that a careful independent assessment of the children, including specification of parental handling of the incident, be done. Studies of this sort could contribute greatly to our knowledge, have some studies of the casualties of encounter groups (Liberman, Yalom, & Miles, 1973).

As we move up the developmental ladder to adolescence, other considerations emerge. No longer are we concerned solely with the formation of sexual attitudes. Now, the effects of erotica upon overt sexual behavior become highly relevant. Will such materials lower the teenagers' threshold for sexual excitation, already highly stimulated from within and without, such that he or she will be more likely to engage in heterosexual intercourse? Will exposure to models of atypical sexual behavior (e.g., homosexuality, rape, group sex) stimulate imitation of these behaviors with others? These seem to be the two major issues related to teenage exposure to erotic materials.

In regard to the first question, we should all remind ourselves of the enormous variety of sexual stimuli impinging upon the average teenager. Friends, movies, TV, books—all highlight sexuality in one form or another. And we should not overlook the erotic power of the physical appearance and presence of the opposite sex. Thus, erotic materials encountered during adolescence are experienced amid a plethora of active sexual stimuli. Their potency probably arises from written and graphic depictions of nudity and the sexual act, as well as the projections of inner states during sexual relations, including sex fantasies. It is here that erotica may provide access to material rarely shared with others or discussed in sex education classes. In our interviews with controls, who were reasonably normal young adults, there were frequent reports that erotic materials contained two themes not found elsewhere—detailed descriptions of the mechanics of sex and equally detailed descriptions of the inner feeling of people, particularly those of the opposite sex, prior to and during sexual relations.

When we examined the frequency and quality of exposure to erotic materials of sex offenders and controls in our sample, the results were surprising. In Figure 1, we can see that the sex offenders, on the average, had less exposure to erotic materials, particularly material

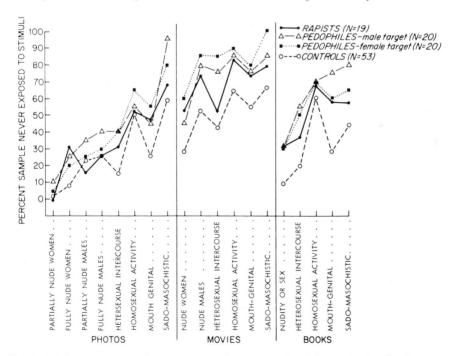

Fig. 1. Adolescent reports of exposure to various erotic stimuli for institutionalized sex offenders vs. controls.

portraying heterosexual intercourse, than did our controls. Similarly, a contrast of controls with sexually atypical samples (homosexuals and transsexuals), as seen in Figure 2, revealed even sharper differences in the same direction. So, if there was any relationship between frequency or type of exposure to erotica and sexual deviance or atypicality in adults, it was an inverse one and not a positive one.

We spent considerable time trying to evaluate two things as well as we could from retrospective reports. Did erotic stimuli release sexual behaviors not previously existent? Our data were complex. Erotic material clearly aroused sexual desire, but the other emotions aroused depended upon the respondent's sex guilt, which was uniformly greater in the sex offender than in the controls. Did the respondent actually try out some of the sexual behavior portrayed in the erotic material seen in adolescence? By and large they report that they did, but there were few differences between sex offenders and controls, except for the rapist sample, which had a significantly lower rate of imitation. In Table I we see the percent of subjects in each

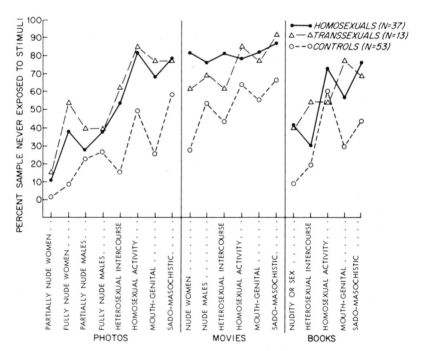

Fig. 2. Adolescent reports of exposure to various erotic stimuli for homosexuals and transsexuals vs. controls.

TABLE I. RESPONDENTS WHO REPORTED SUBSEQUENT IMITATION OF EROTICA AND TIME OF IMITATION

		When imitation occurred		
	Percent reporting imitation	Right away	Shortly after	Months– years after
Rapists	57	12	63	25
Male object, pedophiles	77	10	40	50
Female object, pedophiles	87	0	57	43
Controls	85	16	53	31

sample who reported imitation and how long after exposure it occurred. We can see that most of the reported imitation occurred some time after the exposure to erotica, suggesting that a type of latent learning took place which was not expressed until a later time when an appropriate partner was available.

In regard to the second issue of whether exposure to deviant models is likely to stimulate experimentation with these deviant patterns of sexual behavior, the evidence for the sexual offenders, homosexuals, and transsexuals was quite clear. By and large, they do not report exposure to erotica portraying their atypical sexual pattern during their formative years. Thus, erotic material does not appear to play a significant role in atypical sexual development. These behavior patterns clearly arise from other developmental sources. However, in the current era of greater availability of erotica portraying atypical sexual patterns we must ask whether such material could reinforce or accelerate the trends begun by these other developmental precursors.

On a more subtle level, we can question whether exposure to erotica affects attitudes toward one's own sex, the opposite sex, or sexual relationships in general in socially undesirable ways. Criticisms of erotica have arisen in many quarters, from the antipornography forces to the women's liberation movement. Whether it be the unrealistic portrayal of the female anatomy in *Playboy* or the reification of sex for its own sake devoid of meaningful relationships, the propagation of undesirable sexual values stimulates a core anxiety. We did attempt to get at this issue in our in-depth interview but found the results very complex. First, reactions to erotica were typically filtered through the previously established sex identity and general value orientations of the viewer. Thus, if one put a high value on human relationships and commitment to others, he paid little attention to erotica which glamorized transitory one-night stands. Or, he might find a casual sexual experience a stimulating idea but it had nothing to do with his desire to get married someday. Second, the attitudes derived from erotica were as often positive as negative, viewed from a general societal viewpoint. One person might learn the details of sexual technique, which he viewed as a positive learning experience; another might learn rather unrealistic ideas about what it takes to satisfy a member of the opposite sex, as one respondent reported: "I wanted to get a full climax. One that would leave her as this girl was [in the erotic material], a throbbing soaking mess, just lying there half dead." Still another man might learn that women have sexual needs which require considerate lovemaking. As one reported, recalling an adolescent experience with erotica, "It was the first time that I became aware of the notion that women could like sex—that it wasn't just something that they did as a duty for a man. I decided then that I would try to learn to be a good lover."

It is unfortunately the case that many of these subtle sexual attitudes are learned through some type of media and not either in the home or in school. If we wish to see the proper inculcation of humanistic sexual values, then we shall have to be willing to talk about things both at home and at school which go beyond the biology of human reproduction. Despite our concern in this area, our data were not congruent with the hypothesis that sexual attitudes and values portrayed in erotica are automatically absorbed into the value system of the young teenager.

Issue 3. Exposure to erotica will lower the threshold for antisocial sexual behavior in individuals predisposed to such behavior.

Here, we are no longer referring to the impact of erotica upon the average man, but on individuals who either by virtue of past behavior or latent tendencies could be a rapist, exhibitionist, or child molester. Would free access to erotic materials release whatever weak inhibitions of such behavior might exist in the minority of individuals in our society who might be so inclined? Actually, the question has two components, one dealing with erotic material which portrays culturally sanctioned sexual behavior, broadly defined, and one dealing with erotic material which models antisocial sexual behavior such as sadism, rape, and pedophilia. Most of the data bearing on this question are based on erotic materials of the first type, since there has only recently been any widespread circulation of erotica portraying antisocial acts. It is with the latter that researchers on aggression and researchers on sexuality deal with similar issues. Both are concerned with the impact of symbolic models of antisocial behavior upon the overt behavior of the viewer. In the case of the former, special issues arise because the sexual act, portrayed according to sanctioned cultural norms, is not an inherently antisocial act.

Unfortunately, we lack research on the direct impact of erotica on actual or potential sex offenders. That is, we have nothing analogous to the studies carried out with students and married couples (Mosher, 1973; Mann, Sidman, & Starr, 1973), in which systematic behavioral reports of sexual feelings and behavior were obtained following exposure to erotic films. The data from these studies are quite clear, however. Erotic films arouse sexual desires, which are experienced as comfortable or uncomfortable depending upon the person's sex guilt. The sexual behavior during the ensuing 24 or 48 hours was strongly dependent upon the availability of sanctioned sexual partners. Behavioral change was not seen in either single males and single females who did not have readily available and sanctioned partners. Married couples in both studies did show more frequent instances of sexual activity in the 24 hours following exposure when compared to the control group. The effect was evidently short-lived as there were no differences beyond 24 hours. Also, the type of sexual behavior reported by the married couples did not vary greatly from their normal practices.

However, these data relate to the average man or woman and not to the potential deviant. The only data available here are of a retrospective nature derived from our interview study, in which we directed additional questions to respondents concerning their adult experiences with erotica. One way that we attempted to determine if a relationship existed between the commission of repeated antisocial sex acts and experience with erotica was by comparing the reports of frequency of exposure of convicted sex offenders and nondeviant community controls. In Figure 3 we see data very similar to those presented earlier on adolescence, in which the convicted sex offenders reported significantly less exposure to erotica than did the controls. Thus, it was not possible to find a direct relationship between the frequency of contact with erotica and the probability of engaging in antisocial sexual behavior; in fact, a curious inverse relationship is suggested by the data.

We also attempted to determine what types of sexual behavior were precipitated by erotica. Generally, we found that immediate precipitation of sexual activity by erotica was rare. If there was any tendency to attempt imitation of sexual activity depicted in erotica, it occurred some time after the exposure.

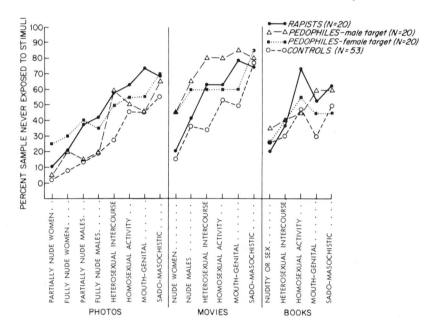

Fig. 3. Recent reports of exposure to various erotic stimuli for institutionalized sex offenders vs. controls.

A stimulus need not elicit direct sexual behavior to be significant. In many instances, behavior described in erotica became incorporated into the sex fantasy life of the person. Here a sharp difference between the sex offenders and the community controls was noted, whereby a larger percentage of the sex offenders (55% rapists, 25% child molesters, vs. 9% controls) noted that themes from erotica turned up in their sex fantasies or daydreams. It appeared that the sex offenders continued atypical adolescent patterns of deriving fantasy sex objects from the media while the controls drew theirs from real-life sexual encounters. It was interesting that one class of sex offenders, the rapists, had a particularly obsessive preoccupation with sexual matters and that they transformed many nonerotic materials into grist for their sex fantasies. For example, one rapist reported becoming very sexually excited and desirous of carrying out a sexual assault after reading a report of rape by a rape victim—the more the victim described the terror, the more excited he became. Incidentally, this potent erotic stimulus appeared in the *Ladies' Home Journal*!

The utilization of erotica to nourish sexual fantasies by sex offenders appeared compatible with a general pattern of sexual and personal immaturity. Generally, our research indicated that all groups of males used masturbation as an outlet during the teenage years. During the adult period, this declined for the controls but remained high for sex offenders, who utilized material from erotica for fantasy stimulation. The controls, on the other hand, were more likely to turn to actual sex partners as the substance for their sex fantasies.

While erotica appeared to play a special role in the life of the sex offender, there appeared to be little evidence that these fantasies directly stimulated antisocial sexual behavior. They did, however, form one class of stimuli contributing to an obsessive and often distorted preoccupation with sex in this group.

Most of these findings relate primarily to erotica depicting "normal" sexual relations, broadly defined. Ready access to erotica portraying sadomasochism, pedophilia, and similar behaviors is a very recent phenomenon, and it is still not clear what impact these materials may have in releasing antisocial sexual behavior in predisposed individuals. Clearly this is an area warranting more careful study. However, lacking further evidence on this matter, it appears from our studies and others carried out on similar populations for the Commission on Obscenity that erotic materials play a minimal role in releasing antisocial sexual behavior in predisposed individuals.

FUTURE DIRECTIONS IN RESEARCH

The research carried out to date has not suggested that free access to erotica poses serious public health problems to our communities. However, as stated earlier, this conclusion is probably specific to the relatively relaxed sexual values of our time. Should a period of sexual repression arise, then, the significance of erotica must be reevaluated. However, most of the conclusions in this chapter are based upon studies carried out during the period 1967–1969, which was the period in which the U. S. Commission on Obscenity and Pornography was in existence. The research was carried out on a "crash" basis and involved strategies adapted to this extreme time pressure. Since the termination of the commission, little research on the impact of erotica has been, or is being, carried out. It is true that the results of the studies done are consistent in their findings, but there are still significant issues remaining. Here are some of those neglected areas.

Sex Differences in Response to Erotica. Except for some early data on the Kinsey report on sex differences in reaction to erotica, most experimental and field studies have focused largely upon males. As the role of the woman in our society is changing, particularly in regard to sexuality, there is a need for systematic studies of response to erotica among younger females.

The Incidence of Young Children's Contacts with Erotica. The availability of magazines such as *Playboy, Penthouse,* and similar publications in supermarkets and drugstores means that young children have relatively free access to materials portraying full nudity and, more recently, simulated sexual relations. It would be helpful to know how many children glance through such materials and the frequency of such contacts. It would also be helpful to get a picture, analogous to what is being done with regard to media portrayals of aggressive behavior, of the total amount of sexual stimuli children encounter in all media. Detailed, in-depth interview studies of children are also needed to determine the nature of their reactions to such material, behavioral and attitudinal. Evidence regarding the incidence of contacts with sexual material, the type of material experienced, and subjective reactions to it would be most helpful in clarifying the impact on children and youth of current social policy regarding erotica.

The Incidence of Psychological and Psychiatric Casualties Related to Experiences with Erotica. As alluded to earlier, there is a need to document, as carefully as possible, psychiatric casualties in children and youth associated with some specific erotic stimulus. While much speculation abounds concerning such reactions, we, in fact, have few hard data concerning the incidence of such reactions, the people likely to manifest them, the duration of the reaction, and its severity. These data could be of great assistance in evaluating the hazards of a policy which permits relatively free access to erotic materials for adults.

The Nature of the Consumers of Erotica and the Role That Such Material Plays in Their Lives. In our previous research, we did attempt to sample respondents who were extensive consumers of erotic materials. While our results were provocative, there is need for much wider sampling to determine the incidence of individuals who (a) purchase erotic materials for home use and (b) go to adult movie theaters. Particularly in regard to the latter, some evidence concerning the frequency of such experiences would be most valuable. Is the audience largely a one-time group or is there a substantial number of repeat attenders of X-rated movies? In one sense, some estimates of the magnitude of the demand provides a clue to the magnitude of the social issue. If X-rated films cater primarily to a one-time audience, then they serve primarily a novelty effect of portraying something unique. There may be little desire, on the part of the average man or woman, to repeat it often. If, on the other hand, the consumers of X-rated films represent a small minority of repeat customers, then we know something about the target groups needing further study.

Positive Social Effects of Erotic Materials. All of the above research directions operate upon the assumption that erotic materials have potentially damaging effects which must be documented. In a sense, this is a proper orientation; as with a new drug, dangerous side effects had better be detected early in the game. But, following our analogy, what of the potential therapeutic effects of erotic materials? In our own research, the adult sex offender had fewer contacts with erotica during his formative years than did the normally developing male. Many adult sex education programs utilize erotic films as part of a process of desensitization to sexual matters. Both of these suggest that free access to materials portraying sexual relations may have positive impact on sexual attitudes and behavior. However, there is little systematic evidence on this point and we need more, and of a more specific nature. If there are positive benefits in viewing portrayals of sexual relations, how are these benefits mediated? Do they extinguish anxiety about sexuality, improve knowledge and skills, set new norms of performance, raise or lower personal expectations as well as those of sexual partners? At the present time, many university students are taking human sexuality courses which involve the presentation of sexually explicit films. Yet, the students who take such courses are not followed systematically for any substantial period. These cohorts represent very valuable samples for researchers in answering some of the questions raised regarding the potential positive effects of contact with sexually explicit materials.

RELATIONSHIP BETWEEN RESEARCH DATA AND LEGAL POLICY

The previous data and discussion have been based upon the unverbalized assumption that such data are relevant in some fashion to the legal system. The relevance may derive from the capacity to influence new legislation or to influence the actual implementation of legislation currently on the books. However, the relationship between social facts and social policy, as expressed through legal mechanisms, has not always been a simple one. Issues of values, passions, and nonempirical assumption may play a critical role in the development and implementation of laws. There has been movement recently toward a more rational formation of laws so that the data of the social scientists play an increasingly important role in debates about the law. The issue of the deterrent value of capital punishment considers data on such deterrence; commitment laws for the mentally ill consider data on the actual dangers to the patient and others of community versus hospital care. So, data concerning the dangers, or lack thereof, from pornography might be considered in legislation or court decisions regarding this social issue.

Now, this is not to say that the data of the social scientist should be accepted uncritically; strong efforts should be made to punch holes in them wherever possible. Honest and often acrimonious debate exists about data within the social sciences so it would not be surprising that such information would be scrutinized very carefully by the community at large when it forms one part of an argument regarding legislation. Such argument is very productive for a field because it sends us back to the drawing board for better studies and better data. However, all of this interchange assumes that we are willing to play by certain rules—rational rules, if you will—in which the canons of logic and reason take precedence over passion and prejudice.

Therefore, it is extremely interesting to examine the 1973 Supreme Court decision on obscenity, a decision which followed the completion and distribution of the many studies carried out for the U. S. Commission on Obscenity and Pornography. This decision, which really involved three decisions (*Kaplan* v. *California*, 71-1442; *Paris Adult Theater I* v. *Slaton*, 71-1051; and *Miller* v. *California*, 70-73), subtly implied that the rules of the game outlined in the above paragraph could be voided. In *Kaplan*, the court states, "A State could reasonably regard the 'hard core' conduct described by *Suite 69* as capable of encouraging or causing anti-social behavior, especially in its impact upon young people. States need not wait until behavioral experts can provide empirical data before enacting controls of commerce in obscene materials unprotected by the First Amendment or by a constitutional right to privacy. We have noted the power of a legislative body to enact such regulatory laws on the basis of unprovable assumptions."

This paragraph starts with the reasonable proposition that the empirical data on the effects of pornography upon a young viewer may not be clear enough to provide guidelines for a reasonable judicial decision. Implied is the need for better data, more comprehensive data, and greater expert consensus. Strong differences of opinion are still well within the ground rules of the rational game. However, in the last sentence of the paragraph a new issue is raised which is intended to appear as a logical consequence of the two preceding sentences. The key word which should, to be consistent with the previous sentences, read "unproved" reads instead "unprovable." Now, a proposition which is unprovable can be neither true nor false; it is incapable of verification by empirical data because it is a tautology or because the terms used are too vague for operational specification. So, the Court can uphold legislation based upon unprovable assumptions. What appears to social scientists as a question of empirical fact is removed from that category to the realm of the unprovable in which facts no longer operate to confuse feelings. Perhaps the clearest statement of this philosophy of *sentio ergo sum* was the statement by Charles Keating in his minority report to the report of the U. S. Commission on Obscenity and Pornography (1970), "I do not have the professional interest of social scientists in the academic world of whether or not obscenity is the direct cause of every anti-social act committed by a person 'addicted to' or the 'reader' of such materials. It is enough for me that a relationship has been found. On this matter my contacts with law enforcement officers over the past thirteen years have confirmed what my own intelligence tells me is so."

Both the *Kaplan* decision and the Keating remarks spring from a similar antiscientific, antirational position in which one's feelings and one's beliefs no longer must be tested against the canons of logic or scientific method but are justified by their own existence. This shift, however, subtly suggests a movement away from rationality to a new set of rules of the game in which fear and prejudice justify the truth or falsehood of beliefs about human behavior.

Lest it appear that too much is being read into the remarks abstracted from the *Kaplan* decision, a closer look at the *Paris Adult Theater I* decision is in order. To quote further: "Although there is no conclusive proof of a connection between anti-social behavior and obscene material, the legislature of Georgia could quite reasonably determine that such a connection does or might exist." This was written in spite of the preponderance of evidence before the Court that was opposed to this conclusion. Thus, the view was supported that, contrary to fact, assumptions regarding human behavior could guide legislation and judicial decisions.

Further along in this opinion, the issue is presented even more forcefully:

> From the beginning of civilized societies, legislators and judges have acted on various unprovable assumptions. Such assumptions underlly much lawful state regulation of commercial and business affairs. . . . If we accept

the unprovable assumption that a complete education requires certain books . . . and the well nigh universal beliefs that good books, plays and art lift the spirit, improve the mind, enrich the human personality and develop character, can we then say that a state legislature may not act on the corollary assumption that commerce in obscene books or public exhibitions focused on obscene conduct, have a tendency to exert a corrupting and debasing impact leading to anti-social behavior? Many of these effects may be intangible and indistinct, but they are nonetheless real. . . . The sum of experience including that of the past two decades, affords an ample basis for legislatures to conclude that a sensitive, key relationship of human existence, central to family life, community welfare and the development of human personality can be debased and distorted by crass commercial exploitation of sex. Nothing in the constitution prohibits a State from reaching such a conclusion and acting on it legislatively simply because there is no conclusive evidence or empirical data.

Once again the concept that certain empirical propositions are inherently unprovable is restated with greater emphasis. In fact, two things are done. First, the data that exist are totally ignored, and second, the issue is placed beyond data into the realm of a priori, unprovable assumptions beyond empirical verification, assumptions which can be legally utilized to form legislation. Rejected are counter-intuitive data which go against the guiding assumptions of the moment. It is not a far cry from this reasoning for the church to reject Galileo's theory because it violated the assumptions of the day, to reject the data on the damaging effects of school segregation because they violate the assumption that the races are happier living apart, to reject data on divorce because they violate the assumption that intact marriages are the norm. If there is a trend associated with the growth of civilization, it is that many of our assumptions are gradually recognized to be merely hypotheses, subject to verification by generally agreed-upon criteria.

Values are never resolved solely by facts, but facts can influence our interpretation of the hazards and benefits associated with different value choices. However, if we reject facts and operate upon the basis of fears and prejudices clothed in the euphemism of "assumptions," then clearly we will never be able to anticipate the costs to society of different courses of action.

REFERENCES

Goldstein, M. J., Kant, H., & Hartman, J. J. *Pornography and sexual deviance.* Berkeley: University of California Press, 1973.

Kinsey, A., Pomeroy, W., & Martin, C. *Sexual behavior in the human male*. Philadelphia: W. B. Saunders, 1948.

Kinsey, A., Pomeroy, W., Martin, C., & Gebhard, P. H. *Sexual behavior in the human female*. Philadelphia: W. B. Saunders, 1953.

Liberman, M. A., Yalom, I. D., & Miles, M. B. *Encounter groups: First facts*. New York: Basic Books, 1973.

Mann, J., Sidman, J., & Starr, S. Evaluating social consequences of erotic films: An experimental approach. *Journal of Social Issues*, 1973, 29(3), 113–131.

Mosher, D. L. Sex differences, sex experience, sex guilt, and explicitly sexual films. *Journal of Social Issues*, 1973, 29(3), 95–112.

U. S. Commission on Obscenity and Pornography. Technical report, 1970.

Improving Comprehension for Jury Instructions

BRUCE DENNIS SALES, AMIRAM ELWORK, and JAMES J. ALFINI

"What happens if a jury misunderstands the judge's instructions and finds a defendant guilty when it really meant to free him? Last week in Washington, D.C., Judge Joseph M. Hannon was confronted with this question—and had precious few precedents to draw on.

The case turned on the fate of Andre Sellars, charged with the murder of an acquaintance, one Epluribus Thomas, during a fight in a grocery-store parking lot. Sellars pleaded self-defense. The jury listened carefully to evidence that Epluribus and his brother Clyde had threatened Sellars's life through a whole weekend of arguments. When testimony ended, the jury heard a half hour's worth of instructions, couched in classic legalese, from Judge Hannon. After deliberating overnight, the nine women and three men announced that they had found Sellars guilty—not of second-degree murder as he was charged, but of manslaughter.

Later, chatting in the jury lounge, several of the jurors discovered that they had really meant to find Sellars innocent, but had misunderstood the judge's instructions. They knew that Sellars had killed

BRUCE DENNIS SALES and AMIRAM ELWORK • University of Nebraska–Lincoln, Lincoln, Nebraska.   JAMES J. ALFINI • American Judicature Society, Chicago, Illinois. The issues spoken to in this chapter are important to both criminal and civil trials. Thus, discussion and examples refer to both settings. This chapter was prepared with the aid of a grant from the National Science Foundation (SOC76-11292).

Thomas, and thought that if they accepted Sellars's self-defense plea, manslaughter was the appropriate verdict.

Baffled, the jurors asked their foreman to write the judge a letter of explanation. Last week, Judge Hannon called the jurors back and questioned them one by one. This time the jurors were split, 9–3 for acquittal. The Judge has asked opposing counsel for legal memorandums. The rule against double jeopardy will bar another murder trial for Sellars, but he could be retried for manslaughter." (*Newsweek*, October 20, 1975, p. 64. Copyright 1975 by Newsweek, Inc. All rights reserved. Reprinted by permission.)

THE STATUS OF JURY INSTRUCTIONS

BACKGROUND

In the course of a jury trial, the jury's exposure to the law by way of instructions from the judge is a critically important event. If the jury is to successfully apply the applicable law to the facts of the case, the instructions must be delivered in language which is understandable to the average juror. Unfortunately, because error in instructing the jury often has been cited as the single most frequent cause for reversal on appeal, the judge is keenly aware of the fact that the language of the instructions must be acceptable to an appellate court, Thus, in phrasing his instructions, the judge may often be encouraged to sacrifice juror understandability for legal accuracy.

For a number of years, the adoption of pattern jury instructions has been viewed as a means of improving this situation. In fact, pattern jury instructions have been touted as "the greatest modern improvement in trial by jury" (McBride, 1969, p. 359). Also referred to as model charges, uniform instructions are intended to provide the judge with a concise, error-free statement of the law which is intelligible to the average juror.

The need for such an innovation has been recognized for some time. Writing in 1930, Jerome Frank took a dim view of the prevailing practices surrounding jury instruction:

> What a crop of subsidiary semi-myths and mythical practices the jury system yields! Time and money and lives are consumed in debating the precise words which the judge may address to the jury, although everyone who stops to see and think knows that these words might as well be spoken in a foreign language—that, indeed, for all the jury's understanding of them, they are spoken in a foreign language. Yet, every day, cases

which have taken weeks to try are reversed by upper courts because a
phrase or sentence meaningless to the jury has been included in or
omitted from the judge's charge (p. 181).

Jerome Frank had touched on a situation which judges and lawyers
had known for some time needed improvement. In fact, upon its
organization in 1922, the Ohio Common Pleas Judges Association
adopted as its first proposal, standardization of jury instructions
(McBride, 1969, p. 340).

Another decade passed, however, before the first complete set of
pattern instructions was compiled and published for use. In 1938, after
laboring for two years, a committee of California judges and lawyers
produced the *Book of Approved Jury Instructions* (hereinafter referred to
as BAJI).[1] In the years that followed it was supplemented, revised, and
finally complemented by a set of criminal instructions (hereinafter
referred to as CALJIC).[2] The success of the California experiment
encouraged other jurisdictions to follow its lead. In 1949, the Nebraska
State Bar published a set of basic instructions for general use (Standardized Instructions to Juries 1953). In the 1950s, the bar associations
of Arizona, Chicago, Idaho, Utah, Nevada, Oregon, and Washington,
D.C., developed sets of instructions based on BAJI, but more limited
in coverage.

Illinois was the first state to produce an official volume of
instructions. The Illinois Judicial Conference in 1957 initiated a pattern
jury instruction project to be carried out under the auspices of the
Illinois Supreme Court. A committee was appointed to draft a set of
civil instructions. The work of the committee was adopted by Supreme
Court Rule,[3] which provides that the instructions must be used when
applicable and that where they are not applicable, any other instructions given must follow the Illinois Pattern Jury Instruction (IPI) Model
(1968, 1971). Thus, the full weight of the authority of the Supreme
Court was behind the Illinois instructions[4] and today they are used
almost exclusively in civil cases (Close, 1964).

[1] The fifth edition of this two-volume work was published in 1969 by West Publishing
Company.
[2] *California Jury Instructions, Criminal* was the first published by West in 1946 and is now
in its third edition.
[3] Illinois Supreme Court Rule 25-1(a), adopted February 1, 1961.
[4] Corboy, "Pattern Jury Instructions—Their Function and Effectiveness," 31 *Insurance
Counsel Journal* 57 (1965) discusses Illinois Supreme Court decisions through the end of
1964 approving IPI instructions.

The judicial policy-making authorities[5] of 17 states have since followed Illinois's example by taking the initiative and ordering the preparation of pattern instructions.[6] To date, published sets of instructions have been produced in 12 of these states.[7] Six of these states have adhered even more closely to the Illinois example by making the use of pattern instructions mandatory pursuant to either a supreme court rule or a court order.[8]

In 9 additional states, bar associations have assumed the prime responsibility for seeing to it that instructions are properly drafted,[9] while in 12 states the responsibility has been assumed by local or statewide judges' associations.[10] In 3 states the work has been a joint project of a judges' association and the state bar.[11] To date, published sets of instructions have been produced in 18 of these jurisdictions.[12]

Thus, 30 states currently have published sets of pattern instructions.[13] In addition, sets of patterns for use in the District of Columbia and in the federal district courts have been published. All of these jurisdictions, except Hawaii, North Carolina, and West Virginia, have sets of criminal patterns.[14]

It is anticipated that, by 1977, at least one set of instructions should be available in 36 states. In addition, 5 more states have made definite plans to draft sets of instructions.[15]

---

[5] Supreme Court, Judicial Conference, etc.

[6] Arizona, Arkansas, Colorado, Delaware, Florida, Idaho, Illinois, Louisiana, Maryland, Michigan, Missouri, Nebraska, New Jersey, New Mexico, Pennsylvania, Washington, and West Virginia.

[7] Arizona, Arkansas, Colorado, Florida, Illinois, Michigan, Missouri, Nebraska, New Jersey, New Mexico, Washington, and West Virginia.

[8] Arkansas, Colorado, Michigan, Missouri, Nebraska, and New Mexico.

[9] Alabama, Iowa, Nevada, Oklahoma, Oregon, South Dakota, Texas, Utah, and Wyoming.

[10] California, Georgia, Hawaii, Indiana, Kansas, Minnesota, Mississippi, Montana, New Hamsphire, New York, Ohio, Tennessee, and Wisconsin.

[11] Connecticut, North Carolina, and North Dakota.

[12] California, Hawaii, Indiana, Kansas, Minnesota, Montana, Nevada, New York, North Carolina, North Dakota, Ohio, Oregon, South Dakota, Texas, Utah, Wisconsin, and Wyoming.

[13] See the bibliography, which also cites published sets of pattern instructions that have been prepared by private individuals in certain of these states and in an additional seven states (Alabama, Connecticut, Kentucky, Mississippi, South Carolina, Tennessee, and Virginia). These sets of instructions have not been included in the totals since it is unlikely that any of them enjoy widespread use in their respective states.

[14] Arizona, California, Colorado, District of Columbia, Florida, Hawaii, Illinois, Iowa, Kansas, Nebraska, New Jersey, North Carolina, North Dakota, Ohio, Oregon, South Dakota, West Virginia, and Wisconsin.

[15] The present status of pattern instruction drafting efforts in the states is summarized in chart form in the appendix.

The Language of Pattern Instructions

Proponents of pattern instructions have ascribed numerous benefits to their use. Principal among these are: (1) They result in significant savings of time for the judge, counsel, and jury; (2) they result in a significant reduction of reversals for erroneous instructions; and (3) they increase the likelihood of juror comprehension of the applicable law (Hannah, 1963).

There is considerable support for the first two propositions. Many judges and lawyers, from states in which patterns enjoy widespread use, have argued that because they no longer are required to research and prepare instructions from scratch, jury trials can be handled more expeditiously (Corboy, 1959). In addition, surveys conducted in states which have adopted patterns have demonstrated that there have been significant decreases in the reversal rate for error in instructions (Corboy, 1965; McKenzie, 1957).

In only one state, however, has there been any effort to empirically demonstrate that pattern instructions can be drafted in a form which can increase the likelihood of juror comprehension of the applicable law (Sigworth & Henze, 1973). In 1971, the Supreme Court of Arizona created a special committee to draft pattern instructions for civil and criminal cases. The committee was chaired by Judge Irwin Cantor, who had been instrumental in the compilation of pattern instructions for use in Maricopa County (Phoenix). Because they had this earlier set of instructions at their disposal, the committee decided upon a novel approach. By applying learning and communications theory and some simple grammatic and semantic analysis, they tested the understandability of the earlier instructions, redrafted them according to theory, and then tested the new instructions to determine whether the scientifically drafted instructions improved juror comprehension. Their data supported the proposition that "jurors understand instructions better if they are phrased in theoretically more comprehensible language" (p. 11–12).

Unfortunately, few drafting committees have been willing to employ or seek the aid of experts to ensure that their instructions are phrased in theoretically more comprehensible language. Two notable exceptions are the drafting committees in Pennsylvania and Florida. The Pennsylvania committee has created a sociolegal subcommittee whose research director is a psychology graduate student. The research of this subcommittee is aimed specifically at discovering, through a series of jury interviews, the extent of juror comprehension of instructions. It is hoped that such efforts not only will result in clearer, more intelligible instructions, but will produce instructions which encourage the judge to deliver his charge in a conversational tone (O'Mara, 1972).

The Florida committee has attempted to increase juror comprehension by eliminating much of the legal jargon from their instructions.[16] For example, many of the problems inherent in proximate cause charges have ostensibly been avoided by referring to "legal cause" and providing the jury with a simple "but for" test.

Although these efforts are commendable, most jury instruction drafting committees continue to be composed solely of judges and lawyers. In drafting the instructions, these committees are much more concerned with legal correctness than with juror understandability. They have neither the means nor the inclination to do otherwise. A good example of this is reflected in a disturbingly comical statement by the authors of BAJI: "The one thing an instruction must do above all else is correctly state the law. This is true regardless of who is capable of understanding it" (as cited in Winslow, 1962).

PROCEDURAL VARIABLES THAT AFFECT THE JURY'S ABILITY TO APPLY THE LAW TO THE FACTS SUCCESSFULLY

Not only have most drafting committees failed to take steps to ensure that their instructions are phrased in theoretically more comprehensible language, but they have failed to consider other factors which could have an effect upon the juror's understanding of their duties and of the applicable law. For the most part, these factors are "procedural" in nature.

For example, consider the timing of presentation of the instructions. The prevailing practice is to instruct the jury on the law at the close of the case—i.e., after argument and just before the jury retires to deliberate. This practice has received some criticism in that it is believed that it leads to juror confusion (Prettyman, 1960; Smith, 1968). Would not the jury be better able to weigh the evidence if they were instructed on the applicable law prior to the presentation of the case? A California judge once unofficially, and with the stipulation of counsel, instituted such a procedure and found the effects to be beneficial (Institute for California Judges, 1959).

---

[16] See "Standardized Jury Instructions," 41 *Florida Bar Journal* 381 (1967). Another interesting approach was employed in Montana where the committee enlisted the services of a journalist to serve as a sounding board on the language used in the instructions. See Lessley, "Montana Jury Instruction Guides," 27 *Montana Law Review* 125, 127 (1966).

What about the manner of presenting the instructions to the jury? Certain commentators have discussed the efficacy of allowing the jury to take copies of the judge's instructions into the jury room (Cunningham, 1958). If the charge is long, as is often the case, is the average juror expected to remember all the critical points of law?

Another procedural consideration relates to what Kalven and Zeisel refer to as the degree of "judicial control" of the jury (1966, p. 418). As Kalven and Zeisel point out, there are essentially three patterns of judicial control to be found in American jurisdictions: (a) The judge may instruct the jury on the law only; (b) in addition, he may summarize the evidence; and (c) in addition, he may comment on the weight of the evidence and the credibility of witnesses (p. 418).

In devoting an entire chapter (chapter 33) to a survey of both the legal power of the judge with regard to his ability to summarize and comment, and the actual use of these powers in each state, Kalven and Zeisel reach certain conclusions concerning the effect which the degree of judicial control has on judge–jury disagreement (p. 427). Unfortunately, they do not inquire into the effect which varying degrees of judicial control have on the jury's understanding of the applicable law and their ability to apply the law to the facts of the case.

Much criticism has been leveled at the overreliance on pattern instructions, (Standardized Jury Instructions, 1949; Applicability of MAI, 1970; Fowler, 1963). One commentator goes so far as to analyze the formality and rigidity of legal procedure inherent in the mandatory use of pattern instructions to the practices surrounding the old common law pleading: "It was thought then that the twisting and straining of the facts of each case in order to fit them into a prescribed pattern was not beneficial." Unfortunately, there has been a trend in recent years toward the imposition of mandatory use.[17]

Unless the drafting committees are provided with the means for improving this situation, pattern instructions may actually contribute to many of the problems which they were intended to alleviate. The purpose of this chapter is to review and organize the psychological and psycholinguistic literature that drafting committees should be aware of in writing, evaluating, and rewriting pattern jury instructions. Each psychological factor that would have import in jury comprehension, memory, and usage of instructions will be separately reviewed and specific suggestions made for using this knowledge.

---

[17] The use of pattern instruction is mandatory in Arkansas, Colorado, Illinois, Michigan, Missouri, Nebraska, and New Mexico.

In the following sections we will identify each variable which prior research, or logic where no research is available, suggests should significantly affect the juror's coding of the instruction. The material on pp. 30–67 sets forth those psycholinguistic variables contained within the jury charge that should directly affect the juror, while that on pp. 67–74 identifies those procedural variables that should affect the juror's ability to accurately apply comprehended instructions to the evidentiary materials.

PSYCHOLINGUISTIC VARIABLES

Jury instructions can only be effective if they are perceived, remembered, comprehended, and followed by the jury in weighing the evidence. The extent to which a jury will follow instructions will be determined by their willingness to do so and by the extent to which they have perceived, remembered, and comprehended the instructions. The purpose of this section is to enumerate those psycholinguistic variables that will affect perception, memory, and comprehension of jury instructions. First, it will be helpful to define these psychological terms.

Perception is defined as the first step in a meaningful interpretation of external objects (Cohen, 1969; Gibson, 1966). It is the point at which one becomes aware or detects that something is out there, and the first few steps during which that something begins to trigger associations and images with past memories. For example, we see a face and immediately recognize it as a face and call it that. This process is called "perceptual recognition" (Paivio, 1971, p. 199). Even though we've never seen that face before, we become aware that it is one through our associations with what other faces look like. Familiar faces are probably recognized faster because their associations are more direct. Generally, stimuli that are perceived quickly are dealt with more efficiently within other cognitive processes. Thus, any variables which affect perception will also tend to affect memory and comprehension.

Memory refers to the extent to which past experiences are retained. The single greatest capability of the mind is that it retains past experiences and then uses them in making judgments about future ones. It is important to isolate those variables which will tend to make jury instructions more memorable. Two ways of testing memory are the multiple choice and the essay test. A factual multiple choice test measures retention by asking for the memorial recognition of the correct answer. This type of recognition must be distinguished from the perceptual recognition discussed earlier. A multiple choice test requires perceptual recognition of all of the choices, and then the memorial recognition of the correct answer. Memorial recognition requires the extra step of associating the answer with a specific question. An essay or short answer examination tests recall. While recognition requires differentiation between given items, recall requires the reproduction of items in their entirety. Generally, the latter is the more difficult task, and the strongest proof that the material is remembered.

The goal of communication is to be understood. Comprehension, in our context, can be defined as the extent to which a person understands another person's intended meaning. It is possible to remember and interpret the meaning of a communication and not understand the communicator's intent. Comprehension can only be tested indirectly, because it is impossible to measure meanings directly. Thus, comprehension tests require interpretations that logically follow from the intended meaning of presented material. Jury verdicts are an example of combined interpretations of evidence and instructions. It is vitally important to control the variables that affect comprehension of jury instructions.

Although we will be discussing perception, memory, and comprehsion when they apply to the variables below, in real life it is difficult to separate them. That is, all three processes interact with and define each other. Perception would not be possible without memory; memory would not exist without perceptual experiences; comprehension would be useless without memory; and so on. It is a well-accepted fact that the more meaningful (or comprehensible) something is, the better it will be remembered (Craik & Lockhart, 1972). With this framework in mind, let us turn to those psycholinguistic variables which most probably will have a significant effect upon a juror's ability to accurately comprehend and apply the law as it is related in the judge's charge. Each of these variables is identified and a review of the relevant literature is provided.

VOCABULARY

High- versus Low-Frequency Words

A complete analysis of the variable of word frequency should be a major step in making jury instructions more effective. High-frequency words are those that are most commonly used, as determined by the frequency of occurrence in magazines and newspapers, and therefore should be the most familiar words in our language.[18] Logically, familiar words should be more easily recognized, recalled, comprehended, and used. Since Thorndike and Lorge (1944) published their frequency counts of 30,000 English words, it became easier for researchers to control this variable and test this hypothesis. Indeed, the hypothesis is now generally supported by literally hundreds of psycholinguistic studies.

Several researchers have undertaken to empirically confirm the statement that high-frequency words are the most familiar words in the language. Noble (1954) demonstrated that subjects could rate meaningless words for subjective familiarity and that these ratings were directly related to the frequency of occurrence of these words in the experiment. Since then, many studies have shown that subjects are able to judge the subjective familarity of real words and that these judgments are highly correlated to objective frequency counts of the same words. O'Neill (1972) found a .65 correlation for nouns, Smith and Dixon (1971a) found a .818 correlation for past tense verbs, Hogenraad (1969) discovered a positive relationship for adjectives, and Carroll (1971) was able to show correlations ranging from .92 to .97 for a mixture of words. Smith and Dixon (1971b) and Begg and Rowe (1972) have also shown that the familiarity increased logarithmically as a function of increasing frequency. Thus, it is safe to assume that high-frequency words are the most familiar words in the language, and familiarity should affect perception, memory, and comprehension. These effects should be considered in the writing of jury instructions.

From the discussion above, it is logical to assert that perception should be somewhat dependent on familiarity. Since familiarity and word frequency are closely related it also follows that perception should be related to word frequency. One test for perception has been the "perceptual recognition task" (see Paivio, 1971, p. 199). In order to test "perceptual recognition," a subject is typically asked to read or repeat material to which he/she has just been exposed for the first time in the experiment. In such tasks, researchers have found that high-frequency words were heard, read, and repeated faster and with fewer errors (Broadbent, 1967; Brown & Rubenstein, 1961; Champagnol, 1971; Klintman, 1968; Morton, 1968; Paivio & O'Neill, 1970; Solomon & Postman, 1952).

---

[18] There is an assumption here that written and spoken frequency is positively correlated.

Landauer and Streeter (1973) showed that high-frequency words were slightly more orthographically confused with other common words than were rare words. Since high-frequency words have been repeatedly shown to be perceptually superior, however, even though they tend to be potentially more orthographically confusing, it must be that frequency of usage is an overpowering variable. Perception is a good indicator of the speed with which a particular item will be cognitively processed. It is safe to assume that the speed of processing is one indicator of the ease with which an item will be processed. Consequently, since high-frequency words are perceived more quickly, it is reasonable to predict that jury instructions will be processed more easily if common words are used.

The use of high-frequency words may also help jurors remember instructions. Again, the same logic applies. Those words most familiar to subjects should be more easily stored and recalled. A recall task is typically one in which subjects are asked to reconstruct and verbalize a previously presented list of words. Most researchers have found a positive relationship between work frequency and recall in short-term and long-term memory tasks (Baddeley & Scott, 1971; Bousfield & Cohen, 1955; Duncan, 1973; Hall, 1954; Murdock, 1960; Postman, 1970). Postman's study was probably the most complete. Three levels of word frequency were used (high, medium, and low) under a short-term task (30 seconds) and a long-term task (7 days). Retention was consistently better for high-frequency words and no differences were found between medium- and low-frequency words. Borude (1971) did a cross-cultural comparison and again found a positive correlation between word frequency and recall.

Obviously, jury instructions should be comprehensible. In trying to understand a printed or heard message, people begin by decoding the denotative (explicit) and connotative (implied) meanings of words. The easier and more meaningful this decoding process becomes, the easier it should be to comprehend the entire message. Familiar words, which also happen to be high-frequency words, are probably those words which are easiest to decode. It should follow then, that the use of high-frequency words in messages should increase comprehension. Several researchers have supported this general notion.

Loewenthal (1969) tested the hypothesis that the denotative meanings of high-frequency words are easier to decode. In an ingenious study where subjects were asked to communicate certain words through the use of clues, while their partners were asked to define the words with the help of the given clue, Loewenthal found that high-frequency words were more successfully communicated than low-frequency words. Klare (1968) summarized several studies and stated that since word frequency is highly correlated ($R = .80$) with word meaningfulness, it is extremely important in reading comprehension. Marks, Doctorow, and Wittrock (1974) hypothesized that by varying the known frequencies of words in elementary school reading materials, comprehension of the meaning of the entire passages could be improved. By doing so with only 15% of the words, comprehension was improved by 25%. Such dramatic results leave no doubt that word frequency is a very important variable which must be considered if jury instructions are to be made more comprehensible.

There is also some evidence that word frequency may be related to evaluative connotations that people place on the meanings of words. Several researchers have found high-frequency words to be less associated with negative feelings than low-frequency words (Dixon & Dixon, 1964; Johnson, Thompson, & Frincke, 1960; Zajonc, 1968). In a more recent study by Smith and Dixon (1971a) it was found that neutral verbs occurred most frequently followed by good and bad verbs in that order.

This research suggests that the use of low-frequency words, so common in legal language, tends to connote more negative meanings than will high-frequency words. Thus, it may be that the charge of "violating the law," as opposed to "breaking the law," may connote a more serious transgression. If so, the choice of particular words and supposed synonyms must be carefully evaluated.

Conclusion. On the basis of these findings it is reasonable to suggest that increasing the use of high-frequency words in jury instructions will increase the ease with which the material will be recalled and comprehended. For example, consider the following instruction:

> Elements of Damage—Husband's Loss of Consortium. The value of the society, companionship, and conjugal relationship with his wife, including services, which the husband:
> a. Has been deprived of to date; and
> b. Is reasonably certain to be deprived of in the future.
> The term "services" means the duties performed by the wife which reasonably devolve upon her in the marriage relation. (Nebraska Jury Instruction 4.08)

The average juror will have difficulty understanding the meanings of at least two and possibly three key words in this instruction. According to Thorndike–Lorge (1944) the words *conjugal* and *devolve* are found in writing less than twice in a million. In addition, although the word *society* is common, here it is used in an unusual context. Such common words as *association, married,* and *fall* could be substituted for *society, conjugal,* and *devolve* and should increase the comprehensibility of the instruction.

Concrete versus Abstract Words

A review of the literature on concrete and abstract words leads to the unmistakable conclusion that concrete words are more effective than abstract words in communicating ideas. Concrete words are remembered better, tend to be more meaningful, and are therefore better comprehended. The exact way in which a concrete lexical item is superior is still an open theoretical question. One explanation is that concrete material allows itself to be visually imagined, and somehow this visual code, which organizes events spatially as well as temporally, enhances memory, meaningfulness, and comprehension. The reader is referred to Paivio (1971) for a review of the different theoretical viewpoints and the empirical data available on imagery and its relation to memory and comprehension of language. Whatever the exact reasons, the effects of concrete words on memory and comprehension have been clearly shown.

The effectiveness of concreteness in increasing retention has been demonstrated in both memorial recognition and recall tasks. When subjects were asked to recognize which word occurred in a previously presented list, concrete words were recognized faster and with more accuracy (Gorman, 1961; Jampolsky, 1950; Olver, 1965; also see Paivio, 1971, p. 184). In tasks where subjects were asked to recall a previously presented list, the results were the same, recall being better for concrete words in both short-term and long-term tasks (Duker & Bastian, 1966; Stoke, 1929; Winnick & Kressel, 1965). If we equate concrete words with those that can be easily visualized (Paivio, Yuille, & Madigan, 1968, found a correlation of .83 between the two) several other researchers have also found that visualization enhances recall (Begg & Robertson, 1973; Bowers, 1931, 1932; Foth, 1973; Gupton & Frincke, 1970; Tulving, McNulty, & Ozier, 1963). Yuille and Paivio (1969) presented subjects with varying levels of concrete passages to read and asked them to recall the words used in the passages. It was found that more words were recalled for the most concrete passages.

As discussed above, one explanation for the superiority of concrete words in memory tasks is that they allow themselves to be cognitively visualized, and that this visual code is more memorable than the verbal code alone. If this is so, then it should be possible to increase recall by simply instructing subjects to use imagery as a mnemonic technique for memorizing a list of words. In such experiments, when lists of concrete words were presented for recall with and without instructions to form mental images of objects named, imagery instructions have been found to enhance recall (Bull & Wittrock 1973; Delin, 1969; Kirkpatrick, 1894; Peterson & McGee, 1974; Schnorr & Atkinson, 1969; Winograd, Karchmer, & Russell, 1971). Moreover, recall of jury instructions should therefore be enhanced with the use of concrete words.

Although the effects of concreteness on meaningfulness and comprehension have not been as well researched as its effects on memory, some conclusions can still be drawn. Bloomer (1961) found that subjects selected synonyms for concrete words more accurately than for abstract words, and on that basis argued that concrete words tend to be more meaningful. O'Neill (1972) had subjects rate a list of nouns on definability (D), imagery (I), concreteness (C), and a few other subjective measures not important to this discussion. A correlation of .703 was found between D and I and one of .640 was found between D and C. In another study by Reynolds and Paivio (1968), where subjects were asked to define words, concrete words were found to elicit longer definitions, shorter latencies between stimuli and responses, and fewer hesitations in responding. It is impossible to measure meaningfulness of words directly. These studies suggest that concrete words are more meaningful than abstract ones.

Several researchers in past years have argued that the level of concreteness in both written and spoken sentences, respectively, was positively related to their comprehensibility (Flesch, 1950; Beighley, 1952). Empirical findings in recent years tend to support this claim. Skehan (1970; see also Paivio, 1971, p. 444) found that the times required to make a true–false judgment of sentences in relation to other sentences were faster for high- and medium-imagery sentences than they were for low-imagery sentences. Begg & Paivio (1969) found that subjects recognized changes in meaning more often than changes in wording when the target sentences were concrete, while the reverse was true when sentences were abstract. These results were interpreted as an indication that concrete sentences are more apt to be coded in terms of meanings rather than strings of words. Finally, two studies have shown that speech becomes more hesitant, which is an indication of difficulty, as it becomes more abstract (Goldman-Eisler, 1961; Lay & Paivio, 1969). Thus, it appears that comprehension of jury instructions should be enhanced with the use of concrete sentences.

Conclusion. Jury instructions often require that jurors understand many abstract concepts. The research cited above suggests that such material is least apt to be remembered or comprehended. Thus, jury instructions that relate concrete ideas or, when that is not possible, contain abstract ideas accompanied by concrete examples should increase comprehension and memory. For example, consider the following instruction:

> Criminal Intent. The intent required by Instruction _____ is a material element of the crime charged against the defendant. Intent is a mental process and it therefore generally remains hidden within the mind where it is conceived. It is rarely if ever susceptible of proof by direct evidence. It may, however, be inferred from the words and acts of the defendant and from the facts and circumstances surrounding his conduct. But before that intent can be inferred from such circumstantial evidence alone, it must be of such character as to exclude every reasonable conclusion except that defendant had the required intent. It is for you to determine from all the facts and circumstances in evidence whether or not the defendant committed the acts complained of and whether at such time he had the criminal intent required by Instruction _____ . If you have any reasonable doubt with respect to either, you must find the defendant not guilty. (Nebraska Jury Instructions, 14.11).

This instruction, describing the criteria by which a jury should decide on whether a crime was committed, uses the abstract notion of "criminal intent." NJI 14.11 attempts to define *intent*. Yet, it serves more to confirm the fact that this criterion is so abstract as to "generally remain hidden within the mind where it is conceived." Such abstractions need to be defined as concretely as possible. The rewritten example below, clarifies the notion of *intent* by relating it to concrete and observable facts. Cautionary statements are inserted at the end of the instruction.

> The intent required by instruction _____ is a material element of the crime charged against the defendant. *Intent is that mental process which guides behavior towards some goal. Every behavior by a thinking person has some intent. Since it is impossible to know directly what is in someone's mind, it is proper to infer a defendant's intent from his words and acts and from the circumstances surrounding his conduct.* It is for you to determine from all of the facts and circumstances in evidence whether or not the defendant committed the acts complained of and whether at such time he had the criminal intent required by Instruction _____ . *Since different intents can be inferred from behaviors it must be of such character as to exclude every other reasonable conclusion.* If you have any reasonable doubt with respect to either, whether or not the defendant committed the acts complained of or whether at such time he had the criminal intent required by Instruction _____ , you must find the defendant not guilty.

Homonyms

In writing jury instructions it is important to use words which will be understood. Some words, however, have more than one meaning, even though they may be spelled alike (homographs), pronounced the same way (homophones), or both (homonyms). For example, the word *converse* could mean to "talk" or could refer to the "reversal" of something. There is enough research now to predict a need for caution in the use of homonyms, homophones, and homographs in jury instructions, by making sure that the intended meaning is a familiar one and that the context of the sentence makes the meaning very clear.

Word encoding is a combination of semantic, syntactic, and phonological features (see section on synonyms). Homonyms share phonological features, but differ in meaning. Since semantic features are strongly encoded, it has been shown that when subjects see or hear a homonym, it immediately evokes the several meanings that the word has (Conrad, 1974; MacNamara, O'Cleirigh, & Kellaghan, 1972; Winograd & Geis, 1974). Thus, possible confusion of intended meanings of homonyms should be carefully anticipated and checked when writing jury instructions.

Obviously, one avenue is to not use homonyms and thus avoid possible misunderstandings. When homonyms are used, however, several adjustments can be made to assure that intended meanings are comprehended. First, since the several meanings of homonyms are not equally often used, it is possible to use only the most common meaning. Secondly, the context in which the homonym is used has been shown to be helpful in the facilitation of recall and comprehension of the intended meanings (Conrad, 1974; MacNamara *et al.*, 1972; Light & Carter-Sobell, 1970; Marcel & Steel, 1973). The context can be intentionally manipulated to enhance the comprehension and memory of an intended meaning in accordance with several methods (Ames, 1966; Artley, 1943; Emans, 1968). Emans categorized context into three categories: meaning, language, and organizational clues. For example, below are five possible types of contextual clues that can be used to enhance comprehension of words.

1. Definition of synonym: "The median or mid-point score was 10.5."
2. Example: "The feline family includes cats, tigers, and lions."
3. Comparison and contrast: "Do not run, but walk."
4. Contextual description: "The dirty, crowded slum."
5. Antonyms: "While she was sociable, he was reserved."

Thus, it is possible to clarify the meanings of words through the use of contextual clues.

*Conclusion.*There are many homonyms in the English language that can cause confusions in comprehension. Consequently, their use in jury instructions should be monitored. Where elimination of the homonym is not possible, we can limit its use to its most common meaning. Secondly, we can manipulate the context to clarify meanings. Such manipulations should make instructions more comprehensible. For example, consider the following instruction:

> Testimony of Accomplice. The state has adduced testimony from a claimed accomplice. His testimony should be closely scrutinized for any possible motives for falsification, and if you find that he has testified falsely in regard to any material matter, you should be hesitant to convict upon his testimony without corroboration, and in no case should you convict the defendant unless you are satisfied of his guilt from the evidence beyond a reasonable doubt. (Nebraska Jury Instructions, 14.58)

The adjective *material* has several meanings. Instead of interpreting it as meaning "relevant," a juror could interpret it in terms of one of its more common meanings such as "economic" or "physical." Such use of homonyms will have debilitating effects on the correct understanding of the instructions. The phrase *relevant to the legal issues in the case* can be substituted for *material* in order to avoid such confusion.

Synonyms

The inexperienced writer often uses synonyms in place of previously used words for stylistic reasons. There is some literature suggesting that this practice might have a debilitating effect on comprehension. The use of synonyms in jury instructions should therefore be carefully controlled.

According to several authors on the art of writing (Flesch & Lass, 1963, p. 124–126; Perrin, 1965, p. 348–350), very few synonyms are totally interchangeable. Synonyms usually have different shades of meaning (connotations) and should not be interchanged unless these differences are known. The only reason to use synonyms, these authors agree, is when different shades of meaning are intended. They should never be used to avoid repetition, as it only achieves artificiality and can create confusion in comprehension. Flesch and Lass used the following two examples to make this argument: (1) "I noticed a *book* with a blue cover and took *it* from the shelf. It was a *book* I had read before." (2) "I noticed a *book* with a blue cover and took the *volume* from the shelf. It was a *work* I had read before." The first example is more natural and simpler to understand. In the second example, the words *volume* and *work* add connotations to the word *book* not intended by the author. A person may interpret the use of synonyms as an intentional attempt to distinguish between shades of meaning. If the communicator does not have any such intent, as in the case where synonyms are used to avoid repetition, the message will be misinterpreted. In addition, both *volume* and *work* are homonyms, by virtue of the fact they have multiple meanings, and for that reason alone, can cause confusions in comprehension (see section on homonyms).

To our knowledge there is no psycholinguistic research directly concerned with the effects of the use of synonyms in communication. However, synonyms have been used to demonstrate the importance of semantic encoding of words in memory. This research has shown another problem with using synonyms. It has been found with subjects who were asked to memorize a list of words that they often mistakenly recorded synonyms in place of the words originally learned (Anisfeld & Knapp, 1968; Cermak, Schnorr, Buschke, & Atkinson, 1970; Clark, 1972; Cramer, 1973; Fillenbaum, 1965; Grossman & Eagle, 1970; Kausler & Settle, 1973; Stark, 1972; Underwood, 1965). This suggests that the use of synonyms in order to communicate different shades of meaning may be less than optimally effective. That is, people may consider the synonyms used in a given message to be interchangeable. In such a case the communicator's intent will be misinterpreted.

Conclusion. The use of synonyms in jury instructions must be carefully studied. We do not know whether people will interpret synonyms as interchangeable or as communicating different shades of meaning. Our hypothesis is that both types of interpretations will occur, depending on the listener-reader and the context in which the synonyms are used. Thus, more research is needed to clarify exactly what impact the use of synonyms does have on juror performance. For example, consider the following instruction:

> Impeachment—Reputation for Truth and Veracity. You have heard testimony as to the general reputation of a witness in his neighborhood or community for truth and veracity. This testimony has been admitted solely for impeachment purposes, that is, to show the character and credibility of the witness. In determining the weight and credibility to be given to his testimony, you should consider his general reputation for truth and veracity. (Nebraska Jury Instructions, 1.71)

The use of strings of synonyms in jury instructions are often used to ensure that the broad intent of the law is fully conveyed. For example, words like *neighborhood-community* and *truth-veracity-credibility* are somewhat synonymous. Since the broad intent of the law is fully conveyed by the word *community*, the word *neighborhood* can be eliminated without any loss of meaning. The words *truth*, *credibility*, and *veracity* do attribute some fine distinctions, necessary to the comprehension of the instruction. Because these words are often used synonymously, however, the necessary distinctions may be less than optimally clear in the above instruction. One way to correct this is to replace *veracity* with the much more common word *accuracy*, and to restructure the sentences in such a way as to make the distinctions between *credibility*, *truth*, and *accuracy* more clear, as below.

> You have heard testimony as to the general reputation of a witness for character and credibility in his community. Even though a person may intend the truth, he may lack the ability to relay it accurately, because of imperfect perception and memory. Thus, credibility is a product of truthfulness and accuracy. In determining the weight and credibility to be given to this witness's testimony, you should consider his reputation for truthfulness and accuracy.

Antonyms

There is cross-cultural evidence that people are more disposed to make favorable rather than unfavorable judgments (Boucher & Osgood, 1969). As a result, there are more favorable adjectives in languages. Antonyms to favorable adjectives are often formed by the addition of negative modifiers (e.g., polite-impolite), while the opposite never occurs. Research has shown that a negatively modified adjective is more difficult to use and comprehend than an antonym with a different root (e.g., polite-impolite-rude). This research should be taken into account in the writing of jury instructions.

Salter and Haycock (1972) ran two studies on negative modifiers. In the first study, the researchers found that children used less negatively modified words than adults. This finding suggests that negatively modified words are more difficult. For example, let us compare two antonyms to the word *polite, rude* and *impolite*. The first one requires a simple comprehension of the negative concept "rude," while the second one requires comprehension for the positive concept "polite" and then a negation of it, making it a two-process operation.

In addition, the word *impolite* is not as definitive as *rude*. Thus, it is easy to see why negatively modified words are more difficult to comprehend and use.

In a second experiment Salter and Haycock asked subjects to think of synonyms to four types of adjectives as exemplified below:

Favorable Adjectives		
X		
e.g., honest		

Antonyms to Favorable Adjectives		
Prefix X	Not X	Y
e.g., dishonest	e.g., not honest	e.g., deceitful

It was found that subjects were able to think of more synonyms to X words than to any others, followed by Y words, and no differences were found between prefix X and not X words. If we assume that those words to which we can think of more synonyms are more meaningful because of associational richness, this study suggests that negatively modified adjectives are less desirable to use than an antonym of a different root word.

In another study by Sherman (1973), comprehension of entire sentences was significantly faster and more accurate when a "prefix X" adjective was used as opposed to a "not X" adjective, even though "not X" adjectives were more frequent in the language. It seems that a "prefix X" adjective sentence simply reverses the meaning of the word, while the use of "not X" has a much broader effect on the entire sentence, making the latter kind of negation more complex. For example, the sentence "The boy was dishonest" requires a two-step negation, but only on the word *honest*. In the sentence "The boy was not honest," it is necessary to first process "The boy was honest" and then to negate the entire sentence. If given a choice, however, a different root antonym is the best possible choice, as in the sentence "The boy was deceitful," because it requires only a one-step process.

Conclusion. On the basis of these findings, it seems reasonable to suggest that drafting committees should avoid negatively modified adjectives and use antonyms with different roots. For example, consider the following instruction:

> Impeachment—Previous Inconsistent Statements. You have heard testimony concerning statements allegedly made by (a witness, witnesses) prior to this trial which may be inconsistent with (his, their) testimony at this trial. This testimony has been admitted solely for impeachment purposes to aid you in estimating the credibility of (the witness, witnesses) and to determine the weight to be given to (his, their) testimony. You may consider it for that limited purpose only and not as evidence of the facts declared in the prior statement. (Nebraska Jury Instructions, 1.72)

The full meaning of the above instruction is totally dependant on a juror's hearing and comprehending the word *inconsistent*. Because *inconsistent* is a negatively evaluated antonym of the root *consistent*, the two words can be easily confused for each other. In place of *inconsistent, contradictory* is probably a better choice because no such confusions are possible.

Negation

There is mounting evidence that people tend to be predisposed to comprehending affirmative sentences better than negative ones. A negative sentence is one which usually has one or two words acting as negators, which modify the entire meaning of a sentence. Since such negation has been demonstrated to make comprehension more difficult under certain conditions, careful control of this variable should aid in making jury instructions more memorable and comprehensible.

A debilitating effect on comprehension has been shown with different types of negations. Several researchers have used the word *not* as negator, and have demonstrated resulting increases in the amount of time it takes to comprehend sentences (Wason, 1959, 1961; Gough, 1965; Slobin, 1966). Such negators as *never* (McMahon, 1963), *less than* (Flores d'Arcais, 1966), and *few, scarcely, minority* (Just & Carpenter, 1971) have also been shown to increase comprehension time when inserted in sentences. The reason for the increases in comprehension time is simply that such negators add one extra step to the comprehension process. For example, when we say something is "not X," we are not evoking a direct opposite to "X," but are instead requiring two steps: (1) a comprehension of what "X" is, and (2) a denial of it. This extra modifying step increases comprehension time.

Several researchers have shown that it is more effective to give affirmative instructions without qualifying negatives. For example, Cornish and Wason (1970) presented subjects with positive and negative clues describing an object. The subjects first identified the object being described and then tried to recall the given clues. More affirmative than negative clues were recalled. In another experiment, Jones (1966) gave subjects a simple timed performance task where they were asked to cross out certain specified numerals from a long list of numerals. One group received straightforward affirmative instructions, while another group received qualifying negations, where they were asked to cross out all numbers "except" specified ones. The group with the negative qualifying instructions were slower and made more errors than the control group. File and Jew (1973) presented airline passengers with emergency landing instructions both visually and verbally. Fewer instructions were recalled when given in the negative form, and regardless of original form, instructions were more often recalled in the active affirmative form.

The difficulty with negative qualifying instructions is that they focus attention on items to which subjects are not expected to respond. Thus, unless the qualifying exceptional situation is bound to occur, such additions to instructions will only tend to make them more complicated than they need be. There are times, however, when an exception needs to be emphasized. For example, the sentence "It is *not* a crime to smoke marijuana, but it is a crime to sell it" has a negative phrase which might clarify an issue. Such an argument has been made by several researchers (Green, 1970; Wason, 1965), and in these cases, negative sentences have been found to enhance comprehension.

Conclusion. It is best to avoid negation by rephrasing sentences in affirmative forms; qualifying negative instructions should only be used in cases where an exception to the rule is relevant in the case. For example, consider the following instruction:

> Liability of Manufacturer, Supplier—Inspection by Third Party. The (manufacturer, supplier) is not relieved of any duty he may have by the fact that he (contracted with, relied upon) (name of third party) to inspect the article before delivery to (name of user). (Nebraska Jury Instructions, 11.07)

When applicable, this instruction is given along with NJI11.03, which describes the liabilities of manufacturers. From our discussion above, it is clear that a negation can only help comprehension if it expresses an exception to a rule, when applicable in a particular case. The above instruction expresses an addition. Thus, the phrase *is not relieved* should make the sentence more difficult to comprehend than if it were expressed in affirmative language. The instruction can be revised in the following manner:

> The (manufacturer, supplier) is bound to all duties even when he (contracted with, relied upon) (name of third party) to inspect the article before delivery to (name of user).

Legal Jargon

The law, like all professions and scientific disciplines, is steeped in jargon. These terms, though sometimes comprehensible to others within the discipline, are often like a foreign language to the uninitiated. When some glimmer of understanding does arise in the layperson-listener, it is likely that the attributed meaning misses the intended meaning. The use of jargon appears so fraught with potential problems it is uncanny that it has not been thoroughly researched. But that is precisely the state of affairs. A review of the literature does not reveal any published research in this area.

Although not formally studied previously, the use of legal jargon should be given careful consideration in drafting jury instructions. It is likely that terms like *proximate cause*, though understandable to the judge and lawyers, and legally correct in case of appellate review, will be confusing to the jurors. We have often heard lawyers and social scientists complain that each other's professional journals are incomprehensible because of the technical jargon. Why then should we expect this terminology to be comprehensible to lay jurors?

Conclusion. The use of legal jargon should decrease the comprehensibility of jury instructions and increase the probability of the jurors incorrectly applying the law. For example, consider the following instruction:

> Proximate Cause. By "proximate cause" is meant. . . . (Nebraska Jury Instructions, 3.41)

The common use of such legal jargon as *proximate cause* can only add confusion to the average juror's mind. *Proximate cause* may be simply replaced by *legal cause*.

GRAMMATICAL CONSTRUCTIONS

Sentence Length and Complexity

The length and complexity of sentences used in instructions will affect the juror's recall and comprehension of them. It would seem logical to assume that the longer and more grammatically complex a sentence becomes, the greater the amount of information that will be contained in it and the greater the amount of logical complexity that will result. Therefore, long and complicated sentences should be more difficult to remember and comprehend than short simple sentences. Psycholinguistic research generally confirms the above hypothesis. It would be misleading, however, to accept the general hypothesis without detailing the effects of length and complexity and understanding the interrelatedness of these two variables.

In order to delineate how length and grammatical complexity affect recall and comprehension, it is necessary to first classify types of sentences; there are four kinds: simple, compound, self-embedded, and compound-self-embedded (Perrin, 1965). A simple sentence contains only one independent clause, or one subject verb message, such as, "She was out of danger." Simple sentences need not be short, as they can be lengthened with prepositional phrase modifiers (e.g., "After a few days of treatment, she was out of danger"), with added adjectives (e.g., "She was out of that horrible danger"), with compound subjects (e.g., "She and I were out of danger"), with two or more verbs (e.g., "She was out of danger and looked happier"), and by similar methods. A compound sentence is made up of two or more independent clauses that would easily make separate sentences were it not for a connecting *and* or *but* or some other connectors (e.g., "I wanted to buy it today, but the store was closed"). A self-embedded sentence is one which contains independent (or main) and dependent (or subordinate) clauses. The main and subordinate clauses may be connected by relative pronouns (e.g., "The boy *whose* toy this is, is crying") or by subordinating conjunctions (e.g., "The boy is crying *because* his toy was taken away"). The compound-self-embedded sentence is a combination of the latter two types of sentences.

Now, let us turn to the effects of length and complexity on recall and comprehension of sentences. Although several researchers have agreed that shorter sentences should be easier to remember (Gerver, 1969; Miller, 1973; Wearing, 1973), the effects of length are not as simple or conclusive as it initially appears. First, because a sentence is qualitatively different from a string of words, the effects of length on memory and comprehension are not continuously linear. Wearing (1973) tested the recall of sentences of varying lengths and found that sentences 9, 11, and 13 words long were equally well remembered, even though as a group they were less well remembered than the shorter sentences of 5- and 7-word lengths. Second, to say that shorter sentences are more easily recalled or comprehended does not mean that two short sentences will be better recalled and comprehended than one long one. Although this is still an empirical question, it is logical to assume that at times one long sentence may be overall shorter than two short sentences, and/or may be easier to recall and comprehend (e.g., "After a few days of treatment she was out of danger" versus "She received treatment. After a few days, she was out of danger"). Third, the distinction between length and complexity is artificial, since in most cases the addition of words also adds phrases and clauses to a given sentence, which in turn makes it more grammatically as well as psychologically complex (Goldman-Eisler & Cohen, 1971; Hamilton & Deese, 1971; Wang, 1970). Sometimes, the addition of words to a sentence changes it from a simple to a self-embedded one, which is inherently more complex (e.g., "Parents may unintentionally retard a child's development" versus "Parents who are not informed about their child's developmental processes may unintentionally retard his development"). As will be discussed below, memory and comprehension are not so much determined by the number of words as by the grammatical complexity of some long sentences. This is the reason why we chose to discuss length and complexity together.

In writing jury instructions, therefore, length should only be a concern when it affects the grammatical complexity of a sentence. Of the types of sentences described, the self-embedded one is the most difficult to recall (Forster & Ryder, 1971; Holmes, 1973; Miller & Isard, 1964) and comprehend (Fodor & Garrett, 1967; Freedle & Craun, 1970; Goldman-Eisler, 1961; Hamilton & Deese, 1971; Wang, 1970). The results have been so dramatic that almost all of the recent research on the effects of grammatical complexity on recall and comprehension has been done with self-embedded sentences.

Several researchers have even differentiated between the different kinds of self-embedded sentences. Holmes (1973) tested the hypothesis that right-branching self-embedded sentences (main clause appears first uninterrupted) are easier to recall than left-branching embedded sentences (subordinate clause appears first uninterrupted) or center-embedded sentences (main clause interrupted by subordinate clause). The following types of self-embedded sentences were used:

Adverbials	Right-branching	The boys listened to the radio while they were working.
	Left-branching	While the driver was repairing the truck he sang loudly.
Relatives	Right-branching	Ann was wearing the pretty frock that her mother made.
	Center-embedded	The truck that Bill was driving crashed into the post.
Complements	Right-branching	The vicar made the claim that church was corrupt.
	Center-embedded	Your suggestion that Alan should conceal the truth alarmed him.

Holmes found that for the adverbials and complements, the right-branching sentences were more easily recalled in a short-term task. On the other hand, it was found that for the relatives, the center-embedded sentences were more easily recalled. Miller and Isard (1964) cautioned that although short center-embedded relative sentences were easily recalled, when the number of subordinate clauses got beyond two, recall became extremely difficult. Other researchers also have found that although short center-embedded relatives were easily comprehended, as the number of subordinate clauses increased, sentences became increasingly more incomprehensible (Blumenthal, 1966; Hamilton & Deese, 1971; Marks, 1968; Stolz, 1967). Right-branching sentences are not as affected by the number of subordinate clauses (Goldman-Eisler & Cohen, 1971; Hamilton & Deese, 1971). Hamilton and Deese explained this phenomenon by proposing that an increase in the number of center-embedded clauses increases the interruption between the subject and the predicate, and that this interruption causes a decrease in comprehensibility. As an added piece of information about self-embedded sentences, several studies (Hakes & Cairns, 1970; Hakes & Foss, 1970) have shown that the use of relative pronouns facilitates recall and comprehension (e.g., "The book *which* I bought is out of print" versus "The book *that* I bought is out of print").

Conclusion. Based on the research cited above, the following suggestions can be made for improving jury instructions. Length of sentences should not be a major concern because sometimes long simple sentences and compound sentences may actually be more memorable and comprehensible than an alternative combination of several shorter sentences. Grammatical complexity, on the other hand, should be a major concern in writing jury instructions. Self-embedded sentences seem to present difficulties in recall and comprehension and should therefore be avoided. When used, right-branching sentences should be preferred over other types, and no more than one subordinate clause should ever be allowed. Although the interaction of length and complexity has been clearly demonstrated in the case of embedded sentences, no such effects have been described for simple and compound sentences. Length, after a point, may have an extreme debilitating effect on these two types of sentences as well, but the exact parameters of this interaction have not been determined experimentally. Miner (1969) and Barlow and Miner (1969) have published a Length-Complexity Index (LCI) which can be used to measure this interaction and to determine at what point extremeness occurs. For example, consider the following instruction:

> Effect of Violation of Statutes and Ordinances. Any violation of a statute (ordinance) regulating the use and operation of motor vehicles upon the highways (streets) does not in and of itself constitute negligence, but any such violation is evidence of negligence which may be considered with all the other facts and circumstances in this case in determining whether or not the person so violating was negligent. (Nebraska Jury Instructions, 7.02)

The instruction suffers because (1) it is too long, (2) it is a compound sentence, and (3) each independent clause has a center-embedded dependent clause. The instruction can be simplified in the following way:

> Any violation of a motor vehicle statute (ordinance) is one type of evidence of negligence, but does not in and of itself constitute negligence.

Verb Structure

Although the effects of differing verb structures on recall and comprehension of sentences still need to be extensively researched, a few general conclusions can be made. Recall and comprehension of sentences are affected by the transitivity of verbs as well as by their connotative meanings. Careful attention to such variables in the writing of jury instructions should prove to make them more effective.

A transitive verb is one which expresses action from the subject to the object, and thus requires a direct object noun phrase (e.g., "Jack arrested the man"). An intransitive verb is one which does not require a direct object (e.g., "Jack said that the man cooperated"). Many verbs take on either form (e.g., "Jack believed the man" versus "Jack believed the man to be innocent"). Several researchers have found that intransitive verbs gave easier sentence recall than transitive verbs (Bacharach, Kellas, & McFarland, 1972; Polzella & Rohrman, 1970; Rohrman, 1970; Segui & Kail, 1972). These findings are explained by the hypothesis that intransitive verbs are psychologically simpler, since they do not denote as complex a relationship between the subject and object as do transitive verbs. Thus, it seems that although sentences with transitive verbs are probably more common, intransitive verbs do not have to be avoided. There is some research, however, which suggests that verbs which can change from transitive to intransitive with the addition of an extra clause make comprehension more difficult (Fodor, Garrett, & Bever, 1968). For example, compare the sentences "John believed the man" and "John believed the man to be innocent." The verb in the latter sentence is intransitive, but that interpretation cannot be made until the last part of the sentence is read. These kinds of constructions may cause some confusion in comprehension. On the other hand, the results of Fodor *et al.* may have really been more of an interaction between intransitivity and self-embedding, which itself causes confusions. Hakes (1971) found less conclusive evidence than Fodor *et al.* for the debilitating effects of verbs which can be transitive or intransitive, with the use of simpler sentences. Until more conclusive research is done, it may be advisable, in writing jury instructions, to avoid the use of verbs which can take either an intransitive or a transitive form in a particular sentence. The sentence "John believed the man to be innocent" can be changed to "John thought the man was innocent" to avoid any possible confusions.

There are several implicit properties of transitive verbs which have been studied that should prove helpful in constructing jury instructions. Several researchers have found that people tend to prefer or find most comprehensible those sentences which have human or at least animate logical subjects with transitive verbs (Brown, Cazden, & Bellugi, 1969; Clark, 1965; Clary & Begun, 1971; Jarvella & Sinnott, 1972). Below are four examples of logical subjects in decreasing order of comprehensibility:

1. Human animate: "The man showed the way."
2. Animate: "The dog showed the way."
3. Concrete: "The map showed the way."
4. Abstract: "Honesty showed the way."

Thus, to maximize comprehensibility of jury instructions, the use of inanimate logical subjects with transitive verbs should be avoided.

Another property of transitive verbs is that in very simple unmodified sentences, they tend to transfer quantitative meaning to the logical object (Abelson & Kanouse, 1966; Gilson & Abelson, 1965; Kanouse, 1972) by connoting the proportion of the object class to which the verb applies. Kanouse found that "subjective verbs" like *understand* and "negative verbs" like *destroy* tended to apply to a greater proportion of the object class than "manifest verbs" like *buy* or "positive verbs" like *produce*. A sentence like "John buys hats," for example, tends to mean "John buys some hats." The use of explicit modifying quantifiers should counteract these effects. Attention to this variable should aid in avoiding possible misinterpretations of jury instructions.

Some sentences with two or more verbs are subject to temporal or causal confusions. People tend to encode temporal and causal relationships in sentences very quickly, as they are central to the correct comprehension of a sentence (Fillenbaum, 1971). A sentence like "He died and was buried" would not make sense if the order of the verbs was reversed. Other sentences, like "He ate some cake and drank some coffee," do not express any temporal or causal relationship and would not be affected by the order of verbs. It is important, therefore, to distinguish between such sentences and make sure that where temporal and causal relationships are important, the order of verbs should reflect them. Barrie-Blackey (1973) found that some temporal sequences are easier to remember than others. It was found that children understood sentences with "after" temporal links (e.g., "Daddy lies down after he comes inside") more easily than sentences with "before" and "until" temporal links, in that order. This needs to be tested with adults, and if found effective, should be considered in writing jury instructions.

Finally, Gumenik and Dolinsky (1971) found that the evaluative meanings of a verb tend to affect the evaluative meaning of logical subjects. Good verbs tend to change the evaluative meaning of logical subjects in a positive direction and vice versa. When the object is negatively evaluated, however, bad verbs will also tend to change the evaluation of the subject in a positive direction (e.g., "John killed the bandit"). Even though killing is a negative action, John is seen positively because the object was a bandit. There might be times when such connotative effects can be either used or avoided in the writing of jury instructions.

Conclusion. It is important to pay attention to verb structures in the writing of effective jury instructions. The use of particular verb structures should tend to make instructions more comprehensible and easier to recall. In addition, careful choosing of verbs should also refine the connotative meanings which they transmit, making sure that misinterpretations do not occur. For example, consider the following instruction:

> Bailment for Consideration—Liability of Bailor (Lessor to Bailee (Lessee). A person (furnishing, leasing) an article to another for compensation owes a duty to such person to whom the article is supplied, and to all others whom the supplier should expect to use the article with the consent of the person to whom furnished or who may be endangered by its probable use, to exercise ordinary care to see that the article, when

furnished, is in a reasonably safe condition to avoid injury to such persons, and to see that such article is free from defect of which he had knowledge, or should have had knowledge, or which he could have discovered by reasonable inspection or by such simple and available tests as to its condition as the intended use would normally suggest, unless: (1) the person so furnishing had reasonable cause to believe that the user would discover the defect and realize the danger, or (2) the person so furnishing used reasonable care to warn the user of the dangerous condition. (Nebraska Jury Instructions, 11.01)

There are several factors which make the instruction above less than optimally comprehensible. First, the number of self-embeddings, which separate the subject from object, tends to make the sentence difficult to comprehend. Second, the sentence creates temporal and causal confusions because of the sheer number of verbs in it, while the mixture of transitive and intransitive verbs in the same sentence makes it psychologically confusing. By reducing the number of verbs, we are able to reduce temporal and causal confusions. In addition, by replacing such verbs as *exercise* and *see*, with *use* and *make sure*, respectively, we are able to reduce transitive–intransitive confusions.

When (furnishing, leasing) an article for compensation, a person owes a duty to anyone who may be endangered by its probable use. The duty is to *use* ordinary care and to reasonably inspect the article, by simple and available tests, to *make sure* that it is in a reasonably safe condition and free from defects, which might cause injury under intended use. A person is relieved of this duty when he has reasonable cause to believe that the user would discover the defect and realize the danger, or when he used reasonable care to warn the user of the dangerous condition.

Active versus Passive Voice

The effects of the active and passive voice on the memory and comprehension of sentences have been studied for many years, and should be considered in writing effective jury instructions. A passive sentence is different from an active one in that the grammatical subject is really the psychological object. It has been argued by several researchers that because of this, passive sentences may lead to more confusions (Anderson, 1974; Huttenlocker, Eisenberg, & Strauss, 1968; Huttenlocker & Strauss, 1968; Hornby, 1972). These researchers have suggested that the active form is the natural form in which the mind stores propositions, and they hypothesize that passive sentences should therefore take longer to decipher and store. Research has shown that although the inversion of the order of the psychological subject and object in the passive sentence has some effects on memory and comprehension, it cannot be concluded that the active form is superior to the passive form. In fact, as will be discussed below, there are times when the passive voice is more effective in communicating ideas. The question as to whether passive sentences should be used in jury instructions, therefore, does not lend itself to a simple yes or no answer.

Several researchers have found passive sentences to be more difficult to recall than active ones (Coleman, 1965; Prentice, 1966; Savin & Perchonock, 1965; Slobin, 1968). Yet, one researcher has found passive sentences to be recalled better than active ones (Wearing, 1973), and several researchers found no differences between these two types of sentences (Blount & Johnson, 1971; Wearing, 1970). Blount and Johnson used sentences in the context of paragraphs and that factor could explain the findings. We know from previous research that context is a powerful factor in memory (Olson, 1970) and can overcome grammatical complexity.

Some researchers have concluded that passive sentences are more difficult to comprehend (Gough, 1966; Huttenlocker *et al.*, 1968; Huttenlocker & Strauss, 1968; Lippman, 1972). Huttenlocker *et al.* found that children got confused when asked to show what was meant by the sentence "The green truck is being pushed by the red truck." This was interpreted as confusion between the grammatical and logical subjects. Lippman found that reasoning tasks were more difficult and took longer when written in the passive voice. Slobin (1971, p. 36), however, has pointed out that when the subject and object are not logically interchangeable, such confusions do not occur. Thus, for example, a sentence such as "The dog is being chased by the cat" may be confusing, but "The leaves are being raked by the boy" is not confusing. Wright (1969) presented subjects with either passive or active sentences and then asked questions about the sentences to test comprehension. It was found that when the questions were asked in the same form as the original sentences, fewer errors occurred. Thus, if the sentence was, "The dog was being chased by the cat" and the question was, "Who was being chased?" few errors occurred. All of the research cited above suggests that although certain precautions are necessary, passive sentences can be used as effectively as active ones in jury instructions.

In fact, passive sentences have been shown to be extremely effective in emphasizing the participation of the logical object in an event. Carroll (1968) showed that when subjects were questioned as to what happened to a logical subject of a sentence, answers were mostly in the active form. When the questions were about the logical object, however, there was an increase in passive answers. Thus, it seems clear that passive sentences focus attention on the logical object and, in the proper context, can be an effective communicative tool. A sentence like "A policeman was killed by these people" places special emphasis on the fact that an officer of the law was killed. Klenbort and Anisfeld (1974) found that subjects clearly recognized that the focal point in passive sentences was the logical object. Olson and Filby (1972) suggested that when an event warrants emphasizing the receiver of action, people tend to code those events in a passive voice. Other researchers have made similar arguments for the utility of the passive sentence (Enkvist, 1964; Tannenbaum & Williams, 1968; Turner & Rommetveit, 1968).

Grieve and Wales (1973) have suggested that the word *the* in front of the logical object in a passive sentence places special emphasis on a particular object, of which the hearer or reader is presumed to know. For example, the sentence "*The girl* was the guilty one" places special emphasis on a particular person. Slobin (1971, p. 37) has also pointed out that the passive voice can be used effectively when mention of a subject is irrelevant or when a subject is unknown, as in "This person was severely beaten."

Conclusion. Although caution must be exercised, passive sentences are not necessarily more difficult to recall and comprehend, and can be used in jury instructions for stylistic reasons as well as for special emphasis. To avoid possible confusions, passive sentences should only be used if the object and subject cannot be logically reversed or if the context is so clear that the intended subject of a sentence cannot be mistaken. Passive sentences can be effective tools in emphasizing the logical object, as well as in simplifying sentences when a subject need not be mentioned. For example, consider the following instruction:

> Aggravation of a Pre-Existing Disabling or Painful Condition—Proximate Cause. If you find from a preponderance of the evidence that the plaintiff, prior to (date of accident), had a bodily condition which was causing disability or pain, and that this pre-existing condition was aggravated by this accident, then, if your verdict is for the plaintiff, the plaintiff is entitled to recover only for the extent of the aggravation of the pre-existing condition proximately caused by the accident. (Nebraska Jury Instructions, 4.09)

The effectiveness of passive constructions is that they tend to emphasize the logical object. The intent of the instruction above is to focus attention on the "accident" and the damages that result from it. Yet, such phrases as "this pre-existing condition was aggravated by this accident" and "the extent of the aggravation of the pre-existing condition was proximately caused by the accident" do just the opposite. Both of these phrases would be more effective in the active voice as shown below.

> If you find from a preponderance of the evidence that the plaintiff, prior to (date of accident), had a bodily condition which was causing disability or pain, and *that this accident aggravated this preexisting condition,* then, if your verdict is for the plaintiff, the plaintiff is entitled to recover only for the extent of the aggravation *that this accident proximately caused to the preexisting condition.*

Similar versus Varied Grammatical Forms

Anyone who has read or heard material which was monotonous will agree that it is difficult to remain attentive to it. Unless jury instructions are attended to, they will not be comprehended or remembered. In addition to the other variables we have discussed, it is advisable to write jury instructions in such a way as to make them easy and interesting to listen to or read. Most authors on the art of writing suggest that one way of reducing monotony of a composition is to vary the grammatical structure of sentences (Flesch & Lass, 1963; Strunk & White, 1972). To our knowledge there are no psycholinguistic data supporting this hypothesis. Nevertheless, it is important to consider this hypothesis and its possible effects on the comprehension and memory of jury instructions.

Flesh and Lass present the following example of monotonous writing: "There was a lively debate among the students. There was great enthusiasm for the idea. There was hardly a dissenting voice. There was full agreement on the project in the end."

All of the sentences in the example above are similar in form and length. By varying sentences along these two parameters, it is possible to express the same ideas more interestingly: "The debate was lively. Were the students enthusiastic? They certainly were. Hardly a disscenting voice was heard, and in the end, everybody agreed on the project—yes, every one of them."

Grammatical variety is not always more effective than similarity in making a message easy to comprehend and remember. Parallel (similar) grammatical form of words, phrases, and clauses in sentences tends to make meaning easier to comprehend. Perrin (1965) used the following sentences as examples: (1) "One group favors gradual desegregation, while another demands that integration be brought about immediately, and a third group said that it is altogether opposed to integration." (2) "One group favors gradual integration, another demands immediate integration, and a third opposes integration altogether."

Each phrase in the first sentence is grammatically different. It is longer, more complex, and more cumbersome than the second sentence. The parallel construction in the second sentence is an effective way of signaling that each phrase is about a similar topic. Consequently the message in the second sentence is easier to understand.

According to this principle of "parallel construction," a sentence with an article (e.g., *the*) or preposition (e.g., *in*) "applying to all the members of a series must be either used only before the first term or else be repeated before each term" (Strunk & White, 1972). In addition, "correlative" expressions (*both, and, not, but, not only, but also, either, or, first, second, third, and the like*) should be followed by the same grammatical constructions. Strunk and White (1972) offer wrong and right examples of these rules:

WRONG	RIGHT
The French, the Italians, the Spanish and Portuguese	The French, the Italians, the Spanish, and the Portuguese
In spring, summer, or in winter	In spring, summer, or winter
	In spring, in summer, or in winter
It was both a long ceremony and very tedious.	The ceremony was both long and tedious.
A time not for words but action.	A time not for words but for action.
Either you must grant his request or incur his ill will.	You must either grant his request or incur his ill will.
My objections are, first, the injustice of the measure; second, it is unconstitutional.	My objections are, first, that the measure is unjust; second, that it is unconstitutional.

The effectiveness of these parallel constructions is that they make similarities in meaning between phrases easy to recognize and categorize. This principle can also apply to the similarities of meanings between entire sentences. The inexperienced writer may vary the grammatical forms of sentences as was suggested earlier, at times when parallel constructions can be dramatically effective. A good example is Dr. Martin Luther King's "I have a dream" speech (1963), in which the title was repeatedly used to introduce several paragraphs. Dr. King also used parallel constructions within paragraphs very effectively: "But not only that. Let freedom ring from Stone Mountain of Georgia. Let freedom ring from Lookout Mountain of Tennessee. Let freedom ring from every hill and mole hill of Mississippi, from every mountain site. Let freedom ring."

Conclusion. Parallelism and variety, if manipulated effectively, can be helpful in making jury instructions easier to comprehend and remember. This conclusion is based on the commonsense arguments we have presented above. To our knowledge there are no psycholinguistic data on this topic. For example, consider the following instruction:

> Conduct of Passengers—Right of Carriers to Eject. A person riding in (type of common carrier) must abide by usual standards of a reasonable passenger. He must also comply with reasonable rules and regulations of (name of carrier) designed to provide for the safety and comfort of passengers and the proper management of the (type of carrier).
>
> The failure or refusal of a passenger so to conduct himself, or a violation by the passenger of reasonable rules and regulations of the carrier, allows the carrier's employees to request the passenger to leave the (type of carrier) and, upon a refusal to do so, to remove him. If the passenger resists, the carrier's employees may use such force as may be reasonably necessary to remove the passenger, at such place and under such circumstances as would not unreasonably endanger the safety of such passenger.
>
> It is for you to determine whether the passenger did abide by the usual standard of conduct of a reasonable passenger, whether the rules and regulations of (name of carrier) were reasonable, and whether these rules and regulations were violated by the passenger (and whether the force used was reasonable under the circumstances).
>
> It is not necessary that the passenger be given actual notice of such rules and regulations, as he accepted passage subject to all reasonable rules and regulations with which he was or should have been familiar under the existing circumstances. It is sufficient if a general notice of such rules and regulations has been given to the public for such length of time as to make it reasonably certain that all passengers in the exercise of due diligence would have become aware of them.

There is little grammatical variety in the above instructions. Sentences beginning with *A*, *The*, and *It* tend to make such instructions monotonous and difficult to attend to. A more imaginative variety of sentence structures is bound to help make them easier to attend to and comprehend. For example, the third and fourth paragraphs in the above instruction can be easily restructured to leave only one *It*. The switch to a series of questions in the third paragraph is an effective way of adding variety, of setting that paragraph apart from the others, and of using similar constructions to underscore the equal importance of the answers to each of the questions.

> You are to determine the answers to two (three) questions:
>
> 1.   Did the passenger violate the usual standards of conduct of a resonable passenger?
>
> 2.   Where the rules and regulations of (name of carrier) reasonable, and if so, did the passenger violate these rules and regulations?
>
> 3.   Was the force used reasonable under the circumstances?
>
> When a passenger accepts passage, he is subject to all reasonable rules and regulations with which he is or should be familiar under the existing circumstances. Thus, the passenger need not be given actual notice of such rules and regulations. It is sufficient if a general notice of such rules and regulations has been given to the public. The notice must be for such length of time as to make it reasonably certain that all passengers in the exercise of due diligence would have become aware of it.

HOLISTIC ORGANIZATION

Organization of Content

There is no doubt that organization accounts for much of why and what people remember. Several researchers have found that the task of remembering unstructured material (e.g., a list of words) is made easier when we impose a structure on it (Bousfield & Cohen, 1955; Cofer, 1965; Nelson, McRae & Slurge, 1971). It has also been shown that the external organization of material will affect how a person organizes that material in trying to memorize it, and will determine the amount of material finally memorized (Bower, Clark, Lesgold, & Winzenz, 1969; Jenkins & Russell, 1952; Underwood, 1964, pp. 62–65). The organization and categorization of strings of incoming information is clearly a fundamental process in all perception and memory (Hultsch, 1971; Mandler, 1966; Norman, 1971). In writing jury instructions, careful attention should be paid to holistic organizational factors that affect comprehension and memory. The ease and extent to which a juror will comprehend and remember instructions will no doubt be partially a function of their holistic organization.

A paragraph or several paragraphs is more than just a number of sentences stuck together. The structure of paragraphs is such that it combines the meanings of individual sentences into holistic ideas, qualitatively different from the simple sum of its components (Balser, 1972; Bransford & Franks, 1971, 1972; Seliger, 1971). Psycholinguists have not dealt nearly as much with the structure of paragraphs or essays as they have with the structure of sentences. Perhaps this is because, unlike the case of sentences, the structure of paragraphs and essays is nonlinguistic. An analysis of paragraph and essay structure requires knowledge of more universal aspects of the organization of human thinking. Although cognitive psychologists have such expertise, few have applied it to linguistics, and fewer yet to paragraphs and essays. Enough research has been done, however, to enable us to make some suggestions. Below we outline some general guidelines on this issue as summarized by educational psychologists who have the similar problem of organizing material for presentation in the classroom (Cunningham, 1971; Tennyson, 1972).

One way to communicate a high-level concept is to build an understanding of lower level concepts and then integrate them. This "hierarchical" type of structure has been advocated for use in classroom instruction by educational psychologists in order to make material more comprehensible (Briggs, 1968; Gagne, 1970; Gagne & Brown, 1961; Gagne & Rohwer, 1969). Several researchers have shown the effectiveness of such a method in controlled situations (Eustace, 1969; Lee, 1968) and have shown that the more complex the task is, the smaller and simpler the component steps should be (Naylor & Briggs, 1963). As a result of and in addition to making instructional material more comprehensible, this kind of "hierarchical" segmentation tends to make it more memorable. Several researchers have shown that memorization of large amounts of material can be facilitated by segmentation (Pechstein, 1918; Webb & Schwartz, 1959), especially when the material is meaningfully related (Pechstein, 1926; Reed, 1924a,b). Thus, the decision on the number and level of components specified by a particular set of jury instructions should be dictated by the number and level of subconcepts necessary to understand and remember the full intent of the law. This is one fruitful area of investigation.

An effective presentation sequence of the legal points outlined in the "hierarchical" structure should be "logical." The difficulty comes in specifying the explicit meaning of the term *logical sequence* (Tennyson, 1972). Merrill (1971) has proposed that the most logical structure is one in which ideas are changed so that each is necessary for succeeding ones. Such an organization, called "algorithmic," is clearly necessary when causal or temporal relations are expressed. The order of sentences in such cases is thus dictated by the logical occurrence of the events described (Seliger, 1971). Sasson (1971) collected empirical data to show that temporal organizational sequence of sentences helps in recall. Greeno and Noreen (1974) found that when one part of a paragraph led to expectations about the content of later sentences in the paragraph, reading rates of later sentences increased. In contrast, when a sentence contradicted expectations based on earlier sentences, reading became slower.

In the hierarchical organization described above, the best sequence is one where the understanding of each concept will facilitate the understanding of later presented concepts either on the same level or on higher levels. For example, if the question of insanity was being adjudicated, one might construct jury instructions in the following way: As an introduction, one might give a short definition of insanity and identify the key subconcepts necessary to the existence of such a state. Next might be an introduction to the organizational structure of the instructions themselves, by informing the jury that in order to understand the concept of insanity they must first understand the subconcepts used in its definition. This will tend to allow the jurors to better anticipate and categorize each section of the instructions. The definition of each subconcept (e.g., mental disease, irresistible urge, right and wrong, conscience, crime) would follow, and the instruction would conclude with a full definition of insanity.

Conclusion. The exact specification and sequence of subconcepts necessary for an optimal level of comprehension both within each instruction and within a particular set of instructions that make up the charge will have to be empirically determined. This kind of experimental manipulation will lead to more comprehensible and more memorable jury instructions.

Length of Charge

Under given conditions, there are limits to the amount of information that the mind can absorb (Miller, 1956). Langer, Schultz, Meffert, and Tausch (1973) had children learn legal definitions of various crimes and found that the shorter, simpler, and more well-structured definitions were learned best. It appears reasonable to predict that jury instructions should be as short as possible, although tests on this point with adults must be conducted to prove that Langer's finding can be generalized. The answer to the question of exactly how short jury instructions should be is not a simple one. First we must decide on the kind of information that jurors are expected to remember.

Jurors should not be expected to remember the exact wording of jury instructions. Otherwise, the length of instructions will have to be limited to several sentences. Psycholinguistic literature suggests that people generally remember semantic information much better than grammatical or lexical information. In fact, memory for exact wording decays several seconds after the idea or meaning of the sentence has been coded (Bregman & Strasberg, 1968; Brent, 1969; Fillenbaum, 1966; Jarvella, 1971; Sachs, 1967, 1974). Perfetti and Garson (1973) tested retention of prose passages after four time intervals. It was found that even recognition, which is a relatively easy task, of original sentences dropped to chance levels after only 30 minutes. In contrast, memory for semantic information stayed above chance levels even after a week. Kolers (1972) has done experiments showing that people read at a much faster rate than is necessary to read every word of a text. We skim through the words in sentences and abstract the meaning that they are expressing into holistic ideas (Anderson, 1974; Bransford, Barclay, & Franks, 1972; Bransford & Franks, 1971, 1972; Flores d'Arcais, 1974; Francis, 1972; Gamlin, 1968, 1971; Olson, 1970). In short, jurors cannot and should not be expected to remember the exact wording of instructions.

Jurors should, however, remember the ideas expressed in instructions. The number of ideas that jurors will remember will be limited, to a great extent, to the ideas that they will comprehend. Sentences that make logical sense tend to be remembered much better than those that do not make logical sense (Wearing, 1972). Mistler-Lachman (1974) found that deeper comprehension of ideas led to better recall by asking people to fill in the blanks of sentences they were to remember, thus forcing comprehension.

The question of the length of instructions and its effect on comprehension and memory is not a simple one since the length of ideas cannot be defined by counting the number of words, sentences, or paragraphs. Rather, what is of greater concern is the number, complexity, and interrelatedness of crucial ideas expressed in the instructions. One set of instructions, for example, could be found to be physically longer than another, yet could still be comprehended and remembered better, if one set contained fewer or simpler ideas than the other. We may find that the repetition of ideas or the giving of examples, both of which will tend to make instructions longer, may clarify crucial points, and that is the ultimate goal. Therefore, although economy on words is a generally preferred goal (Langer et al., 1973), it must be tempered by the more important goal of making all of the necessary intricacies of the law governing the case totally understood.

Conclusion. It is clear that the more complex the law is, the more difficult it will be for people to understand it (Langer et al., 1973). The goal here is not to make the law less complex, but, given the intricacies of the law, to make it comprehensible in jury instructions. There are limits on the amounts and complexity of information that the mind is capable of handling. Unfortunately, there will also be limits on the brevity and simplicity with which given laws can possibly be explained. These competing variables need to be empirically assessed with actual jury instructions. For example, consider the following instruction:

STATEMENT OF THE CASE—WHERE DEFENDANT FILES COUNTERCLAIM

I.   Plaintiff's Claims

A.   ISSUES

This action involves (here state date, place, and nature of occurrence).
Plaintiff A (name) claims in his petition that defendant B (name) was negligent in one or more of the following particulars:

1.
2.
3.

Plaintiff further claims that he was injured (his property was damaged) as a proximate result of that negligence, and he therefore prays for judgment against the defendant for his damages.
Defendant B (name) admits (here state what he admits in his pleadings or othewise, if anything).
Defendant B (name) denies in his answer (here state what defendant denies).

B.   BURDEN OF PROOF

Before the plaintiff can recover against the defendant on his petition in this action, the burden is upon the plaintiff to prove by a preponderance of the evidence each and all of the following propositions:

1. That the defendant was negligent in one or more of the particulars claimed against him by the plaintiff in his petition;
2. That such negligence, if any, of the defendant was the proximate cause or a proximately-contributing cause of the collision;

3. That as the direct and proximate result of said negligence and resultant collision, the plaintiff sustained damages; and

4. The nature, extent, and amount of the damages thus sustained by the plaintiff.

C.   EFFECT OF FINDINGS

If the plaintiff has failed to establish any one or more of the foregoing numbered propositions by a preponderance of the evidence, your verdict will be for the defendant.

On the other hand, if the plaintiff has established by a preponderance of the evidence all of the above numbered propositions, then you must consider the defendant's defenses.

II.   Defendant's Defenses

A.   ISSUES

In defense to the plaintiff's claim, the defendant alleges that:

(a) Plaintiff was himself negligent in one or more of the following particulars:

1.
2.
3.

(b) Plaintiff assumed the risk of his own injury.

(c) (Here state such other defenses as may be pleaded, such as release, etc.)

(d) The sole proximate cause of the plaintiff's injuries if any, was an Act of God.

Plaintiff admits (here state what the plaintiff admits).
Plaintiff denies (here state what the plaintiff denies).

B.   BURDEN OF PROOF

In connection with the assertion of the plaintiff's negligence, the burden is upon the defendant to prove by a preponderance of the evidence each and all of the following propositions:

1. That the plaintiff was negligent in one or more of the particulars claimed against him by the defendant; and

2. That such negligence, if any, of the plaintiff was the proximate cause or a proximately-contributing cause of the plaintiff's (injuries, damages).

C.   EFFECT OF FINDINGS

If the defendant has failed to establish either of these proposition by a preponderance of the evidence, and the plaintiff has established by a preponderance of the evidence that the defendant was negligent in one or

more of the particulars claimed against him by the plaintiff, and that such
negligence was the proximate cause or a proximately-contributing cause of
the (injuries, damages), your verdict will be for the plaintiff on the
plaintiff's petition for such damages resulting from the defendant's negligence.

If the defendant has established by a preponderance of the evidence
that the plaintiff was negligent in one or more of the particulars claimed
against the plaintiff and that such negligence was a proximate cause or a
proximately-contributing cause of plaintiff's (injuries, damages), then you
should compare their negligence as to degree as explained to you in the
instruction on comparative negligence.

D.   COMPARATIVE NEGLIGENCE

The plaintiff cannot recover in this case if you find from the evidence
that the negligence of the plaintiff, when compared with that of the
defendant, was more than slight.

Neither can the plaintiff recover if you find from the evidence that the
negligence of the defendant, when compared with that of the plaintiff, was
less than gross.

If you find that the plaintiff was guilty of slight negligence when
compared with the negligence of the defendant, and that the negligence of
the defendant in comparison with the plainfitt's negligence was gross, it is
then your duty to deduct from the whole amount of damages, if any,
sustained by the plaintiff such proportion thereof as the contributory
negligence as shown by the evidence, and return a verdict for the balance
only.

E.
(Insert here other affirmative defense instructions.)

III.   Defendant's Counterclaim

A.   ISSUES

Defendant B (name) has made a counterclaim against plaintiff A
(name). To support this counterclaim he alleges that the plaintiff was
negligent in one or more of the following particulars:

1.
2.
3.

Defendant further claims that he was injured (his property was
damaged) as a proximate result of that negligence, and he therefore prays
for judgment against the plaintiff for his damages.

Plaintiff admits (here state what he admits in his pleadings or
otherwise, if anything).

Plaintiff denies (here state what he denies).

B.   BURDEN OF PROOF

Before the defendant can recover against the plaintiff on defendant's counterclaim in this action, the burden is upon the defendant to prove by a preponderance of the evidence each and all of the following propositions:

1. That the plaintiff was negligent in one or more of the particulars claimed against him by the defendant;

2. That such negligence, if any, of the plaintiff was the proximate cause or a proximately-contributing cause of the collision;

3. That as a direct and proximate result of said negligence and resultant collision, the defendant sustained damages; and

4. The nature, extent, and amount of the damages thus sustained by the defendant.

C.   EFFECT OF FINDINGS

If the defendant has failed to establish any one or more of the foregoing numbered propositions by a preponderance of the evidence, your verdict will be for the plaintiff on the defendant's counterclaim.

On the other hand, if the defendant has established by a preponderance of the evidence all of the above numbered propositions, then you must consider the defenses of the plaintiff to the defendant's counterclaim.

IV.   Plaintiff's Defenses to Counterclaim

A.   ISSUES

In defense to the defendant's counterclaim the plaintiff alleges that:

(a) Defendant was himself negligent in one or more of the following particulars:

1.
2.
3.

(b) Defendant assumed the risk of his own injury.

(c) (Here state such other defense as may be pleaded, such as release, etc.)

(d) The sole and proximate cause of the defendant's injuries, if any, was an Act of God.

Defendant admits (here insert what the defendant admits).
Defendant denies (here insert what the defendant denies).

B.   BURDEN OF PROOF

In connection with the assertion of the defendant's negligence as a defense to the defendant's counterclaim, the burden of proof is upon the plaintiff to prove by a preponderance of the evidence each and all of the following propositions:

1. That the defendant was negligent in one or more of the particulars charged against him by the plaintiff; and

2. That such negligence, if any, of the defendant was the proximate cause or a proximately-contributing cause of the defendant's (injuries, damages).

C.   EFFECT OF FINDINGS

If the plaintiff has failed to establish either of these propositions by a preponderance of the evidence, and the defendant has established by a preponderance of the evidence that the plaintiff was negligent in one or more of the particulars charged against him in the counterclaim and that such negligence was the proximate cause or a proximately-contributing cause of the collision, your verdict will be for the defendant on the defendant's counterclaim for such damages resulting from plaintiff's negligence.

If the plaintiff has established, by a preponderance of the evidence, that the defendant was negligent, and that such negligence was the proximate cause or a proximately-contributing cause of the collision, then you should consider whether the defendant's negligence was of such a degree that it is sufficient to diminish or defeat his recovery as explained to you in the instruction on comparative negligence.

D.   COMPARATIVE NEGLIGENCE

The defendant cannot recover in this case if you find from the evidence that the negligence of the defendant, when compared with that of the plaintiff, was more than slight.

Neither can the defendant recover if you find from the evidence that the negligence of the plaintiff, when compared with that of the defendant, was less than gross.

If you find that the defendant was guilty of slight negligence when compared with the negligence of the plaintiff, and that the negligence of the plaintiff in comparison with the defendant's negligence was gross, it is then your duty to deduct from the whole amount of damages, if any, sustained by the defendant such proportion thereof as the contributory negligence chargeable to the defendant bears to the entire negligence as shown by the evidence, and return a verdict for the balance only.

E.

(Insert here other affirmative defense instructions.)

(Nebraska Jury Instructions, 2.03)

The presentation of sections I, II, III, and IV, with each of their subsections, unnecessarily lengthens and complicates the instructions. A more comprehensible, shorter, and simpler way of presenting these instructions would be to present everyone's claims and counterclaims under section A, everyone's burden of proof under section B, and similarly for sections C and D.

PROCEDURAL VARIABLES

If the psycholinguistic variables are manipulated effectively within jury instructions, then each juror would be able to comprehend successfully the intended meaning of each instruction as well as the intended meaning of the jury charge taken as a whole. Although this is a necessary first step, it is not sufficient to ensure that the comprehended instructions will be remembered and utilized appropriately during the course of jury deliberations. Several procedural alternatives in the way instructions are presented may have a significant effect upon how well instructions are remembered and how effectively they are used. In this section, these variables will be identified and a review of the relevant literature provided.

Spoken versus Written Mode

Educational psychologists, who are constantly concerned with whether students learn better from lectures or from reading texts, have done experiments comparing reading and listening. Several researchers have found that when students are given written texts, they comprehend and remember material much better than when they listen to lectures (Beighley, 1952; Corey, 1934; Siegel, 1973). This difference should not be attributed to any superiority of visual perception over auditory perception. Young (1973) showed this not to be the case by controlling (matching) the reading rates of subjects under a reading condition with the auditory presentation rate for subjects under the listening condition, and finding no differences between the two groups. When people are given written texts they in fact are given a chance to go over material several times. It is this factor which explains the superiority of written material to lectures on comprehension and memory.

One way to increase the probability that a juror will comprehend and remember instructions should be to present them in written form as well as in the auditory mode. In effect, this will give jurors a chance to study the instructions several times, thereby giving jurors a chance to fully comprehend and memorize them. The longer and more complex the jury instructions are, the more justification there is for presenting them in written form. Several experimenters have shown that vocalization of written material facilitates memory (Murray, 1966; Tell & Ferguson, 1974). Having the judge read the jury instructions assures that each juror pays attention to them at least once. Giving the jurors a written version of instructions allows easy access to them anytime clarification is needed.

An alternative approach to increasing juror memory for the instructions is to tape-record them and then allow the recording to go into the deliberation room. This procedure was tried with apparent success by Judge Luther M. Swygert sitting in Hammond, Indiana, Federal Court in 1958. Empirical studies of its effectiveness, however, have never been undertaken.

Conclusion. Research is needed with jury instructions to test the comparative effectiveness of spoken presentation alone versus spoken-plus-written presentation versus spoken-plus-written presentation which can be kept and looked at again during deliberation. Research should also be conducted to test the efficacy of note-taking during instructions and evidence. This procedure is in use in several jurisdictions. In others (e.g., New Jersey Model Jury Instructions—Civil, 1.12.), note-taking is not permitted on the theory that

> [it] is distracting, . . . few jurors would take complete notes—and fragmentary notes would be apt to attach undue weight during the jury's deliberations to certain facts or circumstances, to the disregard or slighting of other facts or circumstances of equal significance. Experience has shown that it is better to depend upon the combined recollections of all the jurors than upon the notes taken by one or more of them.

These assumptions need to be tested.

TIME OF PRESENTATION

The presentation of instructions to jurors at the end of a trial is psychologically suspect for two reasons. First, it assumes the jurors have perfect memories and, once charged with instructions, can selectively recall and evaluate all of the appropriate evidence. In addition, it assumes that until the instructions are given, the jurors will passively listen to all of the evidence without evaluating it. As will be discussed below, neither of these assumptions is supported by research literature.

It is clear that people do not have perfect memories, because when given a mass of facts to be remembered, they will remember some and forget some. People do, however, have the ability to select which information to remember and which to forget. Learning psychologists have for years made distinctions between incidental and intentional learning. When given instructions as to what material they are expected to learn, people will learn it more effectively by concentrating on the relevant material and paying less attention to irrelevant material. This effect has been shown empirically with many different types of materials and in many situations (Dawley & Dawley, 1974; Duchastel & Brown, 1974; Kaplan & Rothkopf, 1973; Marton & Sandquist, 1972; Mechanic, 1962; Meunier, Kestner, Meunier, & Ritz, 1974; Wolk, 1974; Wolk & Du Cette, 1974; Postman & Adams, 1957; Zerdy, 1971). If jurors knew what is relevant to their verdict at the beginning of a trial, they would be better able to focus in on relevant evidence as it is being presented, and later remember it. This is one argument for presenting jury instructions at the beginning as well as at the end of a trial.

As stated earlier charging a jury at the end of a trial assumes that the jurors have been passively listening to all of the evidence without evaluating it. For years psychologists made similar assumptions about people who participated in their experiments. Recently, an entire area of research under the heading of "demand characteristics" has refuted that assumption. Many researchers have shown that people in psychological studies do their best to figure out what the experiment is about and what the experimenter is trying to prove, and then proceed intentionally to make the experiment a success, although some do just the opposite (Orne, 1962, 1973; Page, 1971, 1972, 1973; Patty & Page, 1973; Rosenthal, 1963, 1966). In any case, this entire area of research asserts that people are never passive receivers of information, but rather are constantly actively interpreting information and trying to find its meaning.

If people are not passive in an experimental study, we have no reason to assume that jurors can be passive during a trial, a social situation in which human emotion is constantly displayed. Psychological knowledge would suggest that jurors are, like everyone else, active and selective receivers of information. Because instructions are most often given at the end of a trial, jurors probably select and evaluate evidence in terms of their own sense of morality, and what they perceive to be the morals of the judge and lawyers. By presenting instructions at the beginning of a trial as well as at the end, we should increase the likelihood that jurors will evaluate evidence in light of the law instead.

Conclusion. Students are not expected to remember lectures without being able to take reference notes. Written jury instructions might

70 BRUCE DENNIS SALES ET AL.

increase their effectiveness in that jurors might be more apt to refer to them in deciding on a verdict. Students are often told ahead of time what they will be tested on. By presenting instructions at the beginning of a trial, we should increase the probability that jurors will evaluate evidence and decide cases under the law. Tests need to be conducted comparing the efficacy of instructions presented at the beginning and the end of the trial versus at the end alone. In addition, time of presentation should be manipulated with mode of presentation, spoken versus written, to find the optimal presentation of instructions. Finally, medial presentation should be tested to see if jurors' comprehension and memory is aided, inasmuch as the judge has the right to read instructions during the course of the trial. This might be especially appropriate in trials lasting more than two days.

ROLE OF JUDGE, JURY, AND SUBSTANTIVE LAW INSTRUCTIONS

Instructions may be broken down into instructions that elucidate the role of the jury during the course of the trial, the role of the judge during the course of the trial, and the substantive law that will guide the jury in terms of weighing the evidence in reaching a decision. The first two types of instructions, the role of judge and the role of jury instructions, are often referred to collectively as preliminary instructions. In many jurisdictions it is often the case that some of the substantitive law instructions are also included within these preliminary instructions, only to be repeated later at the end of the trial.

When people drawn from the jury pool first enter the courtroom, they usually have very little idea what is going to happen during their stay within the courtroom and during the course of the trial. It is the purpose of the preliminary instructions to inform the jurors what role they and the judge should play. The preliminary instructions include such things as the jurors' conduct during the trial, their need for impartiality, what duties they will have as triers of fact, their responsibilities for avoiding newspapers, radio, and TV, and what behaviors they should exhibit during the course of the trial, such as not discussing the case among other jurors during recess. Similarly, it is important that the jurors fully understand the role of the judge during the proceedings. They must be instructed as to his duty to make decisions as to the appropriate law controlling the case, his duty in instructing the jurors as to the law that they must decide the case under, and his general responsibility for the conduct of the entire proceeding. As Judge Robert L. McBride, chairman of the Jury

Instruction Committee of the Ohio Judicial Conference (1969, p. 61) has noted, "Preliminary instructions constitute a neglected area of trial administration which is worthy of serious consideration by every trial judge."

Most jurisdictions leave the giving of the role of judge and jury instructions to the discretion of the presiding judge, but as psychologists can attest, the effect of set on subsequent performance can be enormous. Thus, with instructions on the role of the judge and the jury, a jury which is instructed as to its duty to determine facts solely on the basis of evidence, on how it shall determine the believability of evidence, and its obligation to give each party a fair and impartial consideration without sympathy or prejudice, should have a much better orientation, understanding, and set from which to listen to the evidence and cognitively organize it in such a way as to be much more usable at a later point in the proceeding, when the judgment must be reached. Furthermore, the combination of these instructions being given both before the evidence and at the end of the trial after all the presentation of the evidence, but before the presentation of the substantive law instructions, should greatly increase the probability that the evidence will be weighed and organized in such a fashion as to maximize the probability of effective usage. Similarly, where substantive law instructions are contained in these preliminary instructions, they should increase the ability of the jurors to organize the information to be presented during the course of the trial (see section on time of presentation).

Conclusion. Jurors should remember the evidence better and have greater recall for the material facts of the case when they have been presented with preliminary instructions. In addition: (1) A juror's ability to organize, remember, and utilize the material facts of the case should significantly increase when role of the judge and jury instructions are given both at the beginning of the trial and at the end of the presentation of the evidence, but before the substantive law instructions are presented; (2) a juror's memory, comprehension, and utilization of both the law and the weighing of evidence in light of the law will be maximized when the roles of judge, jury, and substantive law instructions are presented at both the beginning and the end of the trial.

ALTERNATE FORMS

Inherent in our discussion up to this point is the underlying belief that it is possible to write one form of instructions for a particular issue that will be ultimately effective. The purpose here is to discuss the validity of this belief.

Let us look into how jury instructions are traditionally written. Jury instructions traditionally are made up by each counsel in the case and then submitted to the judge. The judge then either agrees to read the proposed instructions or rejects them, with counsel having the right to object, thereby preserving his argument for appeal. In order to avoid reversals, judges often quote instructions given in appellate decisions or read the sets of instructions proposed by both counsels. It is to this latter practice of reading alternate forms of instructions that we turn our attention here. What sense is there in reading alternate forms of instructions to the same jurors? Our knowledge of linguistic and cognitive processes leads us to the conclusion that it makes no logical sense whatever.

In fact, such reading could have several effects. One, jurors could code different sets of instructions as having identical meaning and not distinguish between the alternate forms at all. People generally remember semantic information much better than grammatical or lexical information. We abstract the meanings in words, sentences, or paragraphs into larger holistic ideas. Psycholinguists have shown that memory for exact wording decays several seconds after the idea or the meaning of the sentence has been coded. As a result, people often mistake paraphrased versions of previously presented materials for the originals in recognition tasks (Anderson, 1974; Bransford *et al.*, 1972; Bransford & Franks, 1971, 1972; Bregman & Strasberg, 1968; Brent, 1969; Fillenbaum, 1966; Flores d'Arcais, 1974; Francis, 1972; Gamlin, 1968, 1971; Jarvella, 1971; Honeck, 1973; Olson, 1970; Paris & Carter, 1973; Perfetti & Garson, 1973; Sachs, 1967, 1974). It has also been shown that those ideas that are more deeply comprehended are most likely to be remembered later (Anderson, Goldberg, & Hidde, 1971; Mistler-Lachman, 1974; Wearing, 1972). Thus, it is possible for jurors to comprehend one of the alternative forms of instructions better than the other, and then to assume that the less well understood form is a paraphrased version of the better understood form. In such cases the distinctions intended by one counsel or the other will not be communicated.

A second possible effect of reading alternate forms of jury instructions to the same jury is that jurors will distinguish between them. The results in such cases will be that jurors will be confused as to which interpretation of the law is appropriate as a basis for a verdict. The additional length of instructions might also place an added strain on jurors' memories, and in turn create more confusion (see section on length of instructions). Alternate forms are often read as a fair solution to differences in legal opinions between lawyers and judges. If they create confusion, however, such practice is not fair either to the jurors or to the person(s) on trial.

In many jurisdictions there are two or more forms of the same instruction considered appropriate for presentation of the law on that issue. In this situation the alternate forms of the same instruction are considered to present the identical information; whether or not that is indeed the case is an open and empirical question. Clearly, the discussion on psycholinguistic variables indicates the problems that arise when we assume certain words and certain wordings are going to be synonymous in the mind of the juror and convey the same amount of information. Thus, this practice must be considered highly suspect. If litigants are to receive trials that are consistent in their procedure, differential results that might arise because of the use of different alternate forms can only be considered unjust.

Conclusion. The use of two alternate forms in the same instruction when the different attorneys believe they have different shades of meaning that are most beneficial to their side will often result in juror confusion and not necessarily in a more accurate weighing of the evidence in light of the law.

COMMENTARY AND SUMMARY OF EVIDENCE

As noted in the section on the status of jury instructions, several jurisdictions allow the judge to either comment on the evidence, summarize the evidence, comment and summarize the evidence, or do neither. The various combinations logically may have differential impact on a juror's decision-making ability to reach a verdict on the basis of the evidence presented at the trial and in light of the law. To the best of our knowledge these procedural variables have never been studied, although the potential for differential impact on the ultimate result of the trial is obvious.

Conclusion. A juror's ability to perceive, remember, comprehend, and utilize both the evidence and the substantive law should be significantly affected by a judge's comment and/or summary of the evidence.

LENGTH OF TRIAL

A jury's ability to interpret testimony in light of the law is dependent on its ability to remember testimony. People do not have perfect memories. It is therefore unreasonable to expect the jury to remember every bit of testimony presented in a case. To a great extent, the length of a trial will determine what percentage of the testimony will be remembered. This is another variable which should be dealt with in order to increase a jury's ability to come to a fair verdict.

There are literally thousands of studies using recognition and recall tasks showing that people forget information with the passage of time. It is such common knowledge that it is unnecessary to cite experimental research. Long trials put a strain on jurors' memories in two ways. First, long trials usually result from a large amount of testimony. The more material there is to remember, the less the chance that jurors will remember all of it. Second, long trials result in long time gaps between early testimony and the jury's deliberation, which may result in their forgetting tremendous amounts of information presented at the beginning of long trials.

The problem is not easy to solve. One possible solution is to make testimony readily available to jurors during their deliberation. A second possible solution is to increase the attentiveness with which jurors listen to testimony. Frequent rest breaks will not only avoid fatigue, but will also allow rehearsal of the most recently heard testimony; such rehearsal is bound to increase memory. Many researchers have found that material learned in small chunks will be remembered better (Bumstead, 1940; Gordon, 1925; Pechstein, 1918; Webb & Schwartz, 1959). A third possible solution is to make it easier for jurors to focus on relevant testimony by presenting them with instructions at the beginning of, during, and at the end of a trial, thus making it possible to select out and organize important testimony consciously.

Conclusion. The length of a trial will be an important variable to consider in terms of its effects on the amount of testimony a juror will remember. We have suggested possible manipulations to increase the amount of relevant information a jury will remember.

CONCLUSION

One of the most troublesome events in a jury trial is the judge's instructions on the law after the evidence has been presented. If the jury is to apply the law successfully to the facts of the case, the instructions must be delivered in language that is understandable to the average juror. Judges have often been criticized, however, for sacrificing juror understandability for legal accuracy to avoid reversal on appeal. This has caused commentators to use such terms as *ritual* and *mythical practice* when referring to the instruction process.

The adoption of pattern jury instructions has been viewed as a means for improving this situation. Touted as the greatest modern improvement in trial by jury, pattern instructions are intended to provide the judge with a concise, error-free statement of the law that is intelligible to the average juror.

Unfortunately, pattern instructions generally have been prepared in a manner that gives close attention to the legal accuracy but pays scant attention to juror understandability. Most drafting committees have been composed solely of lawyers and judges, and few committees have been willing to employ or seek the aid of experts to ensure that their instructions are phrased in more comprehensible language.

It is hoped that this chapter will provide drafting committees with sufficient information to allow them to appraise critically the comprehensibility of their instructions and rewrite them where necessary. This task is critically important if litigants are to receive a fair trial, since due process requires that each juror decide the case in light of the law and not in ignorance of it.

REFERENCES

Abelson, R. P., & Kanouse, D. E. Subjective acceptance of verbal generalizations. In S. Feldman (Ed.), *Cognitive consistency: motivational antecedents and behavior. consequents.* New York: Academic Press, 1966.

Alfini, J. *Pattern jury instructions.* Chicago: American Judicature Society, 1972.

Ames, W. S. The development of a classification scheme of contextual aids. *Reading Research Quarterly*, 1966, *2*, 57–82.

Anderson, J. R. Verbatim and propositional representation of sentences in immediate and long term memory. *Journal of Verbal Learning and Verbal Behavior*, 1974, *13*, 162–194.

Anderson, R. C., Goldberg, S. R., & Hidde, J. L. Meaningful processing of sentences. *Journal of Educational Psychology*, 1971, *62*, 395–399.

Anisfeld, N., & Knapp, N. E. Association, synonymity and directionality in false recognition. *Journal of Experimental Psychology*, 1968, *77*, 171–179.

Applicability of MAI instructions versus substantive law of Missouri. *University of Missouri-Kansas City Law Review*, 1970,*39*, 129–139.

Artley, A. S. Teaching word meanings through context. *Elementary English Review*, 1943, *20*, 68–74.

Bacharach, V. R., Kellas, G., & McFarland, C. E. Structural properties of transitive and intransitive verbs. *Journal of Verbal Learning and Verbal Behavior*, 1972, *11*, 486–490.

Baddeley, A. D., & Scott, D. Word frequency and the unit sequence interference hypothesis in short-term memory. *Journal of Verbal Learning and Verbal Behavior*, 1971, *10*, 34–40.

Balser, E. The free recall and category clustering of factual material presented in complex sentences. *Psychonomic Science*, 1972, *27*, 327–328.

Barlow, M. C., & Miner, L. E. Temporal reliability of length-complexity index, *Journal of Communication Disorders*, 1969, *2*, 241–251.

Barrie-Blackey, S. Six-year-old children's understanding of sentences adjoined with time adverbs. *Journal of Psycholinguistic Research*, 1973, *2*, 153–165.

Begg, I., & Paivio, A. Concreteness and imagery in sentence meaning. *Journal of Verbal Learning and Verbal Behavior*, 1969, *8*, 821–827.

Begg, I., & Robertson, R. Imagery and long term retention. *Journal of Verbal Learning and Verbal Behavior*, 1973, *12*, 689–700.

Begg, I., & Rowe, E. J. Continuous judgments of word frequency and familiarity. *Journal of Experimental Psychology*, 1972, *95*, 48–54.

Beighley, K. C. An experimental study of the effect of four speech variables on listener comprehension. *Speech Monographs*, 1952, *19*, 249–258.

Bloomer, R. H. Concepts of meaning and reading and spelling difficulty of words. *Journal of Educational Research*, 1961, *54*, 178–182.

Blount, H. P., & Johnson, R. E. Syntactic influences in the recall of sentences in prose. *Proceedings of the Annual Convention of the American Psychological Association*, 1971, *6 (pt. 2)*, 529–530.

Blumenthal, A. L. Observation with self-embedded sentences. *Psychonomic Science*, 1966, *6*, 453–454.

Borude, R. R. Immediate recall as a function of frequency of word usage. A replication. *Psychologia: An International Journal of Psychology in the Orient*, 1971, *14*, 184–186.

Boucher, J., & Osgood, C. W. The Pollyanna hypothesis. *Journal of Verbal Learning and Verbal Behavior*, 1969, *8*, 1–8.

Bousfield, W. A., & Cohen, B. H. The occurrence of clustering in the recall of randomly arranged words of different frequencies of usage. *Journal of General Psychology*, 1955, *52*, 83–95.

Bower, G. H., Clarke, N. C., Lesgold, A. M., & Winzenz, D. Hierarchical retrieval schemes in recall of categorized word lists. *Journal of Verbal Learning and Verbal Behavior*, 1969, *8*, 323–343.

Bowers, H. Memory and mental imagery. An experimental study. *British Journal of Psychology*, 1931, *21*, 271–282.

Bowers, H. Visual imagery and retention. *British Journal of Psychology*, 1932, *23*, 190–195.

Bransford, J. D., Barclay, J. R., & Franks, J. J. Sentence memory: A constructive versus interpretative approach. *Cognitive Psychology*, 1972, *3*, 192–209.

Bransford, J. D., & Franks, J. J. The abstraction of linguistic ideas. *Cognitive Psychology*, 1971, *2*, 331–350.

Bransford, J. D., & Franks, J. J. The abstraction of linquistic ideas: A review. *Cognition*, 1972, *1*, 211–249.

Bregman, A. S., & Strasberg, R. Memory for the syntactic form of sentences. *Journal of Verbal Learning and Verbal Behavior*, 1968, *7*, 396–403.

Brent, S. B. Linguistic unity, list length, and rate of presentation in serial anticipation learning. *Journal of Verbal Learning and Verbal Behavior*, 1969, *8*, 70–79.

Briggs, L. J. Sequencing of instructions in relation to hierarchies of competence. Pittsburg: American Institute of Research, 1968.

Broadbent, D. E. Word-frequency effect and response bias. *Psychological Review*, 1967, *74*, 1–15.

Brown, C. R., & Rubenstein, H. Test of response bias explanation of word-frequency effect. *Science*, 1961, *133*, 280-281.

Brown, R., Cazden, C., & Bellugi, V. The child's grammar from I to III. In J. P. Hill (Ed.), *Minnesota symposium on child psychology*. Minneapolis: University of Minnesota Press, 1969.

Bull, B. L., & Wittrock, M. C. Imagery in the learning of verbal definitions. *British Journal of Educational Psychology*, 1973, *43*, 289-293.

Bumstead, A. P. Distribution of effort in memorizing prose and poetry. *American Journal of Psychology*, 1940, *53*, 423-427.

Carroll, J. C. Process and content in psycholinguistics. In *Current trends in the description and analysis of behavior*. Pittsburgh Press, 1968. Pp. 175-200.

Carroll, J. B. Measurement properties of subjective magnitude estimates of word frequency. *Journal of Verbal Learning and Verbal Behavior*, 1971, *10*, 722-769.

Cermak, G., Schnorr, J., Buschke, H., & Atkinson, R. C. Recognition memory as influenced by differential attention to semantic and acoustic properties of words. *Psychonomic Science*, 1970, *19*, 79-81.

Champagnol, R. Genetic evolution of the reading speed of words in relation to their frequency. *Année Psychologique*, 1971, *71*, 407-416.

Clark, E. V. On the child's acquisition of antonyms in two semantic fields. *Journal of Verbal Learning and Verbal Behavior*, 1972, *11*, 750-758.

Clark, H. H. Some structural properties of simple active and passive sentences. *Journal of Verbal Learning and Verbal Behavior*, 1965, *4*, 365-370

Clark, H. H., & Begun, J. S. The semantics of sentence subjects. *Language and Speech*, 1971, *14*, 34-46.

Close, G. Theory and practice of standardized jury instructions. *Insurance Counsel Journal*, 1964, *31*, 490-497.

Cofer, C. N. On some factors in the organizational characteristics of free recall. *American Psychologist*, 1965, *20*, 261-272.

Cohen, J. Sensation and perception: I. Vision. *Eyewitness series in psychology*. Chicago: Rand McNally and Co., 1969.

Coleman, E. B. Learning of prose written in four grammatical transformations. *Journal of Applied Psychology*, 1965, *49*, 332-341.

Conrad, C. Context effects in sentence comprehension—a study of the subjective lexicon. *Memory and Cognition*, 1974, *2*, 130-138.

Corboy, P. H. Illinois system of instructing jurors in civil cases. *DePaul Law Review*, 1959, *8*, 141-164.

Corboy, P. H. Pattern jury instructions—their function and effectiveness. *Insurance Counsel Journal*, 1965, *32*, 57-65.

Corey, S. M. Learning from lectures and learning from reading. *Journal of Educational Psychology*, 1934, *25*, 459-470.

Cornish, E. R., & Wason, P. C. The recall of affirmative and negative sentences in an incidental learning task. *Quarterly Journal of Experimental Psychology*, 1970, *22*, 109-114.

Craik, F. I. M., & Lockhart, R. S. Levels of processing: A framework for memory research. *Journal of Verbal Learning and Verbal Behavior*, 1972, *11*, 671-684.

Cramer, P. Evidence for a developmental shift in the basis for memory organization. *Journal of Experimental Child Psychology*, 1973, *16*, 12-22.

Cunningham, T. J. Should instructions go into the jury room? *California State Bar Journal*, 1958, *33*, 278-289.

Cunningham, D. J. Task analysis and part versus whole learning methods. *AV Communication Review*, 1971, *19*, 365–398.

Dawley, L. T., & Dawley, H. H. Incidental and intentional learning of economic information in beginning typewriting. *Perceptual and Motor Skills*, 1974, *38*, 337–338.

Delin, P. S. The learning to criterion of a serial list with and without mnemonic instructions. *Psychonomic Science*, 1969, *16*, 169–170.

Dixon, T. R., & Dixon, J. F. The impression value of verbs. *Journal of Verbal Learning and Verbal Behavior*, 1964, *3*, 161–165.

Duchastel, P. C., & Brown, B. R. Incidental and relevant learning with instructional objectives. *Journal of Educational Psychology*, 1974, *66*, 481–485.

Duker, W. F., & Bastian, J. Recall of abstract and concrete words equated on meaningfulness. *Journal of Verbal Learning and Verbal Behavior*, 1966, *5*, 455–458.

Duncan, C. P. Storage and retrieval of low frequency words. *Memory and Cognition*, 1973, *1*, 129–132.

Efran, M. G. The effect of physical appearance on the judgment of guilt, interpersonal attraction, and severity of recommended punishment in a simulated jury task. *Journal of Research in Personality*, 1974, *8*, 45–54.

Emans, R. Context clues as an aid to the reader. *Journal of Typographic Research*, 1968, *2*, 369–373.

Enkvist, N. E. On defining style, In J. W. Spencer (Ed.), *Linguistics and style*. London: Oxford University Press, 1964. Pp. 3–56.

Eustace, B. W. Learning a concept at differing hierarchical levels. *Journal of Educational Psychology*, 1969, *60*, 449–452.

File, S. E., & Jew, A. Syntax and the recall of instructions in a realistic situation. *British Journal of Psychology*, 1973, *64*, 65–70.

Fillenbaum, S. Words as feature complexes: Fales recognition of antonyms and synonyms. *Journal of Experimental Psychology*, 1965, *70*, 122–129.

Fillenbaum, S. Memory for gist: Some relevant variables. *Language and Speech*, 1966, *9*, 217–227.

Fillenbaum, S. On coping with ordered and unordered conjuctive sentences. *Journal of Experimental Psychology*, 1971, *87*, 93–98.

Fishman, L., & Izzett, R. R. *The influence of a defendant's attractiveness and justification for his act on the sentencing tendencies of subject-jurors*. Paper presented at Midwestern Psychological Association, 1974.

Flesch, R. Measuring the level of abstraction. *Journal of Applied Psychology*, 1950, *34*, 384–390.

Flesch, R., & Lass, A. H. *A new guide to better writing*. New York: Popular Library, 1963.

Flores d'Arcais, G. B. *On handling comparative sentences*. Unpublished manuscript, Harvard University Center for Cognitive Studies, 1966.

Flores d'Arcais, G. B. Is there a memory for sentences? *Acta Psychologica*, 1974, *38*, 33–58.

Fodor, J., & Garrett, M. Some syntactic determinants of sentential complexity. *Perception and Psychophysics*, 1967, *2*, 289–296.

Fodor, J. M., Garrett, M., Bever, T. G. Some syntactic determinants of sentenial complexity. II: Verb Structure. *Perception and Psychophysics*, 1968, *3*, 453–461.

Forster, K. I., & Ryder, L. A. Perceiving the structure and meaning of sentences. *Journal of Verbal Learning and Verbal Behavior*, 1971, *10*, 285–296.

Foth, D. L. Mnemonic technique effectiveness as a function of word abstractness, and mediation instructions. *Journal of Verbal Learning and Verbal Behavior*, 1973, *12*, 239–245.

Fowler, A. L. Jury instructions: An appraisal by a defendant's attorney. *University of Illinois Law Forum*, 1963, 612–626.

Francis, H. Sentence structure and learning to read. *British Journal of Educational Psychology*, 1972, *42*, 113–119.

Frank, J. *Law and the modern mind*. New York: Brentano's, 1930.

Freedle, R., & Craun, M. Observations with self-embedded sentences using written aids. *Perception and Psychophysics*, 1970, *7*, 247–249.

Friend, R. M., & Vinson, M. Leaning over backwards—juror's responses to defendant's attractiveness. *Journal of Communication*, 1974, *24*, 124–129.

Gagne, R. M. *The conditions of learning* (2nd ed.). New York: Holt, Rinehart & Winston, 1970.

Gagne, R. M., & Brown, L. T. Some factors in the programming of conceptual learning. *Journal of Experimental Psychology*, 1961, *62*, 313–321.

Gagne, R. M., & Rohwer, W. D., Jr. Instructional psychology. *Annual Review of Psychology* (Vol. 20). Palo Alto, California: Annual Reviews, 1969.

Gamlin, P. M. The interaction of meaning and syntax in sentence comprehension. *Child Study*, 1968-69, *30*, 3–13.

Gamlin, P. J. Sentence processing as a function of syntax, short term memory capacity, the meaningfulness of the stimulus and age. *Language and Speech*, 1971, *14*, 115–134.

Gerver, D. Effects of grammaticalness, presentation rate, and message length on auditory short-term memory. *Quarterly Journal of Experimental Psychology*, 1969, *21*, 203–208.

Gibson, J. J. The senses considered as perceptual systems. Boston: Houghton Mifflin, 1966.

Gilson, C., & Abelson, R. P. The subjective use of inductive evidence. *Journal of Personality and Social Psychology*, 1965, *2*, 301–310.

Goldman-Eisler, F. Hesitation and information in speech. In C. Cherry (Ed.), *Information theory*. London: Butterworths, 1961.

Goldman-Eisler, F., & Cohen, M. Symmetry of clauses and the psychological significance of left branching. *Language and Speech*, 1971, *14*, 109–114.

Gordon, K. Class results with spaced and unspaced memorizing. *Journal of Experimental Psychology*, 1925, *8*, 337–343.

Gorman, A. M. Recognition memory for nouns as a function of abstractness and frequency. *Journal of Experimental Psychology*, 1961, *61*, 23–29.

Gough, P. B. Grammatical transformations and speed of understanding. *Journal of Verbal Learning and Verbal Behavior*, 1965, *4*, 107–111.

Gough, P. B. The verification of sentences: The effect of delay on evidence and sentence length. *Journal of Verbal Learning and Verbal Behavior*, 1966, *5*, 492–496.

Green, J. M. The semantic function of negatives and passives. *British Journal of Psychology*, 1970, *61*, 17–22.

Greeno, J. G., & Noreen, D. C. Time to read semantically related sentences. *Memory and Cognition*, 1974, *2*, 117–120.

Grieve, R., & Wales, R. J. Passives and topicalization. *British Journal of Psychology*, 1973, *64*, 173–182.

Griffitt, W., & Jackson, T. Simulated jury decisions: Influence of jury–defendant attitude similarity–dissimilarity. *Social Behavior and Personality*, 1973, *1*, 1–7.

Grossman, L., & Eagle, M. Synonymity, antonymity, and association in false recognition responses. *Journal of Experimental Psychology*, 1970, *83*, 244–248.

Gumenik, W. E., & Dolinsky, R. Effect of verb and object meaning on the connotative evaluation of sentence subject. *Journal of Experimental Psychology,* 1971, *87,* 436–438.

Gupton, T., & Frincke, G. Imagery, mediational instructions and noun position in free recall of noun verb pairs. *Journal of Experimental Psychology,* 1970, *86,* 461–462.

Hakes, D. T. Does verb structure affect sentence comprehension? *Perception and Psychophysics,* 1971, *10,* 229–232.

Hakes,D. T., & Cairns, H. S. Sentence comprehension and relative pronouns. *Perception and Psychophysics,* 1970, *8,* 5–8.

Hakes, D. T., & Foss, D. J. Decision processes during sentence comprehension: Effects of surface structure reconsidered. *Perception and Psychophysics,* 1970, *8,* 413–416.

Hall, J. F. Learning as a function of word-frequency. *American Journal of Psychology,* 1954, *67,* 138–140.

Hamilton, H. W., & Deese, J. Comprehensibility and subject verb relation in complex sentences. *Journal of Verbal Learning and Verbal Behavior,* 1971, *10,* 163–170.

Hannah, H. A. Jury instructions: An appraisal by a trial judge. *University of Illinois Law Forum,* 1963, 627–643.

Herriott, P. The comphrehension of sentences as a function of grammatical depth and order. *Journal of Verbal Learning and Verbal Behavior,* 1968, *7,* 938–941.

Hester, R. K., & Smith, R. E. Effects of a mandatory death penalty on the decisions of simulated jurors as a function of heinousness of the crime. *Journal of Criminal Justice,* 1973, *1,* 319–326.

Hogenraad, R. Disponibilité et fréquence du vocabulaire: Les adjectifs qualificatifs. *Année Psychologique,* 1969, *69,* 407–419.

Holborn, S. W., Gross, K. L., & Catlin, P. A. Effects of word frequency and acoustic similarity on free recall and paired associate recognition learning. *Journal of Experimental Psychology.* 1973, *101,* 169–174.

Holmes, V. M. Order of main and subordinate clauses in sentence perception. *Journal of Verbal Learning and Verbal Behavior,* 1973, *12,* 285–293.

Honeck, R. P. Semantic similarity between sentences. *Journal of Psycholinguistic Research,* 1973, *2,* 137–151.

Hornby, P. A. The psychological subject and predicate. *Cognitive Psychology,* 1972, *3,* 632–642.

Hultsch, D. F. Organization and memory in adulthood. *Human Development,* 1971, *14,* 16–29.

Huttenlocker, J., Eisenberg, K., & Strauss, S. Comprehension: Relation between perceived actor and logical subject. *Journal of Verbal Learning and Verbal Behavior,* 1968, *7,* 527–530.

Huttenlocker, J., & Strauss, S. Comprehension and a statement's relation to the situation it describes. *Journal of Verbal Learning and Verbal Behavior,* 1968, *7,* 300–304.

Institute for California judges-panel discussion part III: Instructing the jury. *California Law Review,* 1959, *47,* 888–903.

Jampolsky, M. Etude de quelques épreuves de reconnaissance. *Année Psychologique,* 1950, *49,* 63–97.

Jarvella, R. J. Syntactic processing of connected speech. *Journal of Verbal Learning and Verbal Behavior,* 1971, *10,* 409–416.

Jarvella, R. J., & Sinnott, J. Contextual constraints on noun distributions to English verbs by children and adults. *Journal of Verbal Learning and Verbal Behavior,* 1972, *11,* 47–53.

Jenkins, J. J., & Russell, W. A. Associative clustering during recall. *Journal of Abnormal and Social Psychology,* 1952, *47,* 818–821.

Johnson, R. C., Thompson, C. W., & Frincke, G. Word values, word frequency and visual duration thresholds. *Psychological Review*, 1960, *67*, 332–342.

Jones, C., & Aronson, E. Attribution of fault to a rape victim as a function of respectability of the victim. *Journal of Personality and Social Psychology*, 1973, *90*, 221–229.

Jones, S. The effect of a negative qualifier in an instruction. *Journal of Verbal Learning and Verbal Behavior*, 1966, *5*, 497–501.

Jurow, G. L. New data on the effect of a "death qualified" jury on the gulit determination process. *Harvard Law Review*, 1971, *84*, 567–611.

Just, M. A., & Carpenter, P. A. Comprehensions of negation with quantification. *Journal of Verbal Learning and Verbal Behavior*, 1971, *10*, 244–253.

Kalven, H., & Zeisel, H. *The American jury*. Boston: Little, Brown, 1966.

Kanouse, D. E. Verbs as implicit quantifiers. *Journal of Verbal Learning and Verbal Behavior*, 1972, *11*, 1141–1147.

Kaplan, M. F., & Kemmerick, G. D. Juror judgment as information integration: Combining evidential and nonevidential information. *Journal of Personality and Social Psychology*, 1974, *30*, 493–499.

Kaplan, R., & Rothkopf, E. Z. The effects of learning prose with parts vs. whole presentation of instructional objectives. *Proceedings of the 81st Annual Convention of the American Psychological Association, Montreal, Canada*, 1973, *8*, 627–628.

Kausler, D. H., & Settle, A. V. Associate relatedness vs. synonymity in the false recognition effect. *Bulletin of the Psychonomic Society*, 1973, *2*, 129–131.

King, M. L. I have a dream. Address delivered at the 1963 March on Washington, D.C. In B. Chambers, *Chronicles of black protest*. New York: Mentor Books, 1968.

Kirkpatrick, E. A. An experimental study of memory. *Psychological Review*, 1894, *1*, 602–609.

Klare, G. R. The role of word frequency in readability. In J. R. Bormuth (Ed.), *Readability, national conference on research in English*. New York: National Council of Teachers of English, 1968. Pp. 7–17.

Klenbort, I., & Anisfeld, M. Markedness and perspective in the interpretation of the active and passive voice. *Quarterly Journal of Experimental Psychology*, 1974, *26*, 189–195.

Klintman, H. Orthographic and frequency factors in verbal reaction time. *Psychological Research Bulletin*, 1968, *8*, 1–10.

Koenig, D. Personal correspondence. 1974.

Koeppel, J. C., & Beecroft, R. S. The conceptual similarity effect in free recall. *Psychonomic Science*, 1967, *9*, 213–214.

Kolers, P. A. Experiments in reading. *Scientific American*, 1972, *227*, 84–91.

Landauer, T. K., & Streeter, L. A. Structural differences between common and rare words: Failure of equivalence assumptions for theories or word recognition. *Journal of Verbal Learning and Verbal Behavior*, 1973, *12*, 119–131.

Landy, D., & Aronson, E. The influence of the character of the criminal and victim on the decisions of simulated jurors. *Journal of Experimental Social Psychology*, 1969, *5*, 141–152.

Langer, I., Schultz, T., & Tausch, R. Characteristics of intelligibility of written information and instruction texts. *Zeitschrift für Experimentelle und Angewandte Psychologie*, 1973, *20*, 269–286.

Lay, C. H., & Paivio, A. The effects of task difficulty and anxiety on heistations in speech. *Canadian Journal of Behavioral Science*, 1969, *1*, 25–37.

Lee, S. S. Transfer from lower-level to high level concepts. *Journal of Learning and Verbal Behavior*, 1968, *7*, 930–937.

Light, L. L., & Carter-Sobell, L. Effects of changed semantic context on recognition memory. *Journal of Verbal Learning and Verbal Behavior*, 1970, *9*, 1–11.

Lippman, M. Z. The influence of grammatical transform in a syllogistic reasoning task. *Journal of Verbal Learning and Verbal Behavior*, 1972, *11*, 424–430.

Loewenthal, K. Semantic features and communicability of words of different classes. *Psychonomic Science*, 1969, *17*, 79–80.

MacNamara, J., O'Cleirigh, A., & Kellaghan, T. The structure of the English lexicon: Simple hypothesis. *Language and Speech*, 1972, *15*, 141–148.

Mandler, G. Organization and memory. In K. W. Spence & S. R. Spence (Eds.), *The psychology of learning and motivation*. New York: Academic Press, 1966.

Marcel, A. J., & Steel, R. G. Semantic cueing in recognition and recall. *Quarterly Journal of Experimental Psychology*, 1973, *25*, 368–377.

Marks, C. B., Doctorow, M. J., & Wittrock, M. G. Word frequency and reading comprehension. *Journal of Educational Research*, 1974, *67*, 259–262.

Marks, L. E. Scaling of grammaticalness of self-embedded English sentences. *Journal of Verbal Learning and Verbal Behavior*, 1968, *7*, 965–967.

Marton, F. I., & Sandquist, G. Learning while typing. *Quarterly Journal of Experimental Psychology*, 1972, *24*, 287–290.

McBride, R. *The art of instructing the jury*. Cincinnati: W. H. Anderson, 1969.

McKenzie, J. C. Standardized instructions—panacea or problem? *Illinois Bar Journal*, 1957, *45*, 350–354.

McMahon, L. E. *Grammatical analysis as part of understanding a sentence*. Unpublished doctoral dissertation, Harvard University, 1963.

Mechanic, A. Effects of orienting task, practice, and incentive on simultaneous incidental and intentional learning. *Journal of Experimental Psychology*, 1962, *64*, 393–399.

Merrill, P. F. *Task analysis: An information processing approach*. Office of Naval Research, NR154- 280, Con. No. N00014-68-A-0494, 1971.

Meunier, G. F., Kestner, J., Meunier, J. A., & Ritz, D. Overt rehearsal and long term retention. *Journal of Experimental Psychology*, 1974, *102*, 913–914.

Miller, G. A. The magical number seven, plus or minus two: Some limits on our capacity of processing information. *Psychological Review*, 1956, *63*, 81–97.

Miller, G. A. Some psychological studies of grammar. *American Psychologist*, 1962, *17*, 748–762.

Miller, G., Bender, D., Florence, T., & Nicholson, H. Real versus reel: What's the verdict? *Journal of Communication*, 1974, *24*, 99–111.

Miller, G. A., & Isard, S. Free recall of self-embedded English sentences. *Information and Control*, 1964, *7*, 292–303.

Miller, J. F. Sentence imitation in preschool children. *Language and Speech*, 1973, *16*, 1–14.

Miner, L. E. Scoring procedures for the length complexity index: A preliminary report. *Journal of Communication Disorders*, 1969, *2*, 224–240.

Mistler-Lachman, J. L. Depth of comprehension or sentence memory. *Journal of Verbal Learning and Verbal Behavior*, 1974, *13*, 98–106.

Mitchell, H. E., & Byrne, D. The defendant's dilemma: Effect of juror's attitudes and authoritarianism on judicial decisions. *Journal of Personality and Social Psychology*, 1973, *25*, 123–129.

Mitchell, H. E., & Byrne, D. *Minimizing the influence of irrelevant factors in the courtroom: The defendant's character, judge's instructions, and authoritarianism*. Paper presented at Midwestern Psychological Association, 1973.

Morton, J. A retest of the response-bias explanation of the word-frequency effect. *British Journal of Mathematical and Statistical Psychology*, 1968, *21*, 21-33.

Murdock, B. B., Jr. The immediate retention of unrelated words. *Journal of Experimental Psychology*, 1960, *60*, 222-234.

Murray, D. J. Vocalization at presentation and immediate recall with varying methods. *Quarterly Journal of Experimental Psychology*, 1966, *18*, 9-18.

Naylor, J. C., & Briggs, G. E. Effects of task complexity and task organization on the relative efficiency of part and whole training methods. *Journal of Experimental Psychology*, 1963, *65*, 217-224.

Nelson, A. K., McRae, B. C., & Slurge, P. T. Recall as a function of instructions and trials. *Journal of Experimental Psychology*, 1971, *90*, 151-153.

Nemeth, C., & Sosis, R. H. A simulated jury study: Characteristics of the defendant and the jurors. *Journal of Social Psychology*, 1973, *90*, 221-229.

Noble, C. E. The familiarity-frequency relationship. *Journal of Experimental Psychology*, 1954, *47*, 13-16.

Norman, D. Human information processing. *Viewpoints*, 1971, *47*, 48-65.

Olson, D. R. Language and thoughts: Aspects of a cognitive theory of semantics. *Psychological Review*, 1970, *77*, 257-273.

Olson, D. R., & Filby, N. On the comprehension of active and passive sentences. *Cognitive Psychology*, 1972, *3*, 361-381.

Olver, M. A. *Abstractness, imagery and meaningfulness in recognition and free recall.* Unpublished master's thesis, University of Western Ontario, 1965.

O'Mara, J. Standard jury charges—findings of pilot project. *Pennsylvania Bar Association Quarterly*, 1972, *January*, 166-175.

O'Neill, B. J. Definability as an index of word meaning. *Journal of Psycholinguistic Research*, 1972, *1*, 287-298.

Orne, M. T. The nature of hypnosis: Artifact and essence, *Journal of Abnormal and Social Psychology.* 1959, *58*, 277-299.

Orne, M. T. On the social psychology of the psychological experiment: With particular reference to demand characteristics and their implications. *American Psychologist*, 1962, *17*, 776-783.

Orne, M. T. Communication by the total experimental situation. Why it is important, how it is evaluated, and its significance for the ecological validity of findings. In P. Pliner, L. Kramer, & T Alloway (Eds.), *Communication and affect: Language and thought.* New York: Academic Press, 1973.

Page, M. M. Effects of evaluation apprehension on cooperation in verbal conditioning. *Journal of Experimental Research in Personality*, 1971, *5*, 85-91.

Page, M. M. Demand characteristics and the verbal operant conditioning experiment. *Journal of Personality and Social Psychology*, 1972, *23*, 372-378.

Page, M. M. Effects of demand cues and evaluation apprehension in an attitude change experiment. *Journal of Social Psychology*, 1973, *89*, 55-62.

Paivio, A. *Imagery and verbal processes.* New York: Holt, Rinehart & Winston, 1971.

Paivio, A., & Madigan, S. A. Noun imagery and frequency in paired-associate learning. *Canadian Journal of Psychology*, 1970, *24*, 353-361.

Paivio, A., & O'Neill, B. J. Visual recognition thresholds and dimensions of word meaning. *Perception and psychophysics*, 1970, *8*, 273-275.

Paivio, A., Yuille, J. C., & Madigan, S. Concreteness, imagery, and meaningfulness values for 925 nouns. *Journal of Experimental Psychology Monograph Supplement*, 1968, *86*(1, pt. 2).

Paris, S. G., & Carter, A. Y. Semantic and constructive aspects of sentence memory in children. *Developmental Psychology*, 1973, *9*, 109-113.

Patty, R. A., & Page, M. M. Manipulations of a verbal conditioning situation based upon demand characteristics theory. *Journal of Experimental Research in Personality*, 1973, *6*, 307-313.

Pechstein, L. A. Whole versus part methods in learning nonsense syllables. *Journal of Educational Psychology*, 1918, *9*, 381-387.

Pechstein, L. A. The whole vs. part methods in learning: Comparison and summary. *Student Education* (Yearbook of the National Society of College Teachers and Educators), 1926, *15*, 181-186.

Perfetti, C. A. Sentence retention and the depth hypothesis. *Journal of Verbal Learning and Verbal Behavior*, 1969, *8*, 101-104.

Perfetti, C. A., & Garson, B. Forgetting linguistic information after reading. *Journal of Educational Psychology*, 1973, *65*, 136-140.

Perrin, P. G. *Writers guide and index to English*. Glenview: Scott, Foresman and Co., 1965.

Peterfalvi, J. M., & Locatelli, F. The acceptability of sentences. *Année Psychologique*, 1971, *71*, 417-427.

Peterson, M. J., & McGee, S. H. Effects of imagery instructions, imagery ratings and number of dictionary meanings upon recognition and recall. *Journal of Experimental Psychology*, 1974, *102*, 1007-1014.

Polzella, D. J., & Rohrman, N. L. Psychological aspects of transitive verbs. *Journal of Verbal Learning and Verbal Behavior*, 1970, *9*, 537-540.

Postman, L. Effects of word frequency on acquisition and retention under conditions of free-recall learning. *Quarterly Journal of Experimental Psychology*, 1970, *22*, 185-195.

Postman, L., & Adams, P. A. Studies in incidental learning: VI. Intraserial interference. *Journal of Experimental Psychology*, 1957, *54*, 153-167.

Prentice, J. Response strength of single words as an influence in sentence behavior. *Journal of Verbal Learning and Verbal Behavior*, 1966, *5*, 422-433.

Prettyman, D. Jury instructions-first or last? *American Bar Association Journal*, 1960, *46*, 1066.

Reed, H. B. Part and whole methods of learning. *Journal of Educational Psychology*, 1924, *15*, 107-115. (a)

Reed, H. B. Part and whole methods of learning. *Journal of Educational Psychology*, 1924, *15*, 389-493. (b)

Report of the Special Commission on the Social Sciences of the National Science Board. Washington, D.C.: National Science Foundation, 1969.

Reynolds, A. & Paivio, A. Cognitive and emotional determinants of speech. *Canadian Journal of Psychology*, 1968, *22*, 164-175.

Reynolds, D. E., & Sanders, M. S. *The effects of defendant attractiveness, age and injury on severity of sentence given by simulated jurors*. Paper presented at Western Psychological Association, 1973.

Roberts, K. H. Grammatical and associative constraints in sentence retention. *Journal of Verbal Learning and Verbal Behavior*, 1968, *7*, 1072-1076.

Rohrman, N. L. More on the recall of nominalizations. *Journal of Verbal Learning and Verbal Behavior*, 1970, *9*, 534-536.

Rosenthal, R. On the social psychology of the psychological experiment. The experimenter's hypothesis as unintended determinant of experimental results. *American Scientist*, 1963, *51*, 268-283.

Rosenthal, R. *Experimenter effects in behavioral research*. New York: Appleton-Century-Crofts, 1966.

Sachs, J. S. Recognition memory for syntactic and semantic aspects of connected discourse. *Perception and Psychophysics*, 1967, *2*, 437–442.

Sachs, J. S. Memory in reading and listening to discourse. *Memory and Cognition*, 1974, *2*, 95–100.

Salter, D., & Haycock, V. Two studies on the process of negative modification. *Journal of Psycholinguistic Research*, 1972, *1*, 337–348.

Sasson, R. Y. Semantic organizations and memory for related sentences. *American Journal of Psychology*, 1971, *84*, 253–267.

Savin, H. B., & Perchonock, E. Grammatical structure and the immediate recall of English sentences. *Journal of Verbal Learning and Verbal Behavior*, 1965, *4*, 348–353.

Schnorr, J. A., & Atkinson, R. C. Repetition versus imagery instructions in the short and long term retention of paired associates. *Psychonomic Science*, 1969, *15*, 183–184.

Segui, J., & Kail, M. The role of lexical verb characteristics in statement retention. *Année Psychologique*, 1972, *72*, 117–130.

Seliger, H. W. The discourse organizer concept as a framework for continued discourse practice in the language classroom. *IRAL: International Review of Applied Linguistics*, 1971, *9*, 195–207.

Sherman, M. A. Bound to be easier: The negative prefix and sentence comprehension. *Journal of Verbal Learning and Verbal Behavior*, 1973, *12*, 76–84.

Siegel, H. B. McLuhan, mass media, and education. *Journal of Experimental Education*, 1973, *41*, 68–70.

Sigall, H., & Ostrove, N. Effects of the physical attractiveness of the defendant and nature of crime on juridic judgment. *Proceedings of 81st Annual Convention of the American Psychological Association, Montreal, Canada*, 1973, *8*, 267–268.

Sigworth, H., & Henze, F. *Jurors' comprehension of jury instructions in southern Arizona.* Unpublished report prepared for the Committee on Uniform Jury Instructions of Supreme Court of the State of Arizona, 1973.

Skehan, P. *The relation of visual imagery to true-false judgment of simple sentences.* Unpublished master's thesis, University of Western Ontario, 1970.

Slobin, D. I. Grammatical transformation and sentence comprehension in childhood and adulthood. *Journal of Verbal Learning and Verbal Behavior*, 1966, *5*, 219–227.

Slobin, D. I. Recall of full and truncated passive sentences in connected discourse. *Journal of Verbal Learning and Verbal Behavior*, 1968, *7*, 876–881.

Slobin, D. I. *Psycholinguistics.* Glenview: Scott, Foresman and Co., 1971.

Smith, G. P. II. Orthodoxy versus reformation in the jury system. *Judicature*, 1968, *51*, 344–346.

Smith, R. C., & Dixon, T. R. Effects of exposure: Does frequency determine the evaluative connotations of words. *Journal of Experimental Research in Personality*, 1971, *5*, 124–126. (a)

Smith, R. C., & Dixon, T. R. Frequency and judged familiarity of meaningful words. *Journal of Experimental Psychology*, 1971, *88*, 279–281. (b)

Solomon, R. L., & Postman, L. Frequency of usage as a determinant of recognition thresholds for words. *Journal of Experimental Psychology*, 1952, *43*, 195–201.

Standardized jury instructions. *University of Pennsylvania Law Review*, 1949, *98*, 223–230.

Stark, K. Synonym responses to 100 free association stimuli. *Psychonomic Monograph Supplements*, 1972, *4*, 269–274.

Stoke, S. M. Memory for onomatopes. *Journal of Genetic Psychology*, 1929, *37*, 594–596.

Stolz, W. S. A study of the ability to decode grammatically novel sentences. *Journal of Verbal Learning and Verbal Behavior*, 1967, *6*, 867–873.

Strunk, W., Jr., & White, E. B. *The elements of style* (2nd ed.). New York: Macmillan, 1972.

Tannenbaum, P. H., & Williams, F. Generation of active and passive sentences as a function of subject or object focus. *Journal of Verbal Learning and Verbal Behavior,* 1968, *7,* 246-250.

Tell, P. M., & Ferguson, A. M. Influence of active and passive vocalization on short term recall. *Journal of Experimental Psychology,* 1974, *102,* 347-349.

Tennyson, R. D. A review of experimental methodology in instructional task sequencing. *AV Communication Review,* 1972, *20,* 147-159.

Thorndike, E. L., & Lorge, I. *The teacher's word book of 30,000 words.* New York: Bureau of Publications, Teachers College, 1944.

Tulving, E., McNulty, J. A., & Ozier, M. Vividness of words and learning to learn in free recall learning. *Canadian Journal of Psychology,* 1963, *66,* 319-327.

Turner, E. A., & Rommetveit, R. Focus of attention in recall of active and passive sentences. *Journal of Verbal Learning and Verbal Behavior,* 1968, *7,* 543-548.

Underwood, B. J. False recognition produced by implicit verbal responses. *Journal of Experimental Psychology,* 1965, *70,* 1, 122-129.

Underwood, B. J. The representatives of rote verbal learning. In A. W. Melton (Ed.), *Categories of human learning.* New York: Academic Press, 1964.

Vidmar, N. Effects of decision alternatives on the verdicts and social perceptions of simulated jurors. *Journal of Personality and Social Psychology,* 1972, *22,* 211-218. (a)

Vidmar, N. *Group-induced shifts in simulated jury decisions.* Paper presented at Midwestern Psychological Association, 1972. (b)

Walster, E. Assignment of responsibilty for an accident. *Journal of Personality and Social Psychology,* 1966, *3,* 73-79.

Wang, M. D. The role of syntactic complexity as a determiner of comprehensibility. *Journal of Verbal Learning and Verbal Behavior,* 1970, *9,* 398-404.

Wason, P. C. The processing of positive and negative information. *Quarterly Journal of Experimental Psychology,* 1959, *11,* 92-107.

Wason, P. C. Response to affirmative and negative binary statements. *British Journal of Psychology,* 1961, *52,* 133-142.

Wason, P. C. The contexts of plausible denial. *Journal of Verbal Learning and Verbal Behavior,* 1965, *4,* 7-11.

Wearing, A. J. The storage of complex sentences. *Journal of Verbal Learning and Verbal Behavior,* 1970, *9,* 398-404.

Wearing, A. J. Remembering complex sentences. *Quarterly Journal of Experimental Psychology,* 1972, *24,* 77-86.

Wearing, A. J. The recall of sentences of varying length. *Australian Journal of Psychology,* 1973, *25,* 155-161.

Webb, W. B., & Schwartz, M. Measurement characteristics of recall in relation to the presentation of increasingly large amounts of material. *Journal of Educational Psychology,* 1959, *50,* 63-65.

Winnick, W. A., & Kressel, K. Tachistoscopic recognition thresholds, paired associate learning, and immediate recall as a function of abstractness, concreteness, and word frequency. *Journal of Experimental Psychology,* 1965, *70,* 163-168.

Winograd, E., & Geis, N. F. Semantic encoding and recognition memory—a test of encoding variability theory. *Journal of Experimental Psychology,* 1974, *102,* 1061-1068.

Winograd, E., Karchmer, M. A., & Russell, I. S. Role of encoding unitization in cued recognition memory. *Journal of Verbal Learning and Verbal Behavior*, 1971, *10*, 199–206.

Winslow, R. L. The instructions ritual. *Hastings Law Journal*, 1962, *13*, 456–473.

Wolk, S. The influence of meaningfulness upon intentional and incidental learning of verbal material. *Memory and Cognition*, 1974, *2*, 189–193.

Wolk, S., & Du Cette, J. Monetary incentive effects upon incidental learning during an instructional task. *Journal of Educational Psychology*, 1974, *66*, 90–95.

Wright, P. Transformations and the understanding of sentences. *Language and Speech*, 1969, *12*, 156–166.

Yngve, V. A. A model and a hypothesis for language structure. *Proceedings of the American Philosophical Society*, 1960, *104*, 444–466.

Young, R. Q. A comparison of reading and listening comprehension with rate of presentation controlled. *AV Communication Review*, 1973, *21*, 327–336.

Yuille, J. C., & Paivio, A. Abstractness and recall of connected discourse. *Journal of Experimental Psychology*, 1969, *82*, 467–471.

Zajonc, R. B. The attitudinal effects of mere exposure. *Journal of Personality and Social Psychology Monograph Supplement*, 1968, *9*, (pt. 2), 1–27.

Zerdy, G. A. Incidental retention of recurring words presented during auditory monitoring tasks. *Journal of Experimental Psychology*, 1971, *88*, 82–89.

BIBLIOGRAPHY

Published Jury Instructions

Abbott, E. L., & Solomon, E. S., eds. 1962. *Instructions for Virginia and West Virginia*. 2nd ed. Charlottesville: Michie Company.

Alexander, G. J. 1953. *Jury instructions on medical issues*. Indianapolis: Burdette, Smith and Company.

Alexander, J. P. 1953. *Mississippi jury instructions*. St. Paul: West Publishing Company.

American Bar Association Section of Antitrust Law. 1965. Committee on Practice and Procedure. Subcommittee on Criminal Prosecution. *Jury instructions in criminal antitrust cases: A compilation of instructions given by United States district courts, 1923–1964*. Chicago: American Bar Association.

Arizona Supreme Court and Arizona State Bar on Uniform Jury Instructions Combined Committee. 1974. *Arizona uniform jury instructions*.

Arkansas Supreme Court Committee on Jury Instructions. 1974. *Arkansas model jury instructions: Civil*. Rev. ed. St. Paul: West Publishing Company.

Baker, H. A. 1966. Illinois pattern instructions on eminent domain. 1966. University of Illinois Law Forum, 174–179.

Bar Association of the District of Columbia. 1966. *Criminal jury instructions for the District of Columbia*. Washington, D.C.: J. L. Ward Company.

Bar Association of the District of Columbia. 1963. *Revised standardized jury instructions for the District of Columbia*. Washington, D.C.: J. L. Ward Company.

Bar Association of the District of Columbia. 1968. *Standardized jury instructions for the District of Columbia*. Rev. ed. Washington, D.C.: Lerner Law Book Company.

Bar Association of Hawaii Committee on Standard Jury Instructions: Criminal. *Hawaii standard jury instructions*. Honolulu: Supreme Court of Hawaii, undated.

Beasley, I. 1966. Pattern charges. 27 *Alabama Lawyer*, 181–192.

Boardman, R. 1964. Pattern jury instructions. 40 *North Dakota Law Review*, 164–172.

Branson, E. R. 1952. *The law of instructions to juries: Rules and approved annotated criminal forms.* Military ed. Indianapolis: Bobbs-Merrill.

Brown, the Hon. Lyle. 1967. Jury instructions: Issues; burden of proof; rules of the road; wilful and wanton conduct; imputed negligence; specific factors affecting negligence and defenses. 21 *Arkansas Law Review*, 104–109.

Chicago Bar Association. 1948. *Standardized jury instructions.* Chicago: Chicago Bar Association.

Colorado Supreme Court Committee on Pattern Jury Instructions. 1969. *Colorado Jury instructions: Civil.* San Francisco: Bancroft-Whitney Company.

Colorado Supreme Court Committee on Uniform Criminal Jury Instructions. 1972. *Colorado jury instructions: Criminal.* Denver: The Printer.

Conway, J. E. 1959. *Wisconsin model jury instructions.* Madison: University of Wisconsin.

Davidson, L. G. 1957. Pattern jury instructions. 45 *Illinois Bar Journal*, 406–418.

Devitt, E. J. 1966. Ten practical suggestions about federal instructions. 38 *Federal Rules Decisions*, 75–79.

Dooley, J. A. 1963. Jury instructions: An appraisal by a plaintiff's attorney. 1963 *University of Illinois Law Forum*, 586–611.

Doubles, M. R., Emroch, E., & Merhige, R. R., Jr. 1964. *Virginia Jury Instructions.* St. Paul: West Publishing Company.

Dowsey, the Hon. J. L. 1968. *Charges to the jury and requests to charge in a criminal case in New York.* 2 vols. Amityville: Acme Law Book Company.

Erisman, F. 1956. *Manual of reversible errors in Texas criminal cases, with suggested instructions to juries.* Longivew: Law Book Publishing Company.

Fess, L. 1952–1953. *Ohio instructions to juries: A treatise on th law of Ohio pertaining to instructions to juries in civil and criminal cases.* Cincinnati: W. H. Anderson Company.

Florida Supreme Court Committee on Standard Jury Instructions. 1970. *Florida standard jury instructions.* Rev. ed. Tallahassee: The Florida Bar Association.

Ford, R., & Clemens, A. 1959. *Trial judges manual of charges.* 3rd ed. Buffalo: Dennis Company.

Haines, the Hon. Edson L. 1968. Criminal and civil jury charges. 46 *Canadian Bar Review*, 48–95.

Hemphill, V. 1951. *Illinois jury instructions: An authoritative forms work with explanatory text and notes.* Chicago: Burdette-Smith Company.

Hodges, G. M. 1959. *Special issue submission in Texas.* Austin: University of Texas Law School Foundation.

Illinois Judicial Conference Committee on Pattern Jury Instructions in Criminal Cases. 1968. *Illinois pattern jury instructions: Criminal.* Chicago: Burdette-Smith Company.

Illinois Supreme Court Committee on Jury Instructions. 1971. *Illinois pattern jury instructions: Civil.* 2nd ed. Chicago: Burdette-Smith Company.

Indiana Judges Association. 1966. *Indiana pattern jury instructions.* Indianapolis: Bobbs-Merrill Company.

Iowa State Bar Association Special Committee on Uniform Court Instructions. 1970. *Revised Iowa uniform jury instructions, annotated.* Des Moines: Iowa State Bar Association.

Joint Committee of the North Dakota Judicial Council and State Bar Association of North Dakota. 1966. *North Dakota jury instructions: Civil and criminal.* Bismarck: State Bar Association of North Dakota.

Jones, W. B. 1953. *Alabama jury instructions with forms.* St. Paul: West Publishing Company.

Kalven, H., Jr. 1960. Work on the Illinois supreme court committee on jury instructions—the elimination of instructions. 9 *University of Chicago Law School Record,* 21, 53–57.

Kansas District Judges Association Committee on Pattern Jury Instructions. 1966. *Pattern jury instructions for Kansas.* San Francisco: Bancroft-Whitney Company.

Kansas District Judges Association Committee on Pattern Jury Instructions. 1971. *Pattern instructions for Kansas: Criminal.* Topeka: R. Sanders, State Printer.

Lottick, C. R., & Ricketts, W. D. 1951. *Indiana instructions to juries in civil cases: Approved and suggested forms.* Indianapolis: Bobbs-Merrill Company.

Los Angeles County Superior Court. 1969. *California jury instructions: Civil.* 5th rev. ed. St. Paul: West Publishing Company.

Los Angeles County Superior Court. 1970. *California jury instructions: Criminal.* 3rd rev. ed. St. Paul: West Publishing Company.

Mathes, W. C., & Devitt, E. J. 1965. *Federal jury practice and instructions.* St. Paul: West Publishing Company.

McBride, the Hon. Robert L. 1969. Standardized jury instructions. 112 *Pittsburgh Legal Journal,* 3–7.

McBride, the Hon. Robert L. 1969. The evil of drifting in jury instructions. 8 *Trial Judges Journal,* 13–14, January.

McClung, P. T. 1959. *Jury charges for Texas criminal practice.* Fort Worth, Texas.

Michie Company editorial staff. 1954. *Instructions: The law and approved forms for Florida.* Charlottesville: Michie Company.

Michigan Supreme Court Committee on Standard Jury Instructions. 1970. *Michigan standard jury instructions: Civil.* Ann Arbor: Institute of Continuing Legal Education.

Minnesota District Judges Association Committee on Jury Instruction Guides. 1963. *Minnesota jury instructions guides: Civil.* St. Paul: West Publishing Company.

Missouri Supreme Court Committee on Jury Instructions. 1969. *Missouri approved jury instructions.* 2nd ed. St. Paul: West Pulishing Company.

Montana Judges Association. 1966. *Montana jury instructions guide.* Montana Judges Association.

Nebraska Supreme Court Committee on Pattern Jury Instructions. 1969. *Nebraska jury instructions.* St. Paul: West Publishing Company.

New Mexico Supreme Court Committee on Uniform Jury Instructions. 1966. *New Mexico uniform jury instructions: Civil.* St. Paul: West Publishing Company.

New York Association of Supreme Court Justices Committee on Pattern Jury Instructions. 1965. *New York pattern jury instructions: Civil.* Rochester: Lawyers' Co-Op.

Nevada State Bar Association. 1966. *Nevada pattern civil jury instructions.* Reno: Nevada State Bar Association.

North Carolina Conference of Superior Court Judges, Committee on Pattern Jury Instructions. 1973. *North Carolina pattern jury instructions for criminal cases.* Raleigh, N.C.: North Carolina Conference of Superior Court Judges and the North Carolina Bar Foundation.

North Dakota Judicial Council and the State Bar Association of North Dakota Joint Committee. 1966. *North Dakota jury instructions: Civil and criminal.* Bismarck: State Bar Association of North Dakota.

Ohio Judicial Conference. 1968. *Ohio standard jury instructions.* Cincinnati: W. H. Anderson Company.

Oregon State Bar Committee on Procedure and Practice. 1966. *Oregon jury instructions for civil cases.* Portland: Oregon State Bar.

Oregon State Bar Committee on Unfirm Jury Instructions. 1966. *Oregon jury instructions in criminal cases.* Portland: Oregon State Bar.

Page, B. 1956. Utah uniform jury instructions. 5 *Utah Law Review,* 149–157.

Palmer, W. J. 1951. Patterns for jury instructions. 29 *Canadian Bar Review,* 256–265.

Palmer, W. J. 1939. Standardized jury instructions succeed. 23 *Journal of the American Judicature Society,* 177–180.

Richardson, J. R. 1954. *Florida jury instructions.* St. Paul: West Publishing Company.

Seventh Circuit Judicial Conference Committee on Jury Instructions. 1965. *Manual on jury instructions in federal criminal cases.* St. Paul: West Publishing Company.

Sinetar, R. J. 1968. A belated look at CALJIC. 43 *California State Bar Journal,* 546–55.

Smith, W. J. 1963. *Tennessee jury instructions: Civil cases.* Charlottesville: Michie Company.

Smith, W. J. 1965. *Tennessee jury instructions: Criminal cases.* Charlottesville: Michie Company.

Snyder, G. C. 1960. Illinois pattern jury instructions. 49 *Illinois Bar Journal,* 230–242.

Snyder, G. C. 1960. Jury instructions revolutionized. 42 *Chicago Bar Record,* 105–111.

Snyder, G. C. 1964. Pattern instructions. 20 *Missouri Bar Journal,* 53–64.

Speiser, S. M. 1961. *Negligence jury charges.* Brooklyn: Central Book Company.

Stanley, O. W. 1957. *Instructions to juries in Kentucky: A treatise on the law relating to instructions to juries in civil and criminal cases.* 2nd ed. Cincinnati: W. H. Anderson Company.

State Bar of South Dakota Committee on Pattern Jury Instructions. 1963. *South Dakota pattern jury instructions: Civil.* Pierre: State Bar of South Dakota.

State Bar of South Dakota Committee on Pattern Jury Instructions. 1970. *South Dakota jury instructions: Criminal.* Pierre: State Bar of South Dakota.

Stevens, G. N. 1966. Pattern jury instructions: Some suggestions on use and the problem of presumptions. 41 *Washington Law Review,* 282–296.

Stottle, B. S. 1962. A step forward in jury instructions. 18 *Journal of the Missouri Bar,* 354–360.

Symposium. 1966. Arkansas model jury instructions. 20 *Arkansas Law Review,* 61–92.

Texas State Bar Pattern Jury Charges Committee. 1969. *Texas pattern jury charges.* Vol. 1 Austin: State Bar of Texas.

Utah State Bar. 1957. *Committee on jury instruction forms for Utah.* Reno:Utah State Bar.

Washington Supreme Court Committee on Pattern Jury Instructions. 1967. *Washington pattern jury instructions: Civil.* St. Paul: West Publishing Company.

Wiehl, L. L. 1961. Instructing a jury in Washington. 36 *Washington Law Review,* 378–406.

Willamette University College of Law. The Willamette Series of Legal Handbooks. 1948–1959. *Instructions to juries as commented upon by the supreme court of Oregon.* Salem: Willamette University.

Wisconsin Board of Circuit Judges Committee on Jury Instructions. 1960. *Wisconsin jury instructions: Civil.* Madison: University of Wisconsin.

Wisconsin Borad of Criminal Court Judges Committee on Jury Instructions. 1962. *Wisconsin jury instructions: Criminal.* Madison: University of Wisconsin.

Wright, D. B. 1960. *Connecticut jury instructions.* 2nd ed. Hartford: Atlantic Law Book Company.

Yerkes, M. S. 1959. Standardized instructions in California. 5 *St. Louis University Law Journal,* 347–355.

3

Dangerousness

SOME DEFINITIONAL, CONCEPTUAL, AND PUBLIC POLICY ISSUES

SALEEM A. SHAH

The administration of criminal justice and related coercive interventions in the lives of citizens present most starkly the many important issues concerning the proper balance between use of the state's authority and power and the rights of individuals. We see exemplified here, as well as in "civil" commitments of the mentally ill, the perennial and fundamental question: Under what circumstances is the state justified in using its power to infringe the liberty of the individual (Allen, 1964; Hart, 1963)?

This paper will focus on the concept of "dangerousness" as it is used, or even misused, in the involuntary commitment of persons officially labeled as mentally ill. Although civil commitment codes in many jurisdictions involve considerations of both dangerousness to self and dangerousness to others, this discussion will be limited to the subject of dangerousness to others. It might be noted, however, that the notion of dangerousness to others is also invoked in some other so-called civil (as contrasted with criminal) commitments, namely, the special and quasi-criminal proceedings pertaining to persons classified as "sexual psychopaths," "sexually dangerous persons," and "defective delinquents" (see, e.g., Brakel & Rock, 1971).

SALEEM A. SHAH • Center for Studies of Crime and Delinquency, National Institute of Mental Health, Rockville, Maryland. This chapter is an expanded version of a paper given at the Law-Psychology Conference, University of Nebraska-Lincoln, October 16-17, 1975.

Since any involuntary deprivation of liberty raises very serious philosophical, public policy, and legal questions, understandably there is much controversy about the precise circumstances that justify such uses of state power, and also about the various safeguards that should be provided. Yet, although there has been considerable judicial scrutiny of criminal laws and procedures in reference to various constitutional questions, issues regarding the involuntary confinement of the mentally ill have traditionally received little attention by the courts. Indeed, only in the past decade has there been much judicial concern with the "massive curtailment of liberty"[1] associated with the commitment of persons involuntarily confined under various civil proceedings, namely, juveniles, sexual psychopaths, and the mentally ill.

A fundamental thesis of this chapter is that the long-standing and continued confusion of *parens patriae* and police power functions of the state with regard to the involuntary commitment of the mentally ill seems to serve the latent purpose of avoiding and disguising the real social control objectives for which such commitments are often used. However, as the logic and reasoning in such landmark cases as *Kent*,[2] *Gault*,[3] and *Winship*[4] have been extended in recent years to the civil proceedings of concern in our discussion, a wider range of procedural due process safeguards are beginning to be accorded. To paraphrase what the Supreme Court pointed out in *Gault* with respect to juveniles, there appears to be a belated recognition that the condition of being mentally ill "does not justify a kangaroo court."[5]

Nevertheless, despite increasing attention to greater procedural due process protections, the courts continue to display a singular avoidance of more basic and *substantive* due process issues involved in the involuntary confinement of the mentally ill on grounds of their presumed dangerousness to others. This discussion will therefore call attention to the fact that while the mentally ill are singled out for preventive detention because of their presumed dangerousness to others, individuals and groups who pose much more obvious and demonstrable dangerousness to others do *not* evoke similar concerns about protecting society.

---

[1] *Humphrey* v. *Cady*, 405 U.S. 508, 509 (1972).

[2] *Kent* v. *United States*, 383 U.S. 541 (1966).

[3] *In re Gault*, 387 U.S. 1 (1967).

[4] *In re Winship*, 397 U.S. 358 (1970).

[5] See note 3 above, at 28.

The discussion begins by emphasizing the critical importance of separating—analytically, conceptually, and in actual practice—the *parens patriae* and police power functions involved in commitment of the mentally ill. Brief reference is then made to a five-point analytic framework which stresses the need for asserted societal values and goals to be supported by appropriate rules and practices. This framework is designed to indicate linkages needed to facilitate better accountability. Then follows a discussion of several problems pertaining to the manner in which key terms and concepts (i.e., *mental illness* and *dangerousness*) are defined and conceptualized in commitment codes. Finally, and perhaps most importantly, several public policy issues and problems are discussed with reference to commitments of the mentally ill based on the police power authority of the state. Although many questions can and indeed are being raised about justifications for involuntary commitment of the mentally ill premised on *parens patriae* objectives, this presentation focuses on police power commitments because these are not founded on care-giving objectives and thus the analytic and public policy problems are clearer and more readily demonstrated. This discussion seeks to demonstrate that the coercive confinement of the mentally ill on presumptions of their dangerousness to others simply does *not* comport with fundamental notions of "what is fair and right and just."[6]

THE CONFUSION OF *PARENS PATRIAE* AND POLICE POWER FUNCTIONS

It would be accurate to say that a great deal of ambiguity, confusion, and societal hypocrisy have for very long typified the commitment and handling of the mentally ill. The most glaring problem pertains to the confusion of the remedial, therapeutic, and care-giving (i.e., *parens patriae)* responsibilities of the state, and the state's obligation and duty to protect the community from danger and harm (i.e., its police power functions). While the former functions may be viewed as involving a moral responsibility of the state, the latter clearly involve an inherent duty.[7]

[6] Justice Felix Frankfurter, in his dissenting opinion in *Solesbee* v. *Blakcom*, 339 U.S. 9, 16 (1950).

[7] See, e.g., S. A. Shah, Crime and mental illness: Some problems in defining and labelling deviant behavior, 53 *Mental Hygiene* 21 (1969); S. A. Shah, Some interactions of law and mental health in the handling of social deviance, 23 *Catholic University Law*

Broadly speaking, there are three major functions of commitment codes for the mentally ill: (1) to provide care and treatment for persons "gravely disabled" as a result of serious mental illness; (2) to prevent danger and harm to oneself as a result of mental disorder, e.g., when manifested by suicidal attempts or by a seriously impaired ability to meet one's basic and essential needs; and (3) to prevent danger to others as a function of an individual's mental disorder. (It has also been suggested that a fourth, but typically unstated and even embarrassing, function exists for the commitment of the mentally ill, namely, to remove from sight persons who make the community uncomfortable [Chambers, 1972].)

The first two objectives of involuntary commitment relate quite clearly to the *parens patriae* responsibilities of the state[8] (although some police power functions are also referred to when seeking to protect persons from endangering their own welfare).[9] However, it is quite obvious that commitments based on the desire to protect others from danger involve primarily and essentially the state's use of its police power. Yet, very typically, commitment codes do *not* make clear distinctions between these two criteria for commitment. Lumping together of the analytically distinct criteria pertaining to dangerousness to self and dangerousness to others is also demonstrated in judicial opinions.[10] As a result, very important substantive and related procedural differences between these two commitment criteria tend to be thoroughly confounded in legislation and in judicial opinions. And, when questions are raised about adequate procedural safeguards for persons facing involuntary confinement in order to protect the community (i.e., police power commitments), it has been easy to

---

Review 674 (1974); Developments in the law—civil commitment of the mentally ill, 87 *Harvard Law Review* 1190, 1207–1212, 1222–1228 (1974) (hereinafter cited as *Developments*).

[8] *Developments*, note 7 above, at 1222–1224.

[9] For example, states employ their police power to prevent people from buying obscene materials, narcotics, and other legislatively prohibited materials. Similarly, certain beneficial measures for individuals are also compelled by the states (e.g., obtaining vaccinations) and to prohibit harmful actions (e.g., riding a motor cycle without a helmet). See, *Developments*, note 7 above, at 1223–1224.

[10] Some significant exceptions do seem to be occurring. See, e.g., *Lynch* v. *Baxley*, 386 F.Supp. 378, 390–392 (1974), where the court noted: "Although dangerousness to self and dangerousness to others are frequently considered together, it is clear that they actually represent quite different state interests. Commitment on account of dangerousness to others serves the police power, while commitment for dangerousness to self partakes of the *parens patriae* notion that the state is the ultimate guardian of those of its citizens who are incapable of caring for their own interests" (at 390).

fudge and to avoid the critical issue by referring to the benevolent *parens patriae* purposes also stated in the statute. Such practices have impeded the development of more forthright and accountable rules and practices which could more clearly relate both substantive and procedural constitutional safeguards to the separate *parens patriae* and police power purposes.[11]

Very desirably, however, the courts have increasingly been rejecting many of the distinctions that have been made between "civil" and "criminal" proceedings even when both could lead to deprivation of liberty. For example, several recent cases have held that a variety of procedural protections must be provided in civil commitment proceedings, e.g., proper notice, right to a hearing, right to counsel, right to be present at hearings, trial by jury, a more demanding standard of proof, written record of the proceedings to facilitate later review, privilege against self-incrimination, consideration of less restrictive alternatives, durational limits on the period of confinement, and more frequent periodic reviews of the person's continuing need for hospitalization.[12] However, it must be emphasized that there are wide variations with respect to the extent to which the above safeguards are required and actually provided in different jurisdictions. For example, even after *Kent*,[13] *Gault*,[14] *Winship*,[15] and *Specht* v. *Patterson*,[16] a state court could still say the following with regard to commitment of the mentally ill: "[P]ersons may be deprived of their liberty for the good of society or themselves. This is not a deprivation of due process of law, but a temporary restraint on liberty, based on the extent of the illness, the need for treatment and hospitalization, as well as the protection of

[11] See also: D. B. Wexler, *Criminal Commitments and Dangerous Mental Patients: Legal Issues of Confinement, Treatment, and Release.* DHEW Publication No. (ADM) 76-331. Washington, D.C.: U.S. Government Printing Office, 1976.
[12] See, e.g., *Lessard* v. *Schmidt*, 349 F.Supp. 1078 (E.D. Wis. 1972), vacated and remanded on other grounds, 414 U.S. (per curiam), modified, 379 F. Supp. 1376 (1974); *Heryford* v. *Parker*, 396 F.2d 393 (10th Cir. 1968); *Bell* v. *Wayne County General Hospital*, 384 F.Supp. 1085 (1974); *Lynch* v. *Baxley*, note 10 above; *State ex rel. Hawks* v. *Lazaro*, 202 S.E. 2d 190 (1974); *Kendall* v. *True*, 391 F.Supp. 413 (1975).
[13] *Kent*, note 2 above, where the Court said: "But the admonition to function in a 'parental' relationship is not an invitation to procedural arbitrariness" (at 555).
[14] *Gault*, note 3 above, where the Court remarked: "Under our Constitution, the condition of being a boy does not justify a kangaroo court" (at 28).
[15] *Winship*, note 4 above.
[16] *Specht* v. *Patterson*, 386 U.S. 605 (1967). This case involved an indeterminate sentence under Colorado's Sex Offender's Act, a so-called civil proceeding. The court pointed out: "These commitment proceedings whether denominated civil or criminal are subject both to the Equal Protection Clause of the Fourteenth Amendment as we held in *Baxstrom* v. *Herold*, 383 U.S. 107, and to the Due Process Clause" (at 608).

society."[17] This statement illustrates very well the manner in which *parens patriae* and police power criteria get lumped together.

A discussion of the various state laws pertaining to the commitment and handling of the mentally ill is beyond the scope of our discussion. For further information in this area the reader is referred to Brakel and Rock (1971) and to the more recent and excellent discussion in the *Harvard Law Revies*.[18] However, since amendments of commitment codes have been continuing apace and very significant revisions have taken place in the last few years, a few of these changes will be noted in subsequent sections of this chapter.

AN ANALYTIC FRAMEWORK TO FACILITATE ACCOUNTABILITY

It has been suggested that numerous and glaring discrepancies are to be found between asserted goals and objectives with respect to commitment of the mentally ill and actual procedures and practices. Elsewhere it has been pointed out that societal systems which permit and even facilitate immense discrepancies between stated intentions and actual practices serve to bring about and even to *institutionalize* societal hypocrisy.[19] In order to have more forthright handling of societal needs and problems it is essential that structures and mechanisms be developed to facilitate better accountability.

Five basic questions provide the essential analytic framework against which societal practices can be evaluated:

1. *What are the fundamental societal values to be protected, the major goals to be attained, and the social harms to be avoided?* These basic values are reflected in broad policy statements, various constitutional provisions (e.g., the Bill of Rights), and in proclamations of legislative purpose and intent.

2. *How clearly have goal values been articulated into policy objectives with appropriate rules to facilitate their implementation?* At this level of analysis it is necessary to ascertain the extent to which the rules (e.g., statutes and administrative regulations) provide a precise and specific reflection of the broad goal values, whether they facilitate proper understanding of the underlying policy objectives, and whether they are formulated in a manner which allows ready implementation.

3. *Have necessary and appropriate resources been allocated to allow attainment of the proclaimed goal values and policy objectives?* The real

[17] *State v. Sanchez*, 457 P.2d 370, 373 (N.M. 1969).
[18] *Developments*, note 7 above.
[19] Shah, 1974, note 7 above.

and true importance of professed values and the sincerity of stated policy objectives can much better be assessed in terms of the resources actually provided than by the extravagance of the rhetoric used to proclaim such benevolent intentions. When the necessary means required for policy implementation are substantially lacking, the values and goals upon which social practices are to be based must be questioned and even challenged. Lacking corrective procedures, hypocrisies will tend to be maintained and public attitudes toward important social values and institutions will tend to be weakened and cynicism generated.

4. *Have appropriate and effective provisions been made to monitor practices and to evaluate compliance with the asserted policy objectives and rules?* Regular, or at the very least periodic, evaluation is essential in order to facilitate better accountability. Lacking meaningful and effective systems to monitor the actual functioning of various social agencies and institutions, the discrepancies between stated goals and actual practices will tend to continue and may increase. Also, we will lack information about the extent to which programs are actually achieving stated policy objectives and goals.

5. *Have appropriate sanctions been provided to encourage compliance with rules and policies and to discourage noncompliance?* Clearly, monitoring systems will have relatively little effect without provision for corrective feedback. Stated differently, unenforced or unenforceable laws and rules will tend to become meaningless. It is essential, therefore, to develop legally proscribed contingencies that will encourage enforcement and provide disincentives and sanctions for noncompliance.

The purpose of the above analytic scheme is simply to provide a framework against which some of our current practices with respect to involuntary commitment of the mentally ill under the police power can generally be analyzed and evaluated.

Broderick (1971) has pointed out that if the basic object of a legal system in a society is to achieve the "idea of justice" for its members, then its success at any given moment *cannot* be measured simply by the values it professes or by the constitutional or legal rules to which it merely pays lip service. Rather, success must be measured in terms of actual achievements, and effective means must be established for repeated evaluations of performance. Failure to take an interest in such matters must surely call into question the sincerity of the professed values and related objectives. And, when social institutions are found to be clearly dysfunctional in reference to professed values and policy objectives, society must either be honest enough to abandon the professed values or, at the very least, modify the relevant institutions and practices to bring them closer to the reality which it wishes to preserve.

SOME DEFINITIONAL ISSUES AND PROBLEMS

Two important concepts that require clarification in commitment codes are *mental illness* and *dangerousness*. As indicated earlier, our concern with the latter concept will be limited to dangerousness toward others.

A critical initial point is that when they appear in various commitment statutes and other laws, the term *mental illness* and the associated concept of *dangerousness to others* have an essentially *legal* meaning. Accordingly, when used in such legal contexts these are *not* medical, psychiatric, or psychological terms, and neither should their interpretation devolve exclusively, or even mainly, on such experts. Whether or not the nature and degree of mental disorder meet the requisite statutory definition of *mental illness* and *dangerousness* should be determined by the triers of fact.[20] However, as the result of the judicial default that commonly occurs, in practice the "experts" often make such crucial legal and public policy determinations.[21]

There is another fundamental point. In order to allow clear and reliable understanding and interpretations of statutory provisions, whether by courts, attorneys, experts, or administrative bodies, it is essential that the key terms and provisions find precise articulation in laws and related regulations. Moreover, explicit statements of legislative intent and purpose are also needed in order to facilitate reliable (i.e., consistent) interpretations of the law.

A major and common problem, however, is that commitment codes rather typically fail to provide statements of intent and purpose. Neither does one find very clearly articulated definitions of key terms. A review of most commitment laws would lead one to agree with Chambers that "the states have articulated [the] purpose [of commitment] through statutory language murkier than the riddles of the witches of Macbeth (Chambers, 1972, p. 1119).

---

[20] See, e.g., *United States* v. *Spaulding*, 293 U.S. 498, 506 (1935); *Washington* v. *United States*, 312 F.2d 847, 850–851 (1962). See also: *Cross* v. *Harris*, 418 F.2d 1095, 1100–1101 (1967).

[21] Shah, 1974, note 7 above, at 681–685, 689–690.

This statutory murkiness is certainly not a function simply of the imprecision of the basic terms and concepts. It is quite evident that lawmakers seem to have no similar difficulty in providing clear statutory definitions and language in other areas, e.g., in the criminal law. Rather, and as suggested by the aforementioned analytic framework, the possibility of judicial findings of "void for vagueness" appears to provide contingencies that influence the drafting skills of legislators. Yet, since we are discussing here situations in which "massive curtailment of liberty" can result through legal proceedings premised on police power objectives, it is most unfortunate that the need for much greater statutory precison has not been apparent to lawmakers and has not elicited stricter judicial scrutiny.

A few examples of statutory definitions of the terms *mental illness* and *dangerousness* will serve to illustrate some remarkably vague and inadequate definitions, while other examples will illustrate much better definitions. No effort has been made to undertake a thorough review of all state commitment codes; rather, the illustrations are taken from those few laws that have been studied for this particular purpose.

MENTAL ILLNESS

The examples that follow indicate some vague and inadequate definitions:

1. "Mentally ill person includes each person afflicted by mental disease to such extent that he requires care and treatment for his own welfare or the welfare of others or of the community, and specifically excludes a person whose sole psychiatric disorder is drug dependence."[22]

2. "The term 'mental illness' as used in this chapter includes every type of mental disease or mental disorder."[23]

3. "'(M)entally ill' or 'mentally ill person' as used in this act, include every species of insanity and extend to every mentally deranged person, and to all of unsound mind, other than mentally handicapped, epileptics, and persons who manifest the general deterioration of mental processes, including disorientation, confusion or

[22] Conn. Gen. Stat. Ann. 17–176, 1958.
[23] Iowa Code Ann. 229.40, 1971.

impairment of memory, associated with senility, but without psychotic implications."[24]

4. "The term mentally ill, as used in this act, shall include persons suffering from any type of mental illness whatsoever, whether hereditary or acquired by internal or external conditions, diseases, narcotics, alcoholic beverages, accident, or any other condition or happening."[25]

In the past few years there have been a number of revisions of several state commitment codes; many of these revisions provide marked improvements in definitions of key terms and in various other provisions.

The 1971 revision of the Massachusetts law does not itself provide a definition of *mental illness*, but a detailed definition is provided in the administrative regulations development by the Massachusetts Department of Mental Health. The relevant definition reads as follows:

> Involuntary commitment of a person to a mental health facility under the provisions of M.G.L. ch. 123 requires a finding that failure to hospitalize such person would create the likelihood of serious harm by reason of mental illness. For purposes of involuntary commitment "mental illness" shall mean a substantial disorder of thought, mood, perception, orientation, or memory which grossly impairs judgment, behavior, capacity to recognize reality, or ability to meet the ordinary demands of life, but shall not include alcoholism which is defined in M.G.L. ch. 123 s. 35.[26]

The recent revision of the Montana commitment laws (effective as of July 1, 1975) provides an explicit statement concerning the *purpose*

---

[24] Mich. C.L.A. 330.54, 1967. Recently, the standard of commitment for mental illness under this old law was attacked as impermissively vague and overbroad. A three-judge district court agreed with the plaintiff on this issue, noting: "Thus, we must conclude that in M.C.L.A. §330.21 and §330.54, the Michigan act sets forth a process under which a person whose affliction, in the view of a given court, falls anywhere within a vast, uncontoured description of mental ills, is subject to both temporary and indefinite commitment, whether his particular ill presents a realistic threat of harm to himself or to others. In our opinion, the standard of commitment for mental illness is fatally vague and overbroad" (*Bell* v. *Wayne County General Hospital*, 348 F.Supp. 1085, 1096, 1974). However, the revised Michigan law is vastly improved and became effective on August 6, 1974.

For other instances in which certain provisions of state commitment laws have been held to be unconstitutional because of vagueness, see: *State ex rel. Hawks* v. *Lazaro* and *Kendall* v. *True*, note 12 above.

[25] Neb. Rev. Stat. 83–306 (3), 1966. [Just as this manuscript was being typed it was learned that this commitment law has been found to be unconstitutional by a three-judge district court for a number of reasons, cf. *Doremus* v. *Farrell*, 407 F.Supp. 509 (D. Neb. 1975).]

[26] Dept. of Mental Health Regulations, Title 4, ch. 2, Sec. 200.01—Mental Illness.

of the act:

> The purpose of this act is: (1) to secure for each person who may be
> seriously mentally ill or suffering from a mental disorder such care and
> treatment as will be suited to the needs of the person, and to insure that
> such care and treatment are skillfully and humanely administered with full
> respect for the person's dignity and personal integrity; (2) to deprive a
> person of his liberty for purposes of treatment or care only when less
> restrictive alternatives are not available and only when his safety or the
> safety of others is endangered, and to provide for due process of law when
> this is done.[27]

Judicial (involuntary) commitment in Montana requires a finding
that the person is "seriously mentally ill," and this term is defined as
follows:

> "Seriously mentally ill" means suffering from a mental disorder which has
> resulted in self-inflicted injury or injury to others, or the imminent threat
> thereof; or which has deprived the person afflicted of the ability to protect
> his life or health. No person may be involuntarily committed to a mental
> health facility nor detained for evaluation and treatment because he is an
> epileptic, mentally deficient, mentally retarded, senile or suffering from a
> mental disorder unless the condition causes the person to be seriously
> mentally ill within the meaning of this act.[28]

It is noteworthy that this revision of the Montana code, in
addition to providing a clearly articulated statement of purpose and a
clear definition of key terms, also requires explicit consideration of
less restrictive alternatives and spells out several procedural due
process rights. The statute also indicates that the standard of proof for
involuntary commitment shall be "proof beyond a reasonable doubt."

Dangerousness to Others

The examples provided above indicate that even in recent revisions of commitment codes, *parens patriae* and police power functions
continue to be confounded. Most jurisdictions which allow involuntary commitment only if the individual is mentally ill and dangerous
to himself or others, or is unable to care for his physical needs,[29]
express the dangerousness standard simply by referring to the likelihood that the individual will injure or harm himself or others. The

[27] Montana Session Laws, ch. 466, Sec. 38-1301, 1975.
[28] Ibid., ch. 466, Sec. 38–1302 (13), 1975.
[29] *Developments*, note 7 above, at 1203, note 11.

1974 revision of the Arizona code, however, provides a more detailed definition of *dangerousness*. And, even more importantly, it provides separate definitions of *danger to others* and *danger to self*.

> "Danger to others" means behavior which constitutes a danger of inflicting substantial bodily harm upon another person based upon a history of having inflicted or having attempted to inflict substantial bodily harm upon another person within twelve months preceding the hearing on court order treatment. . . .[30]

> "Danger to self" means behavior which constitutes a danger of inflicting substantial bodily harm upon oneself, including attempted suicide. Danger to self is not present if the hazards to self are restricted to those which may arise from conditions defined under grave disability.[31]

The 1971 revision of the Massachusetts statute also provides a fairly detailed and precise definition of *likelihood of serious harm*:

> . . . (1) a substantial risk of physical harm to the person himself as manifested by evidence of threats of, or attempts at, suicide or serious bodily harm; (2) a substantial risk of physical harm to other persons as manifested by evidence of homicidal or other violent behavior or evidence that others are placed in reasonable fear of violent behavior and serious physical harm to them; or (3) a very substantial risk of physical impairment or injury to the person himself as manifested by evidence that such person's judgment is so affected that he is unable to protect himself in the community and that reasonable provision for his protection is not available in the community.[32]

The impressive improvements reflected in the 1974 revision of the Rhode Island Mental Health Law provide yet another example of better definitions of the relevant dangerousness criteria:

> "Likelihood of serious harm" means (1) a substantial risk of physical harm to the person himself as manifested by behavior evincing serious threats of, or attempts at, suicide or by behavior which will result in serious bodily harm; (2) a substantial risk of physical harm to other persons as manifested by behavior or threats evidencing homicidal or other violent behavior.[33]

Similarly improved definitions are also to be found, for example, in the revised commitment laws of Maine, Washington, and West

[30] Ariz. Rev. Stat. Ann. ch. 36–501, 3, 1974.
[31] Ibid., ch. 36–501, 4, 1974.
[32] Mass. Gen. Laws, ch. 123, Sec. 1, 1971.
[33] Rhode Island Gen. Laws Ann. ch. 5, 40.1-5-2 (14), 1974.

Virginia. These recent improvements provide clear evidence that only a lack of interest, sensitivity, and judicial prodding have been reflected in the very vaguely worded laws of yesteryear. Nevertheless, there remains the problem of lumping together the *parens patriae* and police power aspects of commitment codes. Ideally, the developing statutory trend toward making distinctions between dangerousness to self and dangerousness to others will progress further toward distinctions with respect to both substantive and procedural due process considerations.

JUDICIAL INTERPRETATIONS

Issues pertaining to vaguely formulated commitment codes could further be illustrated by reference to some judicial interpretations of these provisions.[34] However, such analysis would take us too far afield for purposes of the present discussion. What will be noted is the very useful analytic framework for judicial interpretations that was provided some years back by the United States Court of Appeals for the District of Columbia in cases involving the District's sexual psychopath law.

In 1962 Maurice Millard pleaded guilty to indecent exposure, was subsequently adjudicated as a "sexual psychopath," and was committed for an indeterminate period to Saint Elizabeth's Hospital. In reviewing a subsequent denial of Millard's *habeas corpus* petition, the court of appeals noted that the statute required that "dangerous conduct not be merely repulsive or repugnant but must have serious effect on the viewer."[35]

Two years later, and after more than 6 years of involuntary confinement for an offense for which the maximum criminal penalty would have been imprisonment for 90 days or a $300 fine, or both, Millard again sought his release and once again appealed the denial of his *habeas corpus* petition. In a noteworthy second decision the court of appeals provided an analytic framework for assessing *dangerousness* which deserves wide attention:

> Predictions of dangerousness, whether under the Sexual Psychopath Act or in some other context, require determinations of several sorts: the type of conduct in which the individual may engage; the likelihood or probability

[34] Some brief illustrations are provided in S. A. Shah, Dangerousness and civil commitment of the mentally ill: Some public policy considerations, *American Journal of Psychiatry*, 1975, *132*, 501–502.
[35] *Millard v. Cameron*, 373 F.2d 468, 471 (1966).

that he will in fact indulge in that conduct; and the effect such conduct if engaged in will have on others. Depending on the sort of conduct and effect feared, these variables may also require further refinement.[36]

A few months later in another case involving the District's Sexual Psychopath Act,[37] the same court made some further comments of interest. In this case (*Cross v. Harris*) the offense was also indecent exposure. The court noted that "a finding of 'dangerousness' must be based on a high probability of substantial injury."[38] The court referred to the analytic framework provided in *Millard* to guide lower courts in applying the conclusory term *dangerous to others*, and noted:

> Without some such framework, "dangerous" could readily become a term of art describing anyone whom we would, all things considered, prefer not to encounter on the streets. We did not suppose that Congress had used "dangerous" in any such Pickwickian sense. Rather, we supposed that Congress intended the courts to refine the unavoidably vague concept of "dangerousness" on a case-by-case basis, in the traditional common-law fashion.[39]

The court then proceeded to analyze the case at hand in reference to the aforementioned framework and emphasized that it was

> . . . particularly important that courts not allow this second question [of likelihood of harm] to devolve by default, upon the expert witnesses. Psychiatrists should not be asked to testify, without more, simply whether future behavior or threatened harm is "likely" to occur. For the psychiatrist "may—in his own mind" be defining "likely" to mean anything from virtual certainty to slightly above chance. And his definition will not be a reflection of any expertise, but . . . of his own personal preference for safety or liberty.[40]

This section of the discussion may be concluded by reiterating the point that vagueness and imprecision of terminology tend to typify the vast majority of commitment codes. Considering the fact that "massive curtailment of liberty" is involved in police power based commitments of the mentally ill, it is noteworthy that lawmakers display an odd inability to draft the precisely formulated statutes that typify other police power situations, e.g., criminal laws. Such poorly

---

[36] *Millard* v. *Harris*, 406 F.2d 964, 973 (1968).
[37] *Cross* v. *Harris*, 418 F.2d 1095 (1969).
[38] Ibid., at 1097.
[39] Ibid., at 1099.
[40] Ibid., at 1100–1101, footnotes eliminated.

articulated statutes lead predictably to vagaries and inconsistencies of interpretation. Moreover, loosely worded laws allow an undesirable degree of flexibility and are therefore more vulnerable to the biases and discretion of decision-makers. And, since medical and psychiatric experts typically play a key role in commitment proceedings, vague terms and related provisions allow—even invite—these experts to use their own particular values and preferences in making the relevant legal decisions.

SOME CONCEPTUAL ISSUES AND PROBLEMS

A major problem in efforts to assess, predict, prevent, and treat dangerous behavior pertains to the manner in which behavior is conceptualized. Behavior—be it socially defined as dangerous, peaceful, constructive, or antisocial—is often viewed as stemming largely if not entirely from within the individual, that is, as derived from his personality. Such a conceptualization tends to view behavior as a fairly enduring, consistent, and even persistent characteristic of an individual. Moreover, not only are specific behavioral acts evaluated and labeled as "dangerous," but the related assumption is often made that such samples of behavior are fairly typical of the individual. Hence, through a conceptual short-cut, first certain aspects of an individual's *behavior* are defined as dangerous, and then the *individual himself* comes to be viewed and labeled as dangerous. This, or course, may be misleading and also unnecessarily stigmatizing since physically violent or other dangerous acts are usually rather infrequent, occur in specific situational contexts, and may not be representative of the individual's customary behavior.[41]

It is very important that behavior be viewed and conceptualized in reference to its particular social, situational, and environmental context. Stated differently, behavior should be viewed as involving interactions between the individual (including aspects of his physical and psychological state at a given time) and a particular physical and social environment. Various characteristics of the environment may well exert major influence on the form, frequency, magnitude, and range of likely behaviors. Some situational factors may tend to elicit, facilitate, and even provoke certain behaviors; other setting-related factors may tend to have an inhibiting and suppressive effect on certain behaviors. Similarly, certain violent or other deviant acts may occur only in certain state-dependent situations for a particular indi-

[41] Shah, 1974, note 7 above, at 677–679.

vidual. For example, it is well known that consumption of alcoholic beverages tends to be a facilitating factor in a wide range of criminal and related dangerous acts (see, e.g., Mulvihill & Tumin, 1969; Voas, 1973). Thus, to the extent that certain behaviors are known to be state-dependent, better prevention and regulation of the particular state (e.g., alcoholic intoxication) can provide a means for controlling the associated behaviors.

What is being suggested, in essence, is that efforts to understand, evaluate, predict, prevent, and treat an individual's violent or other "dangerous" behavior should not concentrate *solely* upon discovering or uncovering aspects of an individual's personality and psychodynamics. It is also very important to give very careful attention to the particular physical and social environment and the situational contexts in which certain types of behaviors are displayed, as well as the extent to which such environmental and situational factors might increase the probability of such behaviors being displayed again in the future.

VALUES, POWER, AND THE DEFINITION AND HANDLING OF "DANGEROUSNESS"

There is a final conceptual and also public policy issue which should be noted here. The definition and handling of "dangerous" behavior are very much influenced by the power structures that exist in a society. For example, dangerous persons with economic means and social influence are not very often to be found in institutions for sexual psychopaths, defective delinquents, and other types of involuntarily committed mental patients.

Also, our society tends to impose preventive detention most readily on persons who can be labeled as mentally ill and then are presumed to pose a danger to themselves or others. Many other individuals and groups that clearly pose greater and more readily demonstrated dangers to society (e.g., drunken drivers and persons convicted of felonious crimes against person) do *not* seem to evoke similar concerns about the use of preventive detention to protect the community from danger.[42]

[42] See, e.g., Shah, 1974, note 7 above, at 706–709 and related footnotes.

Schwitzgebel found in 1969 that fully 47 states, including the District of Columbia, had statutes pertaining to habitual offenders, and 28 of these jurisdictions provide indeterminate sentences. It is not known, however, how often these laws are actually used in these various jurisdictions. R. K. Schwitzgebel, *Development and Legal Regulation of Coercive Behavior Modification Techniques with Offenders*. National Institute of Mental Health, Public Health Service Publication No. 2067. Washington, D.C.: U.S. Government Printing Office, 1971, at 24, and Appendix B, at 70–71.

Moreover, our society tends to focus attention more readily on "dangerous" acts of *individuals* than on *social conditions* and *practices* that pose serious hazards to the health, safety, and physical well-being of literally millions of citizens each year, e.g., industrial practices and working conditions which pose serious and preventable hazards of several occupational diseases. For example, in 1972, *The President's Report on Occupational Safety and Health* (1972) indicated that total deaths annually from job-related injuries were estimated to be over 14,000, with an estimated 2.2 million disabling injuries. The incidence of occupational disease is less well known but estimates pointed to "at least 390,000 new cases of disabling occupational diseases each year." It was also estimated by the president's report that there may be as many as 100,000 deaths per year from occupationally caused diseases (p. 111).

Obviously, not all nor perhaps even the majority of such industrial deaths, diseases, and injuries can be avoided. Rather, the point is whether in light of available knowledge of the known dangers from certain occupational hazards, our lawmakers and relevant governmental agencies have done all that they should to reduce such danger and lethality in our society? The information provided in several recent reports suggests that "violence in the work place" has to a large extent and until rather recently escaped serious attention. Moreover, violations by industries of what are considered by many to be rather inadequate safety standards tend to be handled by regulatory agencies with remarkable tolerance and with "kid gloves."[43]

Such tolerance and not-so-benign neglect of the above sources of danger to others stands out in vivid contrast to the long-standing practice of committing the mentally ill. It seems evident that consider-

---

[43] See, e.g., D. Hunter, *The Diseases of Occupation* (London: English Universities Press, 1970); J. A. Page, & M. O'Brien, *Bitter Wages* (New York: Grossman, 1973); P. Brodeur, *Expendable Americans* (New York: Dutton, 1974); D. A. Schanche, Vinyl Chloride: Time bomb on the production line, *Today's Health*, 1974, 52, 16; W. Greene, Life vs. livelihood. *The New York Times Magazine*, Nov. 24, 1974, 17.

Greene writes about the epic struggle between environmental health and economic values in the continuing and immensely costly litigation pertaining to the discharge into Lake Superior by the Reserve Mining Company of ground taconite rock. This ground rock contains particles virtually identical to amosite asbestos—a cancer-causing agent. The issues in this case, both scientific and legal, are very complex. And, as Greene notes, scientific proof is complicated by the fact that it takes 20 to 30 years from the time of initial exposure for asbestos-caused cancer to begin to take its toll. A very profound issue of law is also at stake, namely, ". . . whether full scientific and legal proof of a suspected health threat to a large population is needed before a court can halt the hazard, or whether the probabilities that are the rough terrain of medical science's frontiers will legally serve to avert a potential calamity before irrefutable, corporal proof is established" (at 17).

ations of economic and political power provide much of the explanation for such striking differences in societal efforts to protect the community from serious harm and danger.[44]

SOME PUBLIC POLICY ISSUES

The focus of attention in this section will be upon public policy questions and considerations pertaining to situations in which the police power doctrine is or may properly be invoked to protect the community against the mentally ill. Even though the discussion will include some concepts that have technical legal meanings and interpretations, my concern as a nonlawyer will not be with legal technicalities, but with more general and fundamental notions of equity, fairness, and justice.

It has correctly been pointed out that issues pertaining to the coercive confinement of the mentally ill are much too important to be left only to mental health experts. Similarly, even though fraught with legal questions, such basic issues pertaining to situations that justify deprivations of a person's liberty are much too important to be left only to lawyers.

A basic theme of this discussion has been that *if* the police power of the state is properly to be used for preventive detention of the mentally ill, then, with respect to this exercise of the police power, there should certainly be provided legal procedures and safeguards which conform closely to procedures and safeguards that have been established in uses of the criminal law. The making available of treatment to the committed mental patient, or the provision of various remedial and rehabilitative programs to the incarcerated offender, does *not* alter the fact that the primary purpose of the deprivation of liberty is to protect the community. Thus, in the case of police power commitments of the mentally ill, the full panoply of procedural due process safeguards should be provided and durational limits for the period of confinement established, and it should be required that

[44] In testifying before the House Select Subcommittee on Labor, on May 22, 1974, Paul Brodeur, author of *Expendable Americans,* (note 45 above), made the following statement: ". . . I submit that if a million people in the so-called middle class or professional class were dying each decade of preventable occupational disease, and if nearly four million were being disabled, there would long ago have been such a hue and cry for remedial action that if the Congress had not heeded it vast numbers of its members would have been turned out of office" (as quoted in *Expendable Americans,* p. 274).

"dangerousness to others" be demonstrated by recent overt acts or clearly evident attempts—and *not* merely be presumed. We should note, however, that the requirement of a recent overt act or attempt will *not* solve the basic problems relating to accurate predictions of future dangerous behaviors since, even with such a prior history, very high rates of "false positive" errors will still be expected.[45] To guard against making errors which could result in infringements of an individual's constitutional right to liberty, the applicable standard of proof should certainly be proof beyond a reasonable doubt.[46]

The criminal process provides us with the clearest case where curtailment of liberty is based upon the police power authority of the state. However, the criminal process is initiated only *after* the individ-

---

[45] Even though a requirement of prior and recent overt acts demonstrating dangerous behavior would certainly be preferable to other more vague requirements, empirical studies suggest that even when a history of prior violence is actually present, in every 19 out of 20 times a prediction of future violence will be *incorrect* (i.e., would involve "false positive" errors). E. A. Wenk, J. O. Robison, & G. W. Smith, Can violence be predicted? 18 *Crime and Delinquency* 393, 399-400 (1972). See also, J. M. Livermore, C. P. Malmquist, & P. E. Meehl, On the justifications for civil commitment, 117 *University of Pennsylvania Law Review* 75, 76-77 (1968).

[46] Several courts have required this standard of proof in various "civil" commitment proceedings. See, e.g., *In re Winship*, note 6 above; *Lassard*, note 14 above; *In re Ballay*, 482 F.2d 648 (1973); *United States ex rel. Stachulak* v. *Coughlin*, 520 F.2d 931 (1975).

In *Winship* the Supreme Court pointed out that "the accused during a criminal prosecution has at stake interest of immense importance, both because of the possibility that he may lose his liberty upon conviction and because of the certainty that he would be stigmatized by the conviction" (at 1072). Since mentally ill persons facing police power commitments certainly have a similar "interest of immense importance," because both the loss of liberty and stigmatizing social reactions are the possible consequence of such adjudications, the logic for requiring a very high standard of proof is indicated in order to reduce as much as possible the risk of erroneous deprivations of liberty.

In *Stachulak* the Court noted: "If the disparate opinions of psychiatrists and the vagaries of proof and prediction suggest anything, it is the desirability of the utmost care in reaching the commitment decision" (at 936).

Yet, the courts in *Hawks* v. *Lazaro* and *Lynch* v. *Baxley*, note 14 above, recommend a lower standard of proof ("clear, cogent, and convincing," and "clear, unequivocal, and convincing," respectively), citing the problems of "subjective judgments" and the "inexactitudes of medical science." The logic here is difficult to follow, given the fact that the *error to be avoided* still pertains to inappropriate deprivations of liberty. One would think that, as the degree of reliability and certainty of the evidence *decreases*, the necessity to avoid errors that could lead to deprivations of liberty should commensurately *increase*. Therefore, *higher*—not lower—standards of proof must be required precisely *because* subjective factors, the "inexactitudes of medical science," increase the unreliability of such evidence. This reasoning certainly applies when an insanity defense is invoked to defend against criminal charges.

ual has engaged in some specifically defined and legally proscribed harmful act, that is, he is alleged to have committed a crime. And, the Constitution has generally been interpreted as prohibiting, or at least zealously limiting, the use of preventive detention against persons who are expected to but have not yet engaged in some dangerous act. Just how strong this legal policy is with respect to prohibiting preventive detention will be illustrated by the following case.

THE SAGA OF DALLAS WILLIAMS[47]

Several of the cases involving Mr. Williams are to be found in Katz, Goldstein, and Dershowitz (1967). A prosecutor once described Dallas Williams as a person who "has the worst criminal record for violence I have ever seen" (p. 521, note 1). Lest it be thought that this could simply reflect the not uncommon overstatement by a prosecutor in certain courtroom situations, we might note the statement of a District Court judge concerning Mr. Williams:

> This is the most recent of petitioner's encounters with the law. It follows an almost incredible record since 1933 of criminal charges and convictions, including manslaughter, assault and battery, assault with intent to kill, shooting with intent to kill, assault with a pistol, and other crimes of violence. . . . There is no doubt that he has been a turbulent, dangerous character. . . (pp. 530–531).

The extent to which not only prosecutors but also the courts and several mental health facilities were impressed with Mr. Williams's repeated and amply demonstrated dangerousness is indicated by several efforts that were made to get him civilly committed. However, while pointing to his obvious dangerousness, the psychiatric examiners found that Dallas Williams was not, at that particular time, suffering from any active mental illness. Thus, in granting Mr. Williams's *habeas corpus* petition the district court stated:

> However commendable was the court's purpose to protect the public from the release to society of a man "potentially dangerous to others," there is no District of Columbia statute or inherent equity power permitting commitment to any institution upon that showing alone. *Many persons who are released to society upon completing the service of sentences in criminal cases are just as surely potential menaces to society as is this petitioner, having a*

---

[47] In view of his long criminal career, with more than 100 arrests and at least 10 convictions for crimes of violence, Mr. Williams came to be known as the "Bad Man of Swampoodle." *The Evening Star* (Washington, D.C.), Oct. 24, 1968.

similar pattern of anti-social behavior, lack of occupational adjustment, and absence of remorse or anxiety; yet the courts have no legal basis of ordering their continued confinement on mere apprehension of future unlawful acts, and must wait until another crime against society is committed or they are found insane in proper mental health proceedings before confinement may again be ordered (p. 530, emphasis added).

As a result of this successful petition Dallas Williams was released. However, as had rather clearly been demonstrated by his previous criminal record, as had been predicted by the psychiatrists who had examined him, and as had been feared by the courts who had dealt with him, Mr. Williams was indeed a very dangerous person. On March 15, 1961, Mr. Williams shot and killed two men. Following a trial in which he invoked an insanity defense, Dallas Williams was convicted on two charges of second-degree murder and was sentenced to a term of 20 to 61 years (pp. 534–535).

Readers, and especially nonlawyers, who have not been indoctrinated in certain legal "word games" and in the elastic interpretations and applications of due process protections, are invited to ponder this case and its various public policy implications very carefully.

It is interesting, even astonishing, that the police power authority to protect the community can be so readily invoked for the commitment of the mentally ill, yet similar statutory provisions are typically lacking to safeguard the citizens from known "potential menaces to society." One might expect that since the mentally ill have been selected for such preventive confinement there must certainly be some very clear and convincing evidence showing that they constitute one of the most dangerous groups in our society. However, such evidence does not exist (see, e.g., Gulevich & Bourne, 1970).[48]

It would appear, then, that we must look elsewhere in efforts to understand why the mentally ill are erroneously perceived and handled as though they pose such a serious threat to the safety of the community. Such reasons may be provided by the particular attitudes and feelings in our society toward the mentally ill.

REJECTION OF THE MENTALLY ILL

During the past 15 years a sizable body of research has accumulated concerning social attitudes and opinions about mental illness and toward the mentally ill. The stigmatizing quality of the label of "mental illness" has been demonstrated with much consistency and is

[48] See Shah, 1975, note 34 above.

now well documented.[49] A strong negative halo is attached by our society to the mentally ill and, as found by Nunnally (1961), "they are considered, unselectively, as being all things bad."

Several studies have sought to explicate the factors which appear to influence such attitudes. For example, Phillips (1963) found that rejecting attitudes toward mentally ill persons seemed to vary depending on the kind of help that such persons were thought to have received. Thus, rejecting attitudes increased as the "mentally ill" individual was described as seeking no help, seeing a clergyman, a physician, or a psychiatrist, or as a person with a history of hospitalization. In fact, attitudes of rejection were disproportionately stronger when the ill person was described as utilizing help from a psychiatrist or from a mental hospital. Phillips also found that the social visibility of an individual's deviation from socially prescribed behaviors (i.e., odd and unusual behavior) seemed to determine the strength of the rejection, and not just the nature or severity of the mental disorder as judged from a psychiatric standpoint (Phillips, 1964).

A very interesting study by Bord (1971) demonstrated that two factors, perceived threat and unpredictability, appeared to account for the major patterns as well as the intensity of the rejecting attitudes exhibited toward the mentally ill. The rejection of such persons increased as their behavior was perceived as both unpredictable and threatening.

Even though empirical evidence does *not* support the impression that the mentally ill constitute one of the most dangerous groups in our society, attitudes of apprehension and rejection appear to be as widespread as they are enduring. And, judging from the legislative provisions which allow preventive detention of the mentally ill as

[49] See, e.g., J. G. Rabkin, Opinions about mental illness: A review of the literature, *Psychological Bulletin*, 1972, 77, 153. See also: J. Cummings & E. Cummings, *Closed Ranks: An Experiment in Mental Health Education* (Cambridge: Harvard University Press, 1957); C. D. Whatley, Social attitudes towards discharged mental patients, *Social Problems*, 1959, 6, 313; K. Yamamoto & H. F. Dizney, Rejection of the mentally ill: A study of attitudes of student teachers, *Journal of Counseling Psychology*, 1967, 14, 264; D. Schroeder & D. Ehrlich, Rejection by mental health professionals: A possible consequence of not seeking appropriate help for emotional disorders, *Journal of Health & Social Behavior*, 1968, 9, 222; J. M. Giovannoni & L. P. Ullmann, Conceptions of mental health held by psychiatric patients, *Journal of Clinical Psychology*, 1963, 19, 398; B. Dohrenwend & E. Chin-Shong, Social status and attitudes towards psychological disorder, *American Journal of Sociology*, 1967, 32, 417. But see also: P. V. Lemkau & G. M. Crocetti, An urban population's opinion about mental illness, *American Journal of Psychiatry*, 1962, 118, 692; G. M. Crocetti & P. V. Lemkau, Public opinion of psychiatric home care in an urban area, *American Journal of Public Health*, 1963, 53, 409, and discussion of this article by H. W. Dunham, 415–417.

"dangerous to others," it would seem that these attitudes of rejection are shared by many legislators. Such stereotypical attitudes may also be shared by many courts.

One is led to conclude that rejecting attitudes toward the mentally ill and the *perceptions* of their unpredictability and threat—and *not* their actual and demonstrated "dangerousness"—seem to provide the major basis for public policies authorizing their police power commitments. A fundamental question is therefore raised concerning the justification for singling out the mentally ill for police power commitments or, more accurately, for their preventive detention. This basic issue cannot be addressed simply by the provision of all available procedural due process safeguards. The *substantive* question begs for and requires more careful and forthright scrutiny.

SOME CONSTITUTIONAL PROBLEMS AND THE ROLE OF THE COURTS

In our system of government, courts have the critically important role of interpreting the Constitution and of determining when laws and practices deviate from the constitutionally prescribed boundaries within which state interests and the rights of individuals must be balanced. Stone (1975) has noted that it is not a usurpation of the legislative role for courts to declare what specific rights are possessed by citizens who are placed at risk by state power. He points out that "since the Nation's founding, it has been thought the peculiar duty of the judiciary to serve as a counterweight on the swing of popular passion and legislative will" (p. 17).

Some 25 years ago Justice Felix Frankfurter wrote an excellent description of the fundamental meaning of the due process clause of the Constitution:

> It is now the settled doctrine of this Court that the Due Process Clause embodies a system of rights based on moral principles so deeply embedded in the tradition and feelings of our people as to be deemed fundamental to a civilized society as conceived by our whole history. Due process is that which comports with the deepest notions of what is fair and right and just. The more fundamental the beliefs are the less likely they are to be explicitly stated. But respect for them is of the very essence of the Due Process Clause. . . . In applying such a large untechnical concept as "due process," the Court enforces those permanent and pervasive feelings of our society as to which there is compelling evidence of the kind relevant to judgments on social institutions.[50]

[50] *Solesbee* v. *Blakcom*, 339 U.S. 9 (1950), Justice Frankfurter's dissenting opinion, at 16.

The reader is reminded that the discussion here does *not* pertain to the highly technical legal meanings and fine points attached to the concept of due process of law. Rather, the analysis here is based upon broad notions of fundamental fairness and what Justice Frankfurter described as the "deepest notions of what is fair and right and just."

The issue being addressed here is whether our society's use of preventive detention of the mentally ill for police power objectives can be considered to be "fair and right and just." And whether the judgments on relevant social institutions typically displayed by the courts reflect applications of the "permanent and pervasive feelings" and moral principles of which Justice Frankfurter spoke so eloquently.

Two basic considerations need to be kept in mind: first, whether it is "just" and "right" to use preventive detention and, if so, under what specific and strictly prescribed and regulated circumstances? Second, given that preventive detention is felt to be necessary in certain situations in order to protect the community, what basic requirements of equity and fairness must be used to ensure that individuals and groups posing a danger to the community are handled in very similar and nondiscriminatory fashion? The first question pertains to the due process clause and the second question to the equal protection clause of the Constitution.

Courts have commented from time to time about the problems of and the needs for limitations on legislation that may be based on strong community passions and discriminatory attitudes. For example, with respect to sexual psychopath legislation, Chief Judge David Bazelon has noted:

> But the test of what anticipated conduct must justify preventive detention cannot be simply whether the legislature has power to prohibit such conduct or to attack the evil it portends. Congress may legislate to protect many different interests—psychic and esthetic as well as physical and economic. But while it may prohibit ugly billboards because they give offense, it may not lock up ugly people for the same reason. *The power to control an evil does not remove all restriction on the means that may be employed for that purpose.* This principle is fundamental to the constitutional order.[51]

As noted earlier, in recent years courts have increasingly broadened the range of procedural due process protections that have been

---

[51] *Cross v. Harris*, 418 F.2d 1095, 1102–1103 (1969), footnotes eliminated and emphasis added. See also: *O'Connor v. Donaldson*, No. 74–8, U.S., decided June 26, 1975, where the Court said: "One might as well ask if the State, to avoid public unease, could incarcerate all who are physically unattractive or socially eccentric. Mere public intolerance or animosity cannot constitutionally justify the deprivation of a person's physical liberty" (at 12).

judged to be constitutionally required in various "civil" commitment proceedings.[52] It would appear that courts most typically have tended to analyze due process arguments in terms of procedural due process and, if the minimal requisite safeguards are provided, the due process challenges have generally been dismissed. The disappointing thread in such judicial scrutiny is the failure to recognize and to confront the more basic *substantive* due process problems.

Stated most simply, one aspect of substantive due process demands that all state actions be reasonably related to a valid state goal. Moreover, when such actions involve infringements of other "fundamental interests," e.g., depriving a citizen of his constitutional right to liberty, these actions must be shown to promote not only a valid but a *compelling* state goal. Thus, even though the validity of the state's interest in protecting society cannot be disputed, serious moral (and perhaps equal protection) problems arise if one asks why the mentally ill have been singled out for such preventive confinement in the absence of any clear and convincing evidence that they truly constitute one of the most dangerous groups in our society? As argued earlier, by confounding the *parens patriae* and police power criteria of commitment codes, our society has avoided dealing more forthrightly with the constitutional questions relevant to police power commitments—the treatment objectives seem to be dragged in presumably to remedy and possibly even to avoid addressing the other substantive issue.

A quick examination of a few other instances in which courts have declared certain laws and practices to be unconstitutional may be illustrative of the issues and arguments that may soon be raised with respect to the police power commitment of the mentally ill. In *Shapiro* v. *Thompson*[53] a 1-year residency requirement for welfare benefits was held by the Supreme Court to be unconstitutional since this law created a classification which constituted an invidious discrimination and denied equal protection of the laws. The Court noted in this decision that freedom to travel throughout the United States "has long been recognized as a basic right under the Constitution."[54] The Court acknowledged that the state had a valid interest in seeking to preserve fiscal integrity of its programs, but pointed out that a state "may not accomplish such a purpose by invidious distinctions between classes of its citizens."[55]

---

[52] See notes 2, 3, and 4 above.
[53] *Shapiro* v. *Thompson*, 394 U.S. 619 (1969).
[54] Ibid., at 631.
[55] Ibid., at 633.

In *Dunn* v. *Blumstein*[56] the Supreme Court held that durational residency laws for voters violated the equal protection clause of the Fourteenth Amendment. The Court commented that it was not sufficient to show that durational residence requirements furthered a substantial state interest, and went on to note that

> . . . the State cannot choose means that unnecessarily burden or restrict constitutionally protected activity. *Statutes affecting constitutional rights must be drawn with 'precision'. . . and must be 'tailored' to serve their legitimate objectives.*[57]

In *Hobson* v. *Hansen*[58] the United States District Court for the District of Columbia agreed that the operation of the public school system in the District unconstitutionally deprived black and poor public school children of their right to equal educational opportunity with the white and more affluent public school children. The court noted:

> Orthodox equal protection doctrine can be encapsulated in a single rule: government action which without justification imposes unequal burdens or awards unequal benefits is unconstitutional. The complaint that analytically no violation of equal protection vests unless the inequalities stem from a deliberately discriminatory plan is simply false. Whatever the law was once, it is a testament to our maturing concept of equality that, with the help of Supreme Court decisions in the last decade, we now firmly recognize that *the arbitrary quality of thoughtlessness can be as disastrous and unfair to private rights and the public interest as the perversity of a willful scheme.*[59]

One does not need to be a lawyer to see that the constitutional principles invoked by the courts in the aforementioned decisions are clearly applicable to the police power aspects of commitment codes. In brief, we have seen that invidious and discriminatory classifications including only the mentally ill, and factually unsupported imputations of dangerousness, have led to the singling out of this group for preventive detention. Moreover, quite obviously the mentally ill are *not* afforded equal protection of the laws since civil commitment procedures typically do not provide the full panoply of procedural due process protections. For example, the constitutional right of the mentally ill to liberty can and typically is infringed by meeting

---

[56] *Dunn* v. *Blumstein*, 405 U.S. 330 (1972).
[57] Ibid., at 342–343, emphasis added.
[58] *Hobson* v. *Hansen*, 269 F.Supp. 401 (1967).
[59] Ibid., at 497, footnotes eliminated and emphasis added.

standards of proof lower than beyond a reasonable doubt; e.g., "clear and convincing" and "preponderance of the evidence" standards most typically are involved in civil commitments.

In sum, whether or not the very technical and also seemingly pliable legal requirements for findings of unconstitutionality are met by the aforementioned aspects of commitment codes, such societal practices do *not* comport with fundamental notions of "what is fair and right and just."

CONCLUSION

The major purpose of this discussion has been to indicate some of the very discriminatory and unfair consequences that result for the mentally ill when the analytically distinct state objectives premised on *parens patriae* and police power are lumped together. Such confounding has led to situations in which ostensibly therapeutic objectives can be invoked to justify State interventions that are actually based on the police power. Thus, the fundamental issues pertaining to the use of preventive detention for social control (i.e., police power) purposes do *not* receive candid scrutiny.

Perhaps, as Dershowitz (Katz *et al.*, 1967, p. 588) suggested, the vexing issues pertaining to preventive detention might be more amenable to resolution if the subject were addressed in a more forthright fashion. To the extent that civil commitments and other "surreptitious" uses of preventive detention are discussed more openly, we would have better prospects of escaping from some of the doctrinal straitjackets into which we seem to be locked. At the very least, and as suggested by the 5-point analytic framework presented earlier in this discussion and as pointed out by Broderick (1971), if certain compelling societal needs require that we deviate from asserted goal values and policy objectives, we should admit this more honestly and make the necessary adjustments to reduce glaring discrepancies between asserted values and the practices in which we engage.

The aforementioned discussion indicates that despite the legal technicalities in which such issues might often get cloaked, commitment codes for the mentally ill based on police power objectives involve the use of "suspect classifications."[60] To select for preventive detention an entire class of persons on the basis of the loose and vague

---

[60] Note: Mental illness: A suspect classification, 83 *Yale Law Journal* 1237 (1974). A very thorough and excellent discussion of the topic is provided in this article.

label of "mental illness" and to then ascribe to them, as a group, the characteristics of "dangerousness" should raise very serious questions about the validity of such a classification. Very strict judicial scrutiny of such laws and practices seems long overdue considering the fact that such state interventions affect the constitutionally protected right to liberty.

It also appears that the mentally ill have been treated much like other "discrete and insular minorities."[61] If the legislature's primary purpose is to protect the community from dangerous persons, then obviously it should classify on the basis of dangerousness and should authorize the detention of *all dangerous persons* whether mentally ill or not. It would appear that a law formulated on the basis of dangerousness might better survive judicial scrutiny under the compelling interest of the state to protect the community.[62] However, legislation which is based in reference to all truly "dangerous" persons, and is not directed simply to a rejected and irrationally feared "minority," would not be politically acceptable. This obstacle to more rationally and precisely formulated laws underlines the crucial role of the equal protection clause, namely, to expose legislative purposes to public scrutiny, "a scrutiny customarily missing when laws affect only the voiceless in society."[63]

It is essential, therefore, that courts more conscientiously perform their function of giving stricter scrutiny to the constitutional questions raised by the police power commitment of the mentally ill. This critically important role of the courts was pointed out most eloquently several years ago by Justice Jackson in his famous concurring opinion in the *Railway Express Agency* case:

> [T]here is no more effective practical guaranty against arbitrary and unreasonable government than to require that the principles of law which officials would impose upon a minority must be imposed generally. Conversely, nothing opens the door to arbitrary action so effectively as to allow those officials to pick and choose only a few to whom they will apply legislation and thus escape the political retribution that might be visited upon them if larger numbers were affected. *Courts can take no better measure to assure that laws will be just than to require that laws be equal in operation.*[64]

---

[61] Ibid., at 1254–1259.
[62] Ibid., at 1263.
[63] Ibid., at 1263.
[64] *Railway Express Agency* v. *New York*, 336 U.S. 106, 112–113 (1949). Jackson, J. concurring. Emphasis added.

Acknowledgment

The author would like to acknowledge the helpful comments received from Thomas L. Lalley and R. Kirkland Schwitzgebel on an earlier draft of this chapter.

REFERENCES

Allen, F. A. *The borderline of criminal justice.* Chicago: University of Chicago Press, 1964.

Bord, R. J. Rejection of the mentally ill: Continuities and further developments. *Social Problems,* 1971, *18*, 496.

Brakel, S. J., & Rock, R. S. *The mentally disabled and the law.* Chicago: University of Chicago Press, 1971.

Broderick, A. Justice in the books or justice in action: An institutional approach to involuntary hospitalization for mental illness. *Catholic University Law Review,* 1971, *20*, 547.

Chambers, D. L. Alternatives to civil commitment of the mentally ill: Practical guides and constitutional imperatives. *Michigan Law Review,* 1971, *70*, 1107; 1119.

Gulevich, G., & Bourne, P. Mental illness and violence. In D. Daniels, M. Gilula, & F. Ochberg (Eds.), *Violence and the struggle for existence.* Boston: Little, Brown, 1970.

Hart, H. L. A. *Law, liberty, and morality.* Stanford: Stanford University Press, 1963.

Katz, J., Goldstein, J., & Dershowitz, A. M. *Psychoanalysis, psychiatry, and law.* New York: Free Press, 1967. Pp. 526–535.

Mulvihill, D., & Tumin, M. *12 crimes of violence.* A staff report to the National Commission on the Causes and Prevention of Violence, 1969. Pp. 639–667.

Nunnally, J. *Popular conceptions of mental health: Their development and change.* New York: Holt, Rinehart & Winston, 1961. P. 51.

Phillips, D. L. Rejection: A possible consequence of seeking help for mental disorders. *American Sociological Review,* 1963, *28*, 963.

Phillips, D. L. Rejection of the mentally ill: The influence of behavior and sex. *American Sociological Review,* 1964, *29*, 679.

The Predident's Report on Occupational Safety and Health. Washington, D.C.: U.S. Government Printing Office, 1972.

Stone, A. A. *Mental health and law: A system in transition.* National Institute of Mental Health, DHEW Publication No. (ADM) 75-176. Washington, D.C.: U.S. Government Printing Office, 1975.

Voas, E. Alcohol as an underlying factor in behavior leading to fatal highway crashes. In M. E. Chafetz (Ed.), *Research on alcoholism: Clinical problems and special populations.* Proceedings of the First Annual Conference of the National Institute on Alcohol Abuse and Alcoholism, 1973. P. 324.

4

Criminal Commitment Contingency Structures

DAVID B. WEXLER

INTRODUCTION

Approximately 5 years ago, while conducting an empirical inquiry into the administration of psychiatric justice in Arizona, we learned, from an interview with a superior court judge, of the following interesting incident: A criminal defendent in a rural county had been committed to the Arizona State Hospital as incompetent to stand trial (IST). After the defendant had been confined as IST for a few months, the superior court judge was visited by the County Board of Supervisors, who successfully urged the judge to dismiss the criminal charges and to recommit the patient pursuant to the *civil* commitment process.

The decision to dismiss the charge and to recommit the patient civilly rather than to continue the IST commitment had certain enormous consequences. In addition to avoiding the prospect of eventual criminal trial, confinement pursuant to a "civil" rather than a "criminal" commitment label would have much to do with the patient's security status while in the hospital, influencing, for example, whether he would be housed on an open ward or instead on the far less attractive maximum security unit.

Was the board of supervisors' recommitment request grounded in such humanitarian and clinical considerations? Hardly. Instead, the supreme motivating force, according to the judge who agreed to the

DAVID B. WEXLER • College of Law, University of Arizona, Tucson, Arizona.

recommitment, was the fact that "the cost of hospitalizing an incompetent criminal defendant falls by statute on the county in question, while the comparable cost of maintaining a civilly committed patient is of course shouldered by the state" (Wexler & Scoville, 1971, p. 172, note 126). In that interview, we had stumbled upon a clear-cut example of what today's proponents of mental health unified services systems describe as "decisions affecting care . . . based on jurisdictional jockeying generated by fiscal considerations that are irrelevant to the patient's needs."[1]

Particularly since learning of that incident, we have been interested in structural arrangements and legal contingencies operative in the commitment process, especially insofar as those structures or contingencies focus on nonclinical criteria or tend to produce countertherapeutic effects (e.g., Wexler, 1974, pp. 672–673, note 4). Our interest was further fueled by research involving legal aspects of behavior modification (Wexler, 1973), during the course of which it was learned that the term *contingency* is the password to the Skinnerian executive washroom.

The topic of incentive structures and contingencies in the commitment process is, of course, far too broad to be covered completely here. Indeed, much of it remains in need of first-stage investigation. It would be very useful, for example, to look into the role played by private psychiatric hospitals in the commitment process, to track down rumors that certain of those hospitals retain patients until (but not after) patient hospitalization insurance policies run out, and to learn whether or not financial structures of certain hospitals produce fiscal incentives to admit and retain patients. But since the topic of this book emphasizes issues in the criminal justice system, this chapter will be limited to a selective discussion of contingency structures operative in the *criminal* commitment area (see generally Wexler, 1976).

"SPECIAL" OFFENDERS SUBJECTED TO INDETERMINATE CONFINEMENT

Laws providing for the commitment of "special" offenders—such as "sexual psychopaths" and "defective delinquents"—typically pro-

---

[1] Testimony entitled, "The Need for Unified Services Amendments," presented on behalf of June Jackson Christmas, M.D., Commissioner, New York City Department of Mental Health and Mental Retardation Services, to the Select Committee on Mental and Physical Handicap, Albany, New York, December 3, 1974, p. 1.

vide that the commitment should be for an indeterminate period and should terminate only when the offender may be safely released. These laws have been subjected to heavy criticism by commentators, often on the ground (among many others) that they promote "shamming" rather than genuine rehabilitation.

When viewed from the perspective of a contingency analysis, matters are even worse, for efforts at shamming—and a fortiori at genuine rehabilitation—are often frustrated by the absence of clear-cut criteria for improvement and discharge. Hugo Adam Bedau, a philosopher, has described four possible correctional models which vary from one another in terms of the type of sentence and release standards: (1) a fixed sentence where release is contingent simply upon reaching the expiration date; (2) an indeterminate sentence where release is gauged by objective conditions (e.g., obtaining a high school equivalency diploma); (3) an indeterminate sentence where release is gauged by subjective criteria (e.g., expressing "socially constructive attitudes"); (4) an indeterminate sentence where the inmate population is never informed of the release criteria.[2] While most administrators of special and security institutions operating under an indeterminate sentence probably purport to follow Model 2 (objective release criteria), the indeterminate sentence in practice probably conforms most closely to Model 3 (vague and subjective release criteria) and not infrequently to Model 4 (unspecified release criteria).

If indeterminate confinement is to be continued in any form—which in my opinion is of questionable constitutionality—it ought at least to conform to Model 2. Models 3 and 4 are examples of bad psychology as well as bad law. In a report to the National Prison Project, for example, Bernard Rubin, M. D., criticized on psychological grounds the "Control Unit Treatment Program" at the United States Penitentiary at Marion, a program which is in some ways analogous to an indeterminate sentence program.[3] The Marion control unit program operated to place hostile prisoners in indefinite special confinement (with progressive tiers of increasing privileges) in order to alter their behavior and attitudes so that they might eventually reenter the general prison population. To begin with, Rubin noted that progres-

---

[2] H. A. Bedau, Physical interventions to alter behavior in a punitive environment, American Behavioral Scientist, 1975, 18, 662–663. Cf. Haymes v. Regan, 18 Cr.L. 2177 (2d Cir. 10/29/75), holding that, so long as a prisoner is given reasons for the denial of parole, the parole board is not constitutionally obligated to disclose the release criteria observed in its parole decisions.

[3] The program was also condemned on constitutional grounds by federal court action in Adams v. Carlson, Civ. No. 72-153 (E. D. Ill., Dec. 6, 1973).

124																																																							DAVID B. WEXLER

sion and release had to operate capriciously, for the stated release criterion was simply one which "reflects the committee's confidence that the offender has matured beyond the point of being a probable danger to other persons" (Rubin, 1973, p. 6). The absence of objective criteria for entering or exiting the program and for range progression within the program led Rubin to conclude that the Marion control unit system could not even be rightfully termed a "program" (p. 9). Moreover, in Rubin's view the "program" worked actual *harm*: It corrupted the inmates by encouraging dishonest game-playing and shamming, and the lack of specified objective criteria was demeaning to the inmates and led to feelings of helplessness, frustration, and outright rage (pp. 9–10).

Many observers agree with Rubin's assessment of programs which do not clearly specify behavior necessary to trigger the valued contingency of release. Ralph Wetzel, for example, has noted that the success and efficiency of contingency management programs can be greatly facilitated by the utilization of cues, prompts, and models relating to expected behavior patterns.[4] And Albert Bandura, in a recent provocative piece (Bandura, 1974), notes that contingencies function to motivate and to impart information. Contingencies operate best, then, "after individuals discern the instrumental relation between action and outcome" (p. 860), and "behavior is not much affected by its consequences without awareness of what is being reinforced" (p. 860). In sum, Bandura concludes:

> Not surprisingly, people change more rapidly if told what behaviors are rewardable and punishable than if they have to discover it from observing the consequences of their actions. Competencies that are not already within their repertoires can be developed with greater ease through the aid of instruction and modeling than by relying solely on the successes and failures of unguided performance (p. 862).

These principles are, as Bandura admits, hardly surprising. That they make considerable intuitive sense is reflected in the anecdote about a father who, disturbed by his young son's propensity for foul language, went to a psychologist for advice on how to handle the problem. "Use principles of behavior modification," the psychologist

[4] R. J. Wetzel, *Behavior Modification in the Social Learning Environment*, unpublished manuscript, undated. See also at pp. 3–4: "Cues in learning need to be clear and should specify behavior. When we say to a child 'I want you to be good and behave yourself' we are not giving a very specific behavioral cue. What are the behaviors of 'being good' and 'behaving one's self'? The ability to give clear, specific noncritical and nonprovocative cues for behavior is a quality of a good trainer."

suggested. "Punish your son contingent upon his use of nasty language." Armed with that advice, the father the next morning asked his son what he would like for breakfast. The son replied (expletives have been deleted), "I think I'll have some of those f-----' cornflakes." The father promptly spanked the boy and sent him to his room for an hour of "time-out." At the expiration of that hour, the father brought the boy back to the table and said, "Now, let me ask you again, what do you want for breakfast?" "Well," the boy responded, "I sure as sh-- don't want any of those f-----' cornflakes!"

If we are to expect patients and inmates to learn something other than to forgo cornflakes in order to seek release from indeterminate confinement, it is evident that we must move toward a model of objective and clearly specified criteria for progression and release. Even if indeterminate confinement laws were abolished and if a lid were clamped on the permissible length of confinement, clear and objective release criteria would be necessary if we had any hope of developing a fair system of parole or other type of system allowing for release prior to the expiration of the maximum permissible confinement period.

DEFENDANTS FOUND INCOMPETENT TO STAND TRIAL (IST)

Until very recently, the typical situation involving IST defendants could have been portrayed as follows:

Defendants alleged to be IST would be automatically confined, often in a maximum security institution, for a rather lengthy period of evaluation (Wexler & Scoville, 1971, p. 165; de Grazia, 1974, p. 436, note 14). Ultimately, a court hearing would be held, and those persons judicially found IST would be automatically committed to a security hospital for an indefinite period (until competent to stand trial) (Wexler & Scoville, 1971, pp. 166–167), perhaps to last a lifetime.[5]

Because of a highly significant Supreme Court decision and certain other developments, the IST legal confinement portrait is now undergoing a radical alteration. Invoking equal protection and due process considerations, the Court, in the 1972 case of *Jackson* v.

---

[5] A 1965 study of patients at the Matteawan State Hospital in New York revealed that 645 of the 1,062 IST committees had been hospitalized for longer than 5 years, and one-fifth of the total had been "awaiting trial" for over 20 years. A. Matthews, *Mental Disability and the Criminal Law: A Field Study* (Chicago: American Bar Foundation, 1970), pp. 214–215.

Indiana,[6] ruled unconstitutional the *indefinite* confinement of ISTs pursuant to procedures and substantive standards which fall below the standards employed for the civil commitment of the mentally ill. Accordingly, the mere filing of criminal charges and a determination that a defendant is incompetent to stand trial cannot, without more (such as a civil commitment type hearing or a showing of dangerousness, for example), authorize long-term hospitalization of ISTs. The *Jackson* Court did, however, approve a limited commitment of persons holding IST status.

A related development is a growing awareness that IST *evaluations* need not consume a lengthy period of time and need not generally occur in secure facilities. While IST evaluations have usually been conducted in secure institutions over a 30- to 90-day period, recent studies have concluded that fully 70 percent of those evaluations can adequately be conducted on an outpatient basis (de Grazia, p. 436, note 14). Finally, because of growing acceptance of the "least restrictive alternative" concept, it is becoming increasingly evident that a defendant found to be IST can often avoid hospitalization and can be treated instead as an outpatient.

But now contrast the contingencies of the revised model with the traditional picture of indefinite secure confinement: If there is a prohibition against bringing to criminal trial a person who is IST and if a person who is IST can be treated on an outpatient basis in his home community, psychologists, psychiatrists, and sociologists might be concerned with certain potential antitherapeutic implications of that psycholegal incentive system. Concern could be expressed over what psychologists might call a "contingency structure" which could induce continued IST status, and psychiatrists might refer to the "secondary gain" advantages that could flow from a patient continuing to play what sociologists refer to as the "psychiatric sick role." In other words, by *remaining* clinically IST while at large in the community, a patient may indefinitely postpone "pending" criminal proceedings without sacrificing liberty.

Although it is not specifically aimed at overcoming the secondary gain advantages of outpatient IST status, the interesting Burt and Morris (1972) proposal to abolish the incompetency plea—and to criminally try defendants despite their incompetence—would surely deal a crippling blow to any antitherapeutic aspects of the above-described incentive structure.

---

[6] 406 U.S. 715 (1972).

DEFENDANTS FOUND NOT GUILTY BY REASON OF INSANITY (NGRI)

Traditionally, persons who have been found not guilty by reason of insanity (NGRI) have been subsequently committed, often to secure institutions. Typically, however, NGRI patients have been rather few in number, a fact explained by the relative rarity of cases in which the insanity defense has even been raised, let alone raised with success. And the relative rarity of raising the insanity defense can in turn be explained by the previously prevailing legal disincentives to its assertion: Until rather recently, the "successful" invocation of the insanity defense would often lead to *automatic* and *indefinite* confinement in a secure mental institution. Under those legal contingencies, the practice of criminal defense lawyers was, as might be expected, to recommend raising the defense only to clients charged with the most serious offenses—such as those carrying a possible penalty of capital punishment or lifelong confinement.

But recent years have witnessed a diminishing of the legal disincentives to the defense's assertion. With the realization that an NGRI verdict establishes simply a *reasonable doubt* about sanity at the time of the crime or at best a proof of insanity at that *prior time*, courts have, on due process and equal protection grounds, begun to find unconstitutional those statutes which authorize *automatic commitment* of persons found NGRI.[7] Since commitment should be premised on a finding of *present* mental illness and dangerousness, due process requires, those courts assert, a post-NGRI verdict hearing relating to present mental status, and equal protection requires that that hearing conform roughly to procedural and substantive standards set by law for civilly committed patients.[8] Further, with the emergence of statutory and constitutional limits on the length of commitment, defendants who successfully raise the insanity defense are becoming less concerned with the fear of *indefinite* hospital confinement.[9] Accord-

[7] E.g., *Bolton* v. *Harris,* 395 F2d 642 (D.C. Cir. 1968).

[8] Ibid.

[9] Persons who are found NGRI might, in appropriate cases, be subsequently civilly committed pursuant to a *parens patriae* or a police power rationale, depending upon the particular clinical situation. But even if different durational limits are set for the two classifications (as seems appropriate), and even if an NGRI defendant is committed pursuant to the police power (with an authorized duration that would presumably be lengthier than would be the case with *parens patriae* commitments), the NGRI committee should not be held for a period exceeding the maximum criminal penalty for the charged offense. See R. A. Burt and N. Morris. A proposal for the abolition of the incompetency plea, 40 *University of Chicago Law Review* 74 n. 30 (1972).

ingly, with the emergence of more favorable legal contingencies surrounding the successful assertion of the insanity defense, we should expect to see the defense raised more often, which will increase the number of NGRI verdicts and accordingly force us to pay more attention to procedures relating to the commitment and release of NGRI acquittees.

Typically, state procedures relating to NGRIs have been different from civil commitment procedures. Usually, NGRI acquittees have had an easier route into and a more difficult route out of institutions than have their civilly committed counterparts. As we have seen, NGRI acquittees have often been automatically committed, without a separate civil-commitment-type hearing relating to present mental condition and dangerousness. And NGRI release procedures have often been extremely cumbersome. In Arizona, for example, where civilly committed patients have always been able to be released by the unilateral action of the hospital superintendent, a now-defunct 1968 law provided that NGRI committees could be released not simply in the discretion of the hospital director, but only after two psychiatrists certified the patient to be no longer dangerous, and after a jury, presumably drawn from the county where the crime occurred, found, with the patient bearing the burden of persuasion, that release was warranted.[10] Compared to civilly committed patients, NGRIs had to bear a tremendously heavy release burden, and "the potential for meting out community vengeance by an unforgiving jury"[11] was apparent. For example, in one Arizona case reported in a field study,

> the patient, charged with assault with a deadly weapon, had originally been found NGRI on October 9, 1969, and was committed to the Arizona State Hospital. On July 30, 1970, two psychiatrists filed certificates to the effect that the patient was no longer a danger to herself or others. The release trial occurred on December 7–9, 1970, but the patient failed to meet her burden of proof, and the jury hung six–six. Thus, despite being hospitalized for fourteen months, being certified as recovered by two staff psychiatrists, and obtaining the favorable votes of half the jurors, she was retained at the hospital.[12]

Those serious disparities in procedural treatment between NGRIs and civilly committed patients have recently led courts to hold,

[10] A discussion of the 1968 law and its defects appears in D. B. Wexler and S. E. Scoville. The administration of psychiatric justice: Theory and practice in Arizona, 13 *Arizona Law Review* 154–158 (1971).

[11] Ibid. at 157.

[12] Ibid. at 158.

principally as a matter of equal protection, that NGRIs are entitled to admission and release procedures that are *closely comparable* (though not necessarily identical) to admission and release procedures for the civilly committed.[13] State legislatures have responded by according to NGRIs procedures that are comparable or identical to civil commitment procedures. Thus, spurred on by cases such as *Bolton* v. *Harris*,[14] many jurisdictions are doing away with automatic commitment of NGRIs and are instead funneling those persons through the ordinary civil commitment process. Similarly, many jurisdictions—now including Arizona—currently release NGRIs according to the same release procedures that apply to ordinary civilly committed patients—typically the unilateral discretionary action of the hospital director.

There may be, however, an adverse latent consequence of releasing NGRIs according to procedures *identical* to civil commitment release procedures. According to hospital officials and staff interviewed by this writer in Arizona, where previously existing disparate release procedures for NGRIs and for the civilly committed have now been changed to provide for completely equivalent release procedures for the two groups, the hospital is fearful of the adverse publicity and public reaction that might ensue if an NGRI patient were to be released "too soon" or, worse yet, if a released NGRI patient were to soon commit another violent act. The hospital is thus reluctant to release, *completely on its own say-so*, NGRIs who seem to the hospital clinically capable of uneventful community adjustment following discharge. Although the matter is of course one for empirical investigation, it may be that, because of the reluctance stemming from sole responsibility for release decisions, the average length of time that NGRIs are now held prior to their release may actually *exceed* the average period of time that, under prior law, comparable NGRIs were held before being "certified" by the hospital as ready for referral to a jury charged with making the ultimate release decision. The new procedure, therefore, may not have removed from consideration the visible nonclinical, extralegal, and probably unconstitutional[15] factors that were potentially operative in the jury-release structure, but may

---

[13] For example, *Bolton* v. *Harris*, 395 F2d 642 (D.C. Cir. 1968).

[14] Ibid.

[15] Cf. *Olson* v. *Pope*, No. 8361, Superior Court of Solano County, California, March 28, 1973, p. 9, where the court, in an unpublished opinion, said that "despite all indications in favor of parole the record suggested that the Adult Authority (parole board) had denied parole because of the vindictive attitude of some residents of the community where the offenses were committed and that if this were established as a fact, it was tantamount to the authority's acting on whim, caprice and rumor."

have instead simply concealed them from view by transferring them (or others like them) to the new decision-making structure of unilateral hospital discharge.

Despite the awareness of the operation of nonclinical release-inhibiting factors, it is often difficult to structure a legal system that will remove or lessen the impact of those factors. The establishment of durational limits on commitment will of course help, for those limits will at least ensure that unwarranted delays in release will not continue indefinitely; but a durational limit will only lessen the problem, not solve it, for it will not address the question of unwarranted confinement of a patient who deserves release *before* the expiration of the period of commitment. To the extent that hospitals or therapists might delay or prevent release of particular patients because of the fear of financial liability that might be incurred should such released patients commit violent acts in the community, statutes could—and should—be enacted immunizing institutions and therapeutic staff from liability for release decisions made in the good faith exercise of professional discretion.[16] But the problems—and fears—run deeper than the question of legal liability. Seemingly, the main concern is with taking full responsibility (in a nonlegal sense) for making difficult decisions about future dangerousness in an area where accurate predictive tools are absent and where, when an "incorrect" decision is made, adverse public and press reaction can be very severe. Psychological studies suggest that if a legal decision-making structure could be designed in which NGRI release responsibility is shared or diffused, the decision to release might be made with fewer inhibitions (cf. Bandura, 1974; Fischhoff, 1975).

Ordinarily, strong policy objections exist with respect to taking advantage of the psychological consequences of diffusing responsibility, for diffusion can easily lead to the uninhibited making of *culpable* decisions.[17] But diffusion can more readily be justified where the

---

[16] Cf. Arizona Revised Statutes §36–543 (D): "The medical director of the agency shall not be held civilly liable for any acts committed by the released patient." See also B. Ennis, Civil liberties and mental illness, 7 *Criminal Law Bulletin* 101 (1971).

[17] Thus, Bandura (1974) discusses diffusion with disapproval: "A common dissociative practice is to obscure or distort the relationship between one's actions and the effects they cause. People will perform behavior they normally repudiate if a legitimate authority sanctions it and acknowledges responsibility for its consequences. By displacing responsibility elsewhere, participants do not hold themselves accountable for what they do and are thus spared self-prohibiting reactions. Exemption from self-censure can be facilitated additionally by diffusing responsibility for culpable behavior. Through division of labor, division of decision making, and collective action, people can contribute to detrimental practices without feeling personal responsibility or self-disapproval."

decisions to be made are necessary and difficult, and where diffusion is necessary to weaken or eliminate the contaminating—or even paralyzing—impact of nonclinical, extralegal, and unconstitutional factors—such as the wrath or vindictiveness of the community.

If a case for diffusion can be legitimately made with respect to hospital release decisions, the next matter of concern would be to determine the type of body that should be designated to share release decision-making authority and responsibility with the hospital. A release jury, such as was until recently operative in Arizona,[18] would obviously not be satisfactory, for it would relieve the hospital of unwarranted inhibitions but would, far more patently than the hospital, be itself subject to similar influences. A court, rather than a jury, might, however, be an acceptable authority-sharing institution. Ideally, courts would be less subject than juries to influences of sheer community vindictiveness. If hospitals were required to secure judicial approval prior to releasing NGRI patients, the hospitals would presumably refer to the courts without inhibition those patients deemed by the hospital to be ready for release.[19] In most instances, the courts could be expected to read and rely upon the hospital psychiatric reports and to approve the hospital release decision without holding a full-blown hearing. In selected instances of troublesome cases, the courts might hold hearings and either accept or disapprove the hospital's release recommendation. In any event, the sharing of release responsibility might well work to lessen improper inhibitions: The hospital will know that a court will scrutinize the hospital release recommendation and will know that the court will serve as an additional safety valve in the release process; the court, on the other hand, will know that the hospital's release recommendation is based upon the evaluative judgment of therapeutic professionals who have had a considerable amount of time to observe the patients proposed for release.

---

[18] It is interesting to note that the scheme of jury release of NGRIs was actually proposed by Arizona hospital officials who were reluctant to release unilaterally patients who had been committed as NGRI.

[19] This writer is aware of instances at the Arizona State Hospital where patients with a past history of violence have been deemed by the hospital staff to be ready for release but where the staff was reluctant to exercise its unilateral release authority. In such instances, the staff often advised the patient or the patient's counsel to seek release by petitioning the court for a hearing. At the hearing, the hospital staff would happily testify in favor of the patient's release. See also the recently enacted Arizona statute which, while mechanically involving the courts in some release decisions, actually retains release authority in the hand of the hospital. Arizona Revised Statutes, §36-543.

If court approval, rather than purely unilateral hospital action, is regarded as appropriate with respect to NGRI patients, the question remains whether equal protection would authorize, for NGRIs, a release procedure that differs from the procedure employed with regard to ordinary civilly committed patients. If equal protection were offended by the distinction, it might be necessary, to accomplish court approval of NGRI releases, to require court approval of the release of *all* hospital patients, thus avoiding the problem of unequal treatment of the NGRI group, though perhaps creating a more cumbersome release mechanism than is really desirable.

It is unlikely, however, that equal protection would be read to require the *identical* procedural handling of NGRI and other patients. Equal protection may require close comparability of procedural treatment, but it ought not to be read to require complete equivalency. Thus, even *Bolton* v. *Harris*,[20] the liberal District of Columbia circuit decision which has spoken most forcefully about according NGRI patients procedural rights that compare closely to civilly committed patients, requires only "reasonable" rather than "rigid" application of the equal protection clause.[21] *Bolton* recognized that some differences in procedural treatment between NGRI and civil patients could be warranted. And the propriety of court-approved release can, according to *Bolton*, be one of those warranted distinctions:

> We uphold the release provisions of §24-301 (3) even though they differ from civil commitment procedures by authorizing court review of the hospital's decision to release a patient. We do not think equal protection is offended by allowing the Government or the Court the opportunity to insure that the standards for the release of civilly committed patients are faithfully applied to Subsection (d) [NGRI] patients.[22]

A system of court-approved release of NGRIs may, therefore, be advantageous both to NGRI patients (by reducing the hospital's inhibitions regarding release) and to society (by ensuring that release standards have been "faithfully applied" to patients who escaped criminal conviction only by the successful operation of the insanity defense). If the system is advantageous both to society and to patients with a history of dangerous behavior, however, it seems curious that it should be employed only with NGRIs and with no other patient categories. It would seem that the crucial distinction, for release

[20] 395 F2d 642 (D.C. 1968).
[21] Ibid. at 651.
[22] Ibid. at 652.

structure purposes, ought not to be between NGRI patients and all others, but ought instead to be between *dangerous* and *nondangerous* patient categories or, in more technical legal language, between *police power* patients and *parens patriae* patients. Serious legislative consideration should be given, in other words, to permitting unilateral hospital release of *parens patriae* patients, but to requiring (for the sake of society and for the affected patients) court approval of the hospital release recommendation before discharging patients committed pursuant to the state's police power.

PRISON-TO-HOSPITAL TRANSFEREES

Although most of the legal controversy surrounding prison-to-hospital transfers centers around the procedural trappings that must accompany involuntary transfers, an emerging area of importance concerns *voluntary* transfer procedures for prisoners desirous of obtaining treatment unavailable in the prison context. Voluntary transfers to mental hospitals or prison psychiatric units do not, of course, require the procedural trappings mandated for involuntary commitments or transfer. Nonetheless, the voluntary transfer area is often riddled with problems and is in considerable need of reform. In many (though not all) jurisdictions, for example, voluntary hospital admission, even with the approval of both the prison and the hospital, is simply not a legally available option insofar as prison inmates are concerned: Involuntary commitment is the only permissible route.[23] That in itself constitutes a legal disincentive to seeking transfer, for if transfer can be effectuated only through commitment, a prisoner who seeks commitment will, at least in the bulk of jurisdictions which do not yet have durational limits on the length of civil confinement, be exchanging his definite sentence expiration date for an indefinite therapeutic release date.[24] Add to that the confusing situation regarding good time allotments in mental hospitals, parole board policies disfavoring conditional release of prisoner-patients, and policies in some states mandating maximum security confinement of transferred prisoners (even of those who have served in prison as responsible outside trustees), and virtually all incentive for an emotionally dis-

---

[23] Until recently, such was the case in Arizona. See D. B. Wexler and S. E. Scoville. The administration of psychiatric justice: Theory and practice in Arizona, 13 *Arizona Law Review* 174–188 (1971).

[24] Ibid.

turbed offender to seek treatment is undercut by the contingencies of the legal system.[25]

All of those adverse legal contingencies deserve reconsideration. Surely, there should be no problem regarding the authorization of voluntary admission for prison inmates, so long as the proposed admission is screened by prison and hospital officials to ensure that the applicant is not simply seeking to avoid a term of penal incarceration.[26] Good time credits—both "ordinary" credits and, under some circumstances, "extra" credits—should be made available to prisoner-patients whether those prisoner-patients have been voluntarily or involuntarily transferred.

Since "ordinary" credits are typically earned by a prisoner not only while he is physically in a given state prison, but are earned also while he is standing trial on an out-of-state detainer[27] and while he is serving a given state sentence out-of-state concurrently with the sentence of another jurisdiction (Wexler & Scoville, 1971, p. 185), there seems little reason to deny such credits to a prisoner serving his sentence in a state mental hospital.[28] The availability of "extra" credits is slightly more difficult, for most states reserve those credits for inmates who perform certain assignments or who hold positions of confidence and trust. Nonetheless, some such positions are already available in a mental hospital setting and others could easily be made available (Wexler & Scoville, 1971, p. 185). Transferred prisoners holding such positions should accordingly be entitled to earn those credits. Moreover, if a prisoner was holding such a position—and earning "extra" credits—prior to the worsening of his mental condition that triggered his transfer to a hospital, he should presumably be permitted to continue earning those extra credits at the hospital even if, because of his mental condition, he is now unable to perform the required activities. In that connection, it is significant that the policy

[25] The disincentive structure is extensively discussed in the empirical study of the Arizona situation. Ibid.

[26] See ibid. at 183 and note 167 (discussing the need for voluntary admission procedures). As will be mentioned in greater detail below, Arizona's new mental health law now permits voluntary hospital admission of prisoners.

[27] See *Walsh* v. *State ex rel.* Eyman, 104 Ariz. 202, 450 P2d 392 (1969).

[28] See People *ex rel. Brown* v. *Herold*, 29 N.Y. 2d 939, 280 N. E. 2d 362, 329 N.Y.S.2d 574 (1972). *Brown* involved a suit against the Director of Dannemora State Hospital, challenging the Department of Corrections' policy denying good-time allowances to all mentally ill prisoners. *Brown* held the departmental policy to be violative of the statutory scheme and of the equal protection clause, at least as applied to prisoners who have not been declared legally incompetent, and who thus may be competent to weigh the risks and benefits of electing the New York good time allowance plan.

of many prisons is such that "prisoners who undergo treatment for *physical* problems are not deprived of ["extra"] credits for the period of time they spend at the county general hospital" (p. 186). In fact, a recent federal case found an equal protection violation in the denial of certain credits to a prisoner medically unable to perform prison labor.[29]

The parole problem is easily as troubling to prisoner-patients as is the problem of good time allowances. Parole boards often have a flat policy against authorizing the conditional release of prisoners who are confined in mental hospitals.[30] Such a firm policy, however, seems unwarranted. Especially in the context of *committed* prisoner-patients, it is important to recognize that

> granting the prisoner-patient parole would not in this setting be equivalent
> to setting him free. Rather, the parole from his penal sentence would
> signify simply that, *when* he is discharged by the hospital, he will be
> released rather than returned to the prison—a fact that should surely
> provide a powerful incentive for the patient to take full advantage of the
> psychiatric care available and thus to regain his liberty. (Wexler & Scoville,
> 1971, p. 186, emphasis added).

Indeed, even with respect to *voluntary* patients, where the hospital traditionally has no control over the patient's decision to leave, the parole preclusion policy is unpersuasive, for the board, if it deems a further period of hospitalization to be necessary prior to the patient's discharge to the community, could parole the patient *to the hospital*, leaving in the hospital's hand the ultimate decision whether to release the patient prior to the expiration of his "parole" status.[31]

[29] *Sawyer* v. *Sigler*, 320 F. Supp. 690 (D.Neb. 1970).

[30] E.g., U.S. *ex rel. Schuster* v. *Herold*, 410 F2d 1071 (2d Cir. 1969); People *ex rel. Slofsky* v. *Agnew*, 68 Misc. 2d 128, 326 N.Y.S. 2d 477 (Sup. Ct., Clinton Co., 1971).

[31] The mechanism of parole-to-hospital is not simply a legal euphemism for parole denied. It can significantly affect the "parolee's" living conditions. In Arizona, for example, "transferred prisoners are placed automatically in the Maximum Security Unit of the state hospital and—for security reasons—are usually retained in that unit during their entire stay at the hospital. If a prisoner-patient were granted parole, however, he would seemingly no longer constitute a "special" security or escape risk, and might well be transferred to the general hospital population, where living conditions are less restrictive and more pleasant and where chances for psychiatric recovery seem substantially greater. The possibility of leaving the Maximum Security Ward and entering the general hospital population is raised not only by the granting of parole, but also by the expiration of a transferred inmate's penal sentence—which is another reason why prisoners contemplating transfer to the hospital ought to be concerned with the computation of their "good time" credits" (Wexler & Scoville, 1971, at 186 note 178, citations omitted).

That point was recently underscored by a lower New York court which, on equal protection grounds, declared unconstitutional that state's outright policy against conditionally releasing prisoner-patients, and which ordered the parole to a civil hospital of a Dannemora State Hospital inmate who had been denied parole solely because of his mental patient status.[32] The record in that case contained the testimony of the director of the secure mental hospital, who claimed that a substantial number of prisoner-patients at the facility could be paroled safely to a civil mental hospital or, in some cases, to outpatient treatment in their home communities. He thought, too, that such action would greatly enhance the patients' chances for complete psychiatric recovery.[33] The court, noting that no flat parole prohibition exists with respect to persons suffering from *physical* disabilities, and noting further that physically disabled prisoners are often paroled to general hospitals for treatment, ruled squarely that, whether dealing with the physically or mentally disabled, "self-sufficiency is not a requirement of parole."[34]

Recent statutes in states such as Massachusetts, Michigan, and Arizona have addressed, to varying degrees, the legal problems associated with prison-to-hospital transferees. The Arizona statute addresses specifically the issues of voluntary hospital admission, good time credits (both "ordinary" and "extra"—double time—credits), and parole. The pertinent provisions are set out below:

> E. A prisoner may apply for voluntary admission to the state hospital under the provisions of Section 36-531. His application, when submitted to the prison physician, shall be forwarded to the superintendent of the state hospital by the prison physician together with the report of the prison physician and such material, if any, provided by the prisoner in support or in explanation of his application. A prisoner hospitalized in the state hospital as a voluntary patient shall be in the legal custody of the superintendent of the prison.

> F. All prisoners transferred to the Arizona State Hospital pursuant to this section (relating to commitments and to voluntary admissions) shall remain eligible to accrue [ordinary] good-time credits pursuant to section 31-251. Double-time deductions pursuant to section 31-252 shall be allowed any prisoner who was earning the deductions immediately prior to transfer to the state hospital, and to any prisoner performing any assignment of confidence or trust at the state hospital.

---

[32] People *ex rel. Slofsky* v. *Agnew*, 68 Misc. 2d 128, 326 N.Y.S. 2d 477 (Sup. Ct., Clinton Co., 1971).
[33] See generally 326 N.Y.S. 2d at 479.
[34] Ibid.

G. No prisoner otherwise eligible shall be denied parole solely because he is confined at the state hopsital pursuant to this section.[35]

CONCLUSION—A BEHAVIORAL JURISPRUDENCE

As the present writer has stated elsewhere (Wexler, 1975), it seems that lawyers and behavioral psychologists have reached the stage where they may begin cooperating to formulate a "behavioral jurisprudence." Such a jurisprudence could involve "contingency consciousness raising"[36] with regard to the legal system, applying behavioral principles in analyzing and revising that system, clarifying vague legal concepts by attempting to redefine them in behavioral terms,[37] and explaining from a behavioral perspective the existence of rights and rules (Vargas, 1975).

REFERENCES

Bandura, A. Behavior theory and the models of man. *American Psychologist*, 1974, *29*, 859–869.
Burt, R. A., & Morris, N. A proposal for the abolition of the incompetency plea. *University of Chicago Law Review*, 1972, *40*, 66–95.
de Grazia, E. Diversion from the criminal process: The 'mental-health' experiment. *Connecticut Law Review*, 1974, *6*, 432–523.
Fischhoff, B. F. The silly certainty of hindsight. *Psychology Today*, 1975, *8* (April), 71–76.
Rubin, B. *Report of visit to control unit treatment program*. Unpublished report, November 25, 1973.
Vargas, E. A. Rights: A behavioristic analysis. *Behaviorism*, 1975, *3* (Fall), 178–190.
Wexler, D. B. Token and taboo: Behavior modification, token economies, and the law. *California Law Review*, 1973, *61*, 81–109.

---

[35] Arizona Revised Statutes, §31-224 (E)-(G). A recent amendment preserves the basic provisions quoted in the text but casts them in considerably different language and poses constitutional difficulties with respect to the procedural treatment of *involuntarily* transferred prison inmates. Arizona Revised Statutes, §31-224 (A)-(G) (Supp. 1975).

[36] Economic analysis, which is being increasingly applied to a broad spectrum of legal issues, may help to augment or facilitate contingency analysis. See generally R. A. Posner, *Economic Analysis of Law* (Boston: Little, Brown & Company, 1972). There is, of course, considerable similarity between economics and behavioral psychology, with economists speaking of incentives and information flow while psychologists are speaking of contingencies and cues.

[37] For a valuable example of clarifying legal concepts through behavioral terminology, see I. Goldiamond. Toward a constructional approach to social problems. *Behaviorism*, 1974, *2* (Spring), 60.

Wexler, D. B. Foreword: Mental health law and the movement toward voluntary treatment. *California Law Review*, 1974, *62*, 671–692.

Wexler, D. B. The surfacing of behavioral jurisprudence. *Behaviorism*, 1975, *3* (Fall), 172–176.

Wexler, D. B. *Criminal commitments and dangerous mental patients: Legal issues of confinement, treatment, and release.* Washington, D. C.: U. S. Government Printing Office, 1976.

Wexler, D. B., & Scoville, S. E. The administration of psychiatric justice: Theory and practice in Arizona. *Arizona Law Review*, 1971, *13*, 1–260.

5

Professional Accountability in the Treatment and Release of Dangerous Persons

R. KIRKLAND SCHWITZGEBEL

Before I began writing this chapter, I was physically threatened by a group of teen-agers while walking to my car in an economically depressed area of an East Coast city. A few days later, I witnessed an attack upon a person in a different city. I did what I could to help him, but it was clearly not enough. I held his hand as he died on the sidewalk of the city waiting for an ambulance that arrived 20 minutes too late. As far as I could tell, he was a fairly typical, and none the less important, inhabitant of skid row. His world came to an abrupt and unnecessary end because of the casual cruelty of a few youths.

Although fighting does of course take place among many animals of the same species, it is usually for food, territory, mates, and perhaps occasionally for social position. The frequency with which human beings injure or kill one another out of nonutilitarian aggression is extraordinary within the general biological community. I have arrived reluctantly at last at the conclusion that some people are mean, and a few people are repeatedly mean.

R. KIRKLAND SCHWITZGEBEL • Department of Psychology, California Lutheran College, Thousand Oaks, California. This work was supported in part by Public Health Service Grant 1 R0 1 MH21303-02 from the National Institute of Mental Health, Center for Studies in Crime and Delinquency. R. Kirkland Schwitzgebel was principal investigator and A. Louis McGarry was coprincipal investigator.

The frightening tendency of man to take himself as his own prey has remained largely unabated in recent years in spite of mental health platitudes, political ideologies, and the involuntary civil commitment of persons presumed to be dangerous. My recent experiences have made me less tolerant of interpersonal cruelty whether that cruelty is by individuals toward each other or by mental health institutions toward patients. It is now time for a broad and serious reassessment of the functioning of the mental health system with regard to its treatment of dangerous persons.

The involuntary, indeterminate commitment of patients to mental hospitals was developed with at least two purposes in mind: the treatment of dangerous persons and the protection of society. It was hoped that society would be protected at the same time as offenders were being effectively treated. That hope must now be—as the saying goes—washed in the cynical acid of fact.

INADEQUACY OF TREATMENT

The issue of the right to treatment has recently received much attention. Whether the Supreme Court in *O'Connor* v. *Donaldson*[1] supported or undermined a general right to treatment may not in the long run be as important as the fact that the Supreme Court was willing to look at conditions inside a mental hospital following commitment. In the past, the Court has been reluctant to do this. Once judicial examination begins, the inadequacy of hospital conditions and treatment should become apparent and judicial remedies should, one hopes, be forthcoming.

Methods will have to be used by hospital staffs and legal personnel to assess the adequacy of the treatment provided to the patients. Traditionally, in general medical practice, the adequacy of treatment is assessed by one of three methods. The first method focuses upon the structure of the institution and uses criteria such as staff–patient ratios and per capita expenditures to determine the adequacy of treatment. The second method, the process method, examines the type and amount of treatment delivered to the patients. Patient records are usually examined to determine how often the patients were seen, by whom, and for what purposes. The third method of treatment assessment focuses on outcome. Here information is collected about the results or effects of the treatment provided.

[1] *O'Connor* v. *Donaldson*, No. 74-8, U.S. (June 26, 1975) (Slip Opinion).

Generally, the courts, as in *Wyatt* v. *Stickney*,[2] have relied upon structural criteria for assessing and enforcing adequate patient care or treatment. An adequate staff–patient ratio does not, however guarantee adequate care or treatment. An adequate staff–patient ratio says nothing about the actual performance of the staff with regard to particular patients. The case of *Whitree* v. *State*[3] is illustrative.

Whitree received a suspended sentence for third-degree assault, violated probation, and was sent to Matteawan State Hospital, where he was evaluated as being unable to understand the proceedings against him. He spent the next 14½ years awaiting trial. During this time, he received no psychotherapy. What he did receive, however, was a fractured nose, a fractured right tibia, a fracture of the eighth and ninth ribs, and injury of two cervical vertebrae. Whitree also sustained other injuries, including a permanent peritonitis of the right shoulder, which resulted from beatings by patients and hospital personnel. He suffered untreated rectal bleeding and headaches. He was burned on his face and chest when a patient poured hot coffee on him. In spite of this, his prescription record for the 14½ years of his confinement showed only that he received vaseline and rectal suppositories.

The hospital finally discharged Whitree as "improved." To this the court commented, "We consider the final diagnosis and the use of the word 'Improved' the epitome of cynicism and a symbol in one word of the medical and psychiatric non-treatment received by this man over the greater part of 14½ years."[4] The court awarded Whitree $300,000 in damages. There was a later out-of-court settlement for $200,000.

In Illinois, Rubin (1972) conducted a detailed study of 17 men who were committed to the psychiatric division of Menard Penitentiary. These men were committed because they were found incompetent to stand trial or not guilty by reason of insanity and were considered dangerous. Rubin concluded that only one of the 17 men was dangerous and noted: "The 17 men spent a cumulative 425 years in prison, after legislative remedy should have resulted in their being placed in treatment or community settings" (p. 403). The man considered most dangerous by the psychiatric staff was so categorized because he became infuriated one day after being put off for 22 years about his

---

[2] *Wyatt* v. *Stickney*, 344 F. Supp. 373 (M.D. Ala. 1972), *aff'd sub nom. Wyatt* v. *Aderholt*, 503 F.2d 1305 (5th Cir. 1974).

[3] 56 Misc.2d 693, 290 N.Y.S.2d 486 (Ct.Cl. 1968).

[4] Ibid. at 500.

wishes to be considered for release. In anger, he struck an assistant warden. Following this incident, he remained in handcuffs for 3 years and was overdosed with phenothiazine medication until toxicity (dyskinesias) was readily apparent (p. 404). This is not psychiatric treatment, this is psychiatric revenge.

In Massachusetts, Dr. A. Louis McGarry and this author recently studied 62 patients indefinitely committed to the Center for the Diagnosis and Treatment of Dangerous Persons at the Bridgewater State Hospital.[5] These particular patients were committed because of sexual offenses with children. The average age of these pedophiles was 38. Most of them had worked in unskilled or semiskilled occupations prior to their commitment. The average (mean) IQ was 85. The average age of their victims was 10, and force was used in 54% of the cases.

At the time of our study, this group of patients had already spent an average of approximately 6½ years at the treatment center. The time spent by individual patients ranged from 1 year to over 13 years.[6] The average amount of treatment received by these patients according to reports by the center's own treatment staff was 2.41 hours per month. This time was generously estimated from treatment reports which would be likely to be positively biased toward reporting treatment efforts. This average treatment time means that this group of patients was exposed at maximum to approximately 36 minutes of formal therapy per week. This is roughly comparable to the findings in a study conducted in 1973 by Evenson, Nieuwenhuizen, Sletten, and Cho, who found that the average patient in Missouri state mental hospitals received about 20 minutes of formal psychotherapy per week (calculations by the author).

The quality and effectiveness of the treatment provided at the treatment center at the Bridgewater State Hospital was not well described in the treatment records. In the case of one patient, the records showed "some" or "moderate" progress for over 10 years of treatment. This raises the question of how much "progress" is enough? How much "progress" can one individual make? Is it not reasonable to conclude that after 10 years of "progress" the treatment provided is *de facto* ineffective or inadequate and that the real purpose being served by continued confinement is preventive detention.

---

[5] See p. 149.

[6] This information is based upon 57 rather than 62 patients because 5 official patient records were so incomplete, unclear, or contradictory that the date of their admission could not be reliably determined.

Surely the burden of proving that more treatment would be beneficial should be shifted to the institution.

In a concurring opinion in the *Donaldson* case, Chief Justice Burger observed, "Despite many recent advances in medical knowledge, it remains a stubborn fact that there are many forms of mental illness which are not understood, some which are untreatable in the sense that no effective therapy has yet been discovered for them, and that rates of 'cure' are generally low."[7] The chief justice correctly raised the issue of "effective therapy" for mental patients, but that issue was not resolved in *Donaldson*. Implied promises of effective therapy for involuntarily committed patients are sprinkled like ground glass through many commitment statutes and mental health publications. Patients, judges, and legislators expect or hope for the effective treatment of dangerous persons, but such hopes or expectations, though alluring, are largely illusions. At the very least, a patient who is indeterminately committed should have a right to an honest appraisal of his status and the likelihood of effective treatment. But this brings us to the next problem: the accurate assessment of dangerousness.

INADEQUACY OF RELEASE DECISIONS

In the absence of the accurate measurement of dangerousness, the legislative blending of treatment and social protection goals in commitment statutes encourages a convenient confusion which obscures from the public (and perhaps even from professional personnel) the ineffectiveness of treatment. Under the guise of treatment, patients may spend many years in an institution when the real and primary purpose of their commitment is preventive detention.

Ironically, in many situations not even preventive detention is achieved because in fact no harm to others is being prevented. This is illustrated by the well-known studies by Steadman and others of the Baxstrom patients in New York (Steadman, 1973; see also Steadman & Keveles, 1972). In summary, 967 involuntarily committed, supposedly dangerous patients were released by court order to other hospitals or the community. After 4½ years, only 2.7% of these patients were returned to the hospitals to which they had originally been committed because of their supposed dangerousness. This does not mean, however, that these patients were "paragons of virtue." In a follow-up

[7] Note 1 above, at 7.

study of a subsample of these Baxstrom patients, it was found that 17% were arrested and 7% were convicted in the 4½-year period. (Not all convictions led to reconfinement.) In short, these supposedly dangerous patients, while surely not a group of ideal citizens, were not nearly as dangerous as assumed by the hospital staffs who originally recommended their commitment.

Similar results were found in Massachusetts with Baxstrom-type patients when a new statute in 1967 required the judicial review of involuntarily committed "dangerous" patients. Out of a subsample of 234 men, a 33-month follow-up study found that 93 patients had been released into the community for an average of 13 months (McGarry & Parker, 1974). Out of this group, 15 (16.1%) had appeared in court. There was only one conviction for a felony. All other charges were misdemeanors. The most frequent charge was drunkenness.

These studies, as well as many others, raise the question of how well dangerousness is assessed in usual psychiatric practice. The answer seems generally to be that the clinical prediction of future dangerous conduct of specific individuals ranges from marginally adequate in those extreme cases of people with a history of repeated violent acts to clearly inadequate for the typical patient. Using the usual clinical methods, many nondangerous patients would have to be wrongfully classified as dangerous and then confined to prevent the harmful conduct of one dangerous person.

A noteworthy study has been published by Kozol and his associates which suggested that "dangerousness can be reliably diagnosed and effectively treated" (Kozol, Boucher, & Garofalo, 1972). This assertion was based upon data collected with regard to 435 patients released from the treatment center at the Bridgewater State Hospital at which Kozol is the chief psychiatrist. Some of these patients were recommended for release from the treatment center as no longer dangerous and some patients were not recommended for release by the treatment center staff but were nevertheless released by courts. Among those recommended for release by the staff, only 6.1% later committed serious, assaultive crimes. In contrast, 34.7% of those patients not recommended for release by the staff subsequently committed serious, assaultive crimes.

This difference between 6.1% and 34.7% initially appears to support the clinical ability to predict future dangerous conduct. However, the data in the Kozol paper have been reanalyzed by Evenson and Altman (1975), who found that the amount of recidivism of the total group of the 435 released patients was 11%. Therefore, it would be possible to obtain 89% accuracy in prediction with this group merely by predicting that all of the patients are not dangerous. Correct predictions by the treatment center staff was 86%. Most of the apparent predictive accuracy of the staff came from correctly indentifying the larger number of patients who were not recidivists. If one statistically compensates for the correct predictions occurring merely by chance in this group of patients, one finds that the staff obtained 27% predictive accuracy instead of the claimed 86%. It may also be noted that 65% of those patients considered dangerous by the staff but nevertheless released by courts did not subsequently commit serious assaultive crimes.

Given this much predictive error by those clinicians claiming diagnostic skill, it can be questioned whether rational distinctions are generally being made between dangerous and nondangerous persons or whether society is presumed to be protected through the mass, indiscriminate confinement of mentally ill persons. Kozol and his associates are at least to be complimented on providing information about their performance even though their interpretation of that information may differ from the interpretation by others. One of the first steps in establishing suitable public accountability is the collection of publicly available data on clinical performance.

Ironically, while Kozol and his associates were claiming psychiatric skill in diagnosing and treating dangerousness, the American Psychiatric Association (Area VI) was preparing a brief in *Tarasoff* v. *Regents of University of California*[8] with an opposing opinion. That brief stated that "absent a prior history of violence, no therapist can accurately predict whether his patient is in fact dangerous or not."[9] (In the *Tarasoff* case the Supreme Court of California imposed liability upon psychotherapists for their failure to warn a woman who was later killed by their patient.) The brief just quoted was part of a petition for a rehearing. The brief further asserted: "The newly imposed duty to warn is also inconsistent with the finding of scientific research that no special professional ability or expertise has yet been demonstrated in the prognosis of dangerousness. Instead, the few studies which have been done strongly suggest that psychiatrists are rather inaccurate predictors; inaccurate in an absolute sense, and even less accurate when compared with other professions." This brief thus contains a forthright admission of the inability of psychiatrists to accomplish generally the goal of social protection.

[8] 118 Cal. Rptr. 129, 529 P. 2d 553 (1974) (In Bank).
[9] American Psychiatrist Association (Area VI) *et al.*, brief *amicus curiae* in support of a petition for rehearing, *Tarasoff* v. *Regents of University California*, 1975, 9.

In terms of public accountability and fundamental fairness, psychiatrists should not be permitted to claim expertise in predicting dangerousness when they wish to commit a patient but to claim they have no expertise when a dangerous person commits an offense. Either this professional group has special expertise in generally predicting dangerousness or it does not.

CIVIL LIABILITY FOR INADEQUATE TREATMENT AND DECISION MAKING[10]

Because there has been, and probably will continue to be, much discussion about a constitutionally based right to treatment and right to accurate diagnosis, it might be useful to consider some legal remedies related to inadequate treatment and inadequate decision-making which are not constitutionally based. The following discussion is, at best, only a brief and very speculative survey of some possible theories of civil liability.

One of the most obvious theories of liability is malpractice. The standard of care required of psychiatrists varies considerably from case to case depending upon particular fact situations and jurisdiction. Factors such as the intractibility of the mental illness, the skill required, and the seriousness of the consequences of treatment error seem to influence greatly the legal results. *Hanmer* v. *Rosen*[11] was a case involving the beating of a patient by a psychiatrist. In finding the psychiatrist liable, the court referred to "improper treatment." Likewise, in *Zipkin* v. *Freeman*,[12] a case involving sexual intercourse between the psychiatrist and his patient, the court referred to "proper" treatment as therapy.

The malpractice suit presents special problems for the mentally ill plaintiff. Psychiatric patients must overcome the obvious impications that they are "crazy" or out of touch with reality; thus there is the threshold issue of the plaintiff's credibility. Also, psychiatry as a medical specialty seems to be less vulnerable to malpractice suits than other specialists of medicine because of the diversity of therapeutic techniques, the wide variety of opinion on appropriate treatment modalities, and the uncertainty of "cure." Therefore, recovery for

---

[10] I am very grateful for the participation of attorney Honora Kaplan in the preparation of this section of the chapter. Useful ideas are hers; errors are mine.

[11] 7 N.Y.2d 376, 165 N.E. 2d 756 (Court of Appeals 1960).

[12] 436 S.W.2d 753 (Mo. 1969).

injuries sustained in the course of organic or mechanical therapy such as electroconvulsive shock is more feasible than recovery for nonorganic treatment such as psychoanalysis.

Another potential theory of liability for inadequate treatment is breach of contract. A physician is entitled to payment for his services under either a written or an implied contract. Conversely, there is a contractual duty imposed upon the physician to use at least ordinary skill and care. Unless the physician agrees in writing or verbally to effect a specific cure, there is generally no guarantee by the physician that the patient will be cured or improved.

In *Nicholson* v. *Han*,[13] a couple sought help from a psychiatrist for problems with their marriage. The psychiatrist undertook treatment supposedly to improve the couple's relationship. But over a period of 2 years, the marital situation deteriorated and finally ended in divorce. The court suggested that although an express contract warranting a cure could be made by a psychiatrist, this must be very clear from what was said by the parties at the time of the making of the contract. The court concluded from the fact situation that there had been no such special agreement and that the essential nature of the plaintiff's claim was the alienation of affections.

The few cases dealing with contractual obligations in the area of mental health have generally involved private patients. However, the need to protect the interest of patients in public institutions is even more critical, particularly when they are involuntarily committed. When patients are committed to a mental institution, they are deprived of the opportunity to select freely a different psychiatrist if treatment does not appear to be effective. A patient in the community may select another psychiatrist with perhaps little harm done except the loss of time and money. The institutionalized patient, meanwhile, suffers in addition a loss of the opportunity to earn a livelihood and to participate in family life.

When a treatable patient is given no treatment in an institution or receives only *de minimus* or perfunctory treatment, there would seem to be a clear possibility of a breach of the agreement to perform the treatment task. The issue of the quality of the performance of that task is not even reached. The problem is not how properly the therapist acted, but whether or not he acted at all.

In those jurisdictions which have not permitted or encouraged actions based upon an implied contract, an express agreement between therapist or hospital and the committed patient might be

[13] 12 Mick. App. 35, 162 N.W.2d 313 (1968).

inferred from the language of the commitment statutes, particularly those statutes which provide for "care and treatment." This explicitly stated purpose of commitment might be sufficient to transform an implied contract into an express agreement to provide adequate treatment for those patients who can benefit from it. A patient voluntarily committing himself for treatment in a private mental hospital reasonably expects treatment which will be at least customary and usual. Courts generally enforce this expectation. There is no reason why the process of involuntary commitment should void this reasonable expectation or diminish the obligation of the psychiatrist or hospital to provide treatment.

One of the immediate difficulties in bringing an action in tort or contract against a public hospital or public employee is immunity from liability. Public hospitals, as governmental units, have been protected in large measure by sovereign immunity, while private charitable (eleemosynary) facilities have been sheltered by the concept of charitable immunity. Private proprietary hospitals, as profit-making businesses, have never been doctrinally immune from liability. Increasingly, charitable immunity has been abrogated by state statutes and does not exist or exists in only a very limited form in at least 25 states. In *Tarasoff*[14] the court interpreted a broad immunity statute to permit liability and found that publicly employed therapists were required to provide that quantum of care which the common law requires of private practitioners.

The failure to apply the legal doctrine of *respondeat superior* has also protected hospitals from tort liability which would otherwise be imputed to an employer for his servant's negligence committed within the scope of employment. Physicians, although part of the medical staff, have traditionally been considered "indepedent contractors" rather than "employees" or "servants" of the hospital, and this status legally precluded the vicarious liability of the medical facility. It has been argued that the hospital as an institution simply does not exercise the requisite control over the physician's acts and decisions to make the hospital liable for injuries resulting from his or her negligent treatment.

Implicit, however, in the supervisory and monitoring responsibility of a hospital are affirmative obligations to maintain and control the quality of care within the facility. As *Darling* v. *Charleston Community Memorial Hospital*[15] indicated, hospitals have a direct duty to furnish

[14] Note 9 above.
[15] 33 Ill.2d 326, 211 N.E.2d 253, *cert. denied*, 383 U.S. 946 (1965).

medical care to patients. Psychiatric institutions, no less than purely medical facilities can be viewed as providing treatment to patients. The psychiatric concept of "milieu therapy," sometimes used to evade public accountability, explicitly acknowledges the institution as a treatment provider.

Patients, relatives, and the public have acted in reliance upon certain express and implied promises of treatment made by professional mental health personnel. Increasingly, empirical evidence raises the question as to whether this reliance has been misplaced. Psychiatry seems to be more content with old problems, rather than new solutions.

The violence done from person to person in the streets of our cities is obvious and terrible. The violence done to a person through years of useless confinement is not so obvious but just as terrible. The time has now come—in fact it is long past due—for the mental health professions to render a public accounting and to become accountable to those whom they claim to serve.

REFERENCES

Evenson, R. C., & Altman, H. A re-evaluation of "The diagnosis and treatment of dangerousness." Unpublished paper, Missouri Institute of Psychiatry, University of Missouri School of Medicine, 1975.

Evenson, R. C., Nieuwenhuizen, M., Sletten, I. W., & Cho, D. W. A computerized survey of treatments used in Missouri institutions. Hospital and Community Psychiatry, 1973, 24, 23-26.

Kozol, H. L., Boucher, R. J., & Garofalo, R. F. The diagnosis and treatment of dangerousness. Crime and Delinquency, 1972, October, 371–392.

McGarry, A. L., & Parker, L. L. Massachusetts' operation Baxstrom: A follow-up. Massachusetts Journal of Mental Health, 1974, 4, 27–41.

Rubin, B. Prediction of dangerousness in mentally ill criminals. Archives of General Psychiatry, 1972, 27, 397–407.

Steadman, H. J. Implications from the Baxstrom experience. Paper presented at the American Academy of Psychiatry and the Law, Atlanta, March 16, 1973. (Mental Health Research Unit, New York State Department of Mental Hygiene, Albany, New York.)

Steadman, H. J., & Keveles, G. The community adjustment and criminal activity of the Baxstrom patients: 1966–1970. American Journal of Psychiatry, 1972, 129, 304–310.

6

Who Should Go to Prison

NORVAL MORRIS

> If once a man indulges himself in murder, very soon he comes to think
> very little of robbing and from robbing he comes next to drinking and
> Sabbath breaking, and from that to incivility and procrastination.
>
> *Thomas DeQuincey*

The question of who should go to prison is a serious one, of course,
but occasionally it has its lighter side. Not long ago, Chicago heralded
the opening of a new jail which is in the modern pattern: a 26-story
triangular concrete structure, housing, in relative comfort, people
awaiting trial and others undergoing short-term punishment. The
decor is "prison stark." The security system is controlled by computer, federal prison administrators having decided apparently that
man is fallible but the computer is not. The computer system controls
the elevators in such a way that two elevators cannot arrive at the
same level together and that the same weight of person must get out
the elevator as got into it, lest an alarm bell ring. It is supposedly
foolproof and all very complicated.

The result was that recently the warden, Ray Nelson, was locked
in an elevator for a protracted period, rendered more protracted by the
fact that nobody in Chicago knew how to persuade the computer to
release him. The prison administrators telephoned a man in California
who they believed had influence with the machine, but since he was
out to a leisurely California lunch, the parole of the warden was
delayed. The next achievement of this advanced security system was
to lock the director of the Federal Bureau of Prisons out of the prison

NORVAL MORRIS • University of Chicago Law School, Chicago, Illinois.

for a long while—an event the prison administrators were a bit sensitive about. The new Chicago jail is not alone in its problems with electronic marvels. In Marion, Illinois, five prisoners recently managed to escape by developing an instrument which activated the electronic equipment controlling the gates. It is not surprising to hear that training in electronics has been abandoned at Marion, it no longer being one of the rehabilitative purposes they want to pursue.

What all this illustrates, of course, is that the ideal and the practical do not always jibe, that people do not agree on prison policy, that rhetoric and reality may be at odds. Consider, for example, that the new jail in Chicago is being opened at the very moment when many authorities in the field contend that people should not go to jail anymore but should instead by diverted into other programs. Our present adult male prison population of between 240,000 and 250,000 is likely to increase substantially in the years ahead, though at the same time we are very skeptical about whether it is a good thing to imprison criminals at all.

It is necessary to state at the outset that we ought to experiment with different types of imprisonment. In fact, the author has been personally involved in the opening of a new federal prison in Butner, North Carolina, which had once been the proposed site for behavior modification programs but now has been adapted to a model several of us suggested for repetitively violent prisoners. Butner is innovative in that it will house 200 dangerous prisoners, men aged 18 to 30 who have been convicted of at least two separate crimes of violence during their last 3 years and who have from 1 to 3 years to serve before their earliest parole-release date. These are the dangerous prisoners, not the amenable ones usually chosen by penal reformers. Butner will be innovative, not only by taking the most dangerous prisoners, but also by making all its programs voluntary. Prisoners will stay in Butner only so long as they wish and will participate in treatment programs only if they choose. They will carry a key to their own cells. Those who want to leave Butner will not be punished for doing so. And some might well wish to leave, for quite comfortable federal facilities now exist to accommodate the higher class of offenders who are recently finding their way to prison.

Though the existence of Butner might suggest a new turn in prison policy, the fact is that there is a serious lack of direction in the field, a lot of uncertainty about what to do with criminals. Fads and fashions, heroic cures and simple remedies are peddled by politicians, including presidents in their messages to Congress. Some have advocated mandatory minimum sentences for violent repeaters in order to reduce crimes of violence, despite the fact that our experience with mandatory minimum sentences is dismal, as in New York in connection with drug control.

The disagreement among authorities is such that some people urge the abolition of imprisonment altogether, on the theory that "caging is evil" and that, as some scholars point out, nothing works anyway. Some of us find caging people very sad. We wish we did not have to put people in prison. But unfortunately prisons—that is, places of enforced banishment subject to security—will probably continue to exist, though perhaps changed in size, character, and condition. And that may not be all bad, since imprisonment may offer less serious threats to human freedom than some of the cures now offered to reduce imprisonment.

Some authorities, though not urging the abolition of punishment, do urge that we put a moratorium on prison building. If nothing has worked so far, let us try other things besides caging. These people say, first of all, that the criminal law prohibits too much and the range of criminal sanctions is too great. They would make illegal only injuries and threats of injury to the person, major depredations to property, and serious interference with governmental processes. They contend that by so narrowing the range of illegal acts, we would reduce the number of people going to prison.

These arguments have appeal. As a matter of fact, the criminal law is not much good at controlling acts which are self-injurious or immoral or fattening or whatever. The criminal law is not a good instrumentality by which to compel people to be virtuous. It rarely succeeds in that. But it has succeeded, however, in corrupting the police, increasing the hypocrisy of the system, wasting the time and energy of countless people, and cluttering the courts and jails.

The trouble with these arguments is that eliminating from the criminal process the so-called victimless crimes will not reduce the prison population. It is true that victimless crimes, such as drug use, drinking, and vagrancy, account for half of our arrests each year, but they do not account for a like portion of the prison population. Few drug offenders go to prison as such. Even if we decriminalize drug use, for example, and regulate it much as we do alcohol, by substituting a regulatory system for a criminal one, we will not much change the number of people going to prison.

Another argument of the people who urge a moratorium on prison building is that we ought to divert criminals from prisons to community-based treatment programs. Let us divert people from jails and prisons, from institutions in general; let us find alternatives. For if we divert enough people from our prisons, we will not have to build more prisons.

As appealing as it sounds, this proposal would not reduce the prison population either. In addition to the usual two punishment choices—doing nothing to the criminal or doing something very severe—we would now add a third, doing something moderate. But we would probably not do something moderate to the ones we now send to prison; instead, we would start to punish moderately those we once did not punish at all. If you increase the discretion to punish in an overcrowded system, you reduce the pressure on the system—and increase the number of times the discretion to punish is exercised. This has been tested and tested and retested. For example, where police are allowed to issue a traffic summons instead of making an arrest, the number of arrests stays about the same, but the number of summonses skyrockets—and the number to whom we do nothing is, of course, reduced. Or, to take another example, where prosecutors are permitted to divert a certain number of cases to a pretrial program, the proportion of cases tried to those declined stays about the same. This happened in a study done in the northern district of Illinois, which is a crowded federal prosecution district but one well staffed with good people. The pattern there was that out of 7,000 cases reported, about 1,000 went to trial and 6,000 were declined. One year they diverted about 150 possible cases from the usual system to a pretrial program. Even so, the figures for the year stayed the same, about 1,000 cases tried of 7,000 reported.

The only way to reduce the number of people imprisoned by diversion from prison to other programs is to select for alternative punishment only those who would have gone to prison otherwise and to put numerical ceilings on the prison population. Otherwise alternative punishments would not reduce the prison population but instead would have the unexpected effect of increasing the number of people subjected to some other kind of punishment however moderate.

But would such punishment really be moderate? The danger of the criminal law is its pervasive interference in people's lives. Some of the suggested alternatives to imprisonment involve the greatest interference with the lives of people, even those not in prison. This may not be such a wise trade-off. At least it is an open question and should be taken seriously. Our most important text here is Orwell's *1984*. In his dark disutopia, the criminal law had withered away by 1984, only to be replaced by pervasive and extensive government interference in the life of every citizen.

Another argument of those who want to reduce the prison population is to imprison only the dangerous. But this will not work either. We lack the capacity, the skills, the evaluative techniques to determine who is dangerous. We always overpredict. If you were to visit an ordinary state prison, you would probably think everyone there was dangerous. Ordinary run-of-the-mill prosecutors and judges, to say nothing of politicians, think everyone is dangerous, certainly everyone in prison. But they are wrong. We put more people in prison than just those who are dangerous.

Despite everything, there is no getting round the fact that our prison population will increase. Males aged 20 to 30 characteristically fill the world's prisons, for crime is a young man's game. In this country the population curve for the 20–30 age group is steadily growing and will peak about 1985. Put aphoristically: The baby boom now hits the prisons. Both in absolute numbers and as a proportion of the total population, the larger wave of the prison-prone age group sweeps toward us. Furthermore, of great significance is the fact that that wave is particularly high among the poorer minority males who disproportionately fill our prison cells. Again, aphoristically: The pill came more slowly to the ghetto.

Events, other than population increases, in prison-prone age groups might also swell the number of people going to prison. If police clearance rates rise, if plea bargaining abates and courts speed up their dispensing of justice, and if our attitudes grow more punitive, more prisons will be built and more people will be sent to fill them. Prisons constitute a growth industry.

It should be obvious now that there is a fundamental lack of clarity in what we should be doing in prisons. That confusion is illustrated by the popular question in magazines and newspapers of whether rehabilitation is good or bad. That question is a stupid, thoughtless, mindless one. The Martinson-type studies of rehabilitation pursued by Michael and Adler 40 years ago and by Barbara Wooten 20 years later have been grossly misapplied. We are constantly told that nothing works. That message is imprecise, and unfortunately it can be used to support the most extreme and divergent views—that we should imprison more people longer or not punish them at all or do something in between. The idea that nothing works is mental depression rather than communication.

The truth about rehabilitation, surely, is that our helping programs for convicted criminals, whether in or out of prison, have not overcome the disadvantages of criminals' life situations or the alienation of conviction and imprisonment. Caging is socially disruptive. Some prisoners have been helped to a moral, law-abiding life in the community, and others have experienced spontaneous remission, but how many have been rehabilitated by going to prison?

Rehabilitation—whatever it means, whatever programs it embraces—must cease to be the claimed purpose of a prison sanction. It is silly to lock people up to do them good. But that does not mean that such treatment programs as we now have in prisons should be abandoned. Quite the contrary. They urgently need expansion. No one with any sensitivity to his fellow man can visit a city jail or a state megaprison without recognizing that they contain, as in all countries, inmates who disproportionately to their social groups are illiterate and undereducated, psychologically disturbed, unemployed and vocationally untrained, and socially isolated. However harsh that sounds, it is the truth. It is therefore both humane and practical, both in the prisoners' and the community's best interests, to remedy those deficiencies.

Still, we must not pretend that the purpose of prison is to rehabilitate. That would be hypocritical. We send people to prison for a variety of reasons having nothing to do with rehabilitation— sometimes as punishment for what they have done, sometimes to deter others who are like-minded, sometimes because we know not what else to do with them. Those seem to be the only reasons we have for imprisoning criminals. We cage criminals for what they have done, for the crimes they have committed. It would be a cruel injustice to cage them for what they are, in order to pretend to be able to change or remake them, to cure them coercively. There is a sharp and essential difference between the purposes of imprisonment and the opportunity for training and helping people once they are in prison. When we fail to preserve that distinction, the system is corrupted and our discussion of the problem confused.

Ought we then to conclude that human behavior is unchangeable? That therefore we ought to reject the rehabilitative ideal? This should not be so. After all, if you are sufficiently ruthless in the matter, you can coercively cure criminals. Capital punishment, protracted imprisonment, banishment—all are effective cures of violence. There is very little recidivism after capital punishment. So too with protracted imprisonment, for aging cures all but the most exceptional proclivities to violent crime. If you really want to be safe, just keep all violent criminals in prison until, say, their 50th birthday. By making the community feel secure, such a program might find great popularity.

But you would have built a Gulag Archipelago that would outdo anything Solzhenitsyn described.

The rejection of the model of coercive curing of criminals does not flow from our lack of power or competence to influence human behavior. Rather, it flows from certain centrally important views about the relationship between individual freedom and state authority. We do not force cures on criminals as a matter of social policy. We know the corruptibility of power, the abuses that attend its exercise. At the moment we cannot coercively change people while also preserving proper respect for their human rights and individual autonomy. That is not to say that people are not improvable. We must be optimistic enough to believe that we can diminish human suffering and expand the meaning of brotherhood, even to embrace the criminal. But these changes ought to be pursued only within the framework of human rights. I think we have got to stay well out of the business of forcibly remaking man.

Let us now try to be affirmative rather than negative. Who should go to prison? That question can be answered affirmatively only by keeping in mind certain minimum conditions. Sentencing ought to be principled. Criminal cases ought to be processed efficiently. Judges should be obligated to give reasons for sentences and those sentences should be subject to appeal. (As it is now, one of the greatest powers exercised by judges—the power to sentence—is not subject to appellate remedy, a nonsensical condition which has given rise to a movement in the profession toward judicial reexamination of sentencing.)

Let us assume that we give the accused their constitutional right to a speedy trial, that we impose principled sentences in line with statute and constitution, and that judges give reasons for the sentences they impose. What principles should guide us then in deciding who goes to prison?

The first principle is that we should in all cases impose the least restrictive sanction necessary to achieve defined social ends. We should be parsimonious in sentencing. That may seem to be an obvious statement. Punishment in excess of what is necessary is cruelty, constitutionally prohibited by the Eighth Amendment.

We also ought to send to prison those people who deserve to go there by the nature of their crimes. If any lesser punishment would depreciate the seriousness of the crime, then imprisonment is appropriate. The easiest way to state this is by example. Take the usual spouse-killer. He has solved his problem (in an increasingly popular, way, it might be added) by eliminating his spouse. He is not likely to murder again. Given that truth, we do not need to lock him up to save lives. Suppose, for the sake of argument, that we could show that probation is appropriate here, since imprisonment would not reduce the incidence of spouse-killing. We would still send the spouse-killer to prison. We would impose our maximum punishment as a means of affirming minimum standards of behavior independently of any other social consequences. Every system in the world would impose its maximum punishment in some form or other at this point. Or take a very different example, that of Spiro Agnew, who was not sent to prison. The community did not like that, although Judge Hoffman and Elliott Richardson behaved quite properly in the case. When Agnew railed against what he called the weakness of the American criminal justice system, he had in fact identified its strength—the ability to make a deal. And a deal is what Agnew got. But why was the community outraged? They thought he deserved more. It was not that they thought he was subject to any regenerative cure. What, after all, would he discuss with his probation officer—real estate deals? The public wanted Agnew to get his just deserts and were outranged when he did not receive them. In the context of punishment and social control, the concept of just deserts is a proper one. We send people to prison because, given the nature of their crimes, they deserve it.

We also ought to send some people to prison to deter others. Some people who commit a particular crime must be imprisoned in order to deter the like-minded. An obvious example is in the tax field. Our entire income tax structure rests on principles of deterrence. Every tax felon need not go to prison; it is sufficient if only a few do. In that way the promise of the law is upheld and the rest of us are encouraged to summon up whatever honesty we can in April. This use of deterrence is also, of course, an example of parsimony in imprisonment, as the figures for last year show. Approximately 80 million tax returns were filed. The taxpayers who were convicted of tax fraud numbered 825, and of those, only 43% were imprisoned. Only 400 people had to go to prison in order to keep the other 80 million reasonably honest. It would seem that we are influenced in our behavior by the threat of punishment, by the very possibility of imprisonment when we prepare our tax returns. There are other areas of white-collar crime in which it would be rash to say we cannot deter by example. In any event, it seems certain that every legal system imposes its maximum punishment of imprisonment on the theory that many will be deterred by the confinement of the few.

Another principle to be followed in deciding who should go to prison rests on our not knowing what else to do. If less restrictive sanctions have already been applied to the offender in question, then prison is all that is left. We fall back upon what we might call our *faute de mieux* principle: We have tried everything else, yet here the criminal is back before us again. There has to be a place for the residual sanction of imprisonment when every other sanction in the criminal justice system fails. The criminal law, though it need not be precipitous in doing so, must apply to the incorrigible its final act of retribution.

These principles are sufficient for the foundation of a theory of imprisonment, at least until prisons are no longer necessary. You will note that we have left out any principle of predicting whether or not a criminal is particularly dangerous. We should not make such predictions. We should not use our power over criminals like that, for we do not predict accurately. Perhaps the statement needs qualification. It is very difficult to tease out of the principles of just deserts, deterrence, and parsimony our implied assumptions about dangerousness, but such assumptions are there. We are incapable of predicting what a particular person will do, but we do have certain expectations about the level of recidivism in particular groups of criminals. On that basis we try to predict who will be dangerous, as when we commit the mentally ill, treat the sexual psychopaths, and identify the habitual criminals. But by overpredicting, as we always do, we commit injustice.

To recapitulate, our system of punishment ought to be a simple one. We should be hesitant and parsimonious in the use of criminal sanctions, especially imprisonment. We should struggle in the coming decades to build a principled system of punishment. We should imprison only those who do such evil to us that we can no longer tolerate their presence among us. Those chosen for prison should deserve it, should deserve being used to deter others, should deserve even our failure to know what else to do with them. Unpopular as it is for academics to admit it, our knowledge is limited and we should therefore act accordingly.

One final point: We must blend what we learn through social science with the values of our country. The great values are not those evoked by the bicentennial; the great values are those embodied in the Bill of Rights. Minimum standards of individual freedom and autonomy under an orderly government must not be engulfed by the criminal justice system. Here is the cutting edge of tyranny. If we abuse our power over criminals, we will abuse it elsewhere.

7

Prison Environments and Psychological Survival

HANS TOCH

We all know—or we all presume we know—that prison is hell. We know this through Goffman's (1961) indictment of total institutions. We know it from prison studies (such as Sykes, 1966; Clemmer, 1940; Ward & Kassebaum, 1965)—studies that catalog "pains of imprisonment" and list extreme adjustments required of inmates to cope with captivity. We even know it from the laboratory, where Zimbardo (1972) has "brutalized" students in simulated cells.

Some of our work helps the familiar theme along. Our most recent book (Toch, 1975) catalogs psychological breakdowns of prison inmates, and presents horrifying self-portraits of suffering and noncoping.

What is missing is the other side of the coin. We need to know what it is that inmates require in prisons that is being supplied to them, or that can be supplied. We need to know about types of inmate coping that are not just defenses against stress. And we need a more discriminating picture of stresses. We need data that tell us which

HANS TOCH • State University of New York at Albany, Albany, N.Y. The research reported in this chapter is supported by Grant No. 75NI-99-0030 ("Interventions for Inmate Survival") from the National Institute of Law Enforcement and Criminal Justice. The project enjoys the collaboration of the New York State Department of Correctional Services, and we are indebted to Commissioner Edward Elwin and Dr. Robert Rommel. My associates are (or have been) James Fox, John Gibbs, Robert Johnson, Daniel Lockwood, and John Seymour. John Gibbs is responsible for the statistical analysis of PPI data.

inmates suffer and which do not, and that pinpoint aspects of the prison environment that are stressing and nonstressing. Such data are needed, because prisons—no matter what we may feel about them—are here to stay. And while we may cheer the "diversion" of inmates into the community, we cannot ignore the obligation we have to ameliorate the lot of those who remain undiverted. To this end, we must find who the inmates are that most need our help, and we must find features of prisons, or "niches" within prisons, that ease the fate of such inmates.

Our current research addresses and explores this concern. We attack the problem in various ways, including through study of vulnerable inmates and of protective prison subsettings. Within a year or so, we hope to get closure on the data we are collecting. In the interim, we are sharing first impressions with prison administrators and staff, and hoping to improve classification and management systems.

This chapter will discuss some of the more generic aspects of our work. These are aimed at mapping differential environmental requirements of the average inmate and the corresponding attributes of prison environments. Our general assumption is that different inmates want or require different features of prison, and that prison environments or subenvironments vary more than we think in the degree to which they can respond to inmate needs. The exploration generally falls under the heading of social ecology, which is a burgeoning area these days.

THE SELF-ANCHORING SCALE

We started work by experimenting with a prison-rating system. We wanted an instrument that could allow us to quantify prison rankings while preserving the unique individual premises on which rankings were based. We chose to adapt the so-called Self-Anchoring Striving Scale which has been used to chart the aspirations of different political and national groups (Cantril, 1965). Our version of this instrument (which we administer orally, as part of an interview), reads as follows:

> A. Everyone who serves time in prisons prefers some types of institutions to others. When you think about what really matters to you when you have to serve time, what would the *best possible* prison be like, for you? In other words, if you have to be confined for a time, what would

the institution have to look like—what would it have to offer, for you to be happy there? Take your time answering; such things aren't easy to put into words.

PERMISSIBLE PROBES: What would you need in an institution to serve the easiest bit, or have the most profitable time? What is missing in some places you have been in (besides women) that could have made you happier?

OBLIGATORY PROBE:Anything else?

B. Now, taking the other side of the picture, what are the things you *hate most* about some prisons? If you imagine the *worst possible* institution, as far as *you* are concerned, what would it be like? What qualities would it have? What would it look like, and feel like?

PERMISSIBLE PROBES:What would make you most miserable in prison? What would make it hardest to do time? What would be your idea of a nightmare prison?

OBLIGATORY PROBE: Anything else?

Here is a picture of a ladder. Suppose we say that the top of the ladder (POINTING) represents the best possible institution for you, and the bottom (POINTING) represents the worst possible institution for you.

C. Where on the ladder (MOVING FINGER RAPIDLY UP AND DOWN LADDER) would you place (NAME OF PRISON) as far as you personally are concerned?

D. Why wouldn't you place (NAME OF PRISON) lower than you have? In what ways is it better than the worst institutions?

E. Why wouldn't you place (NAME OF PRISON) higher than you have? In what ways is it worse than the best institutions?

F. One last question. When you *first* began to serve time, would you have ranked (NAME OF PRISON) *higher* or *lower* than you have now? (IF HIGHER OR LOWER) Where would you have ranked it?

Why is that?

We have not yet content-analyzed the scale anchors, but we have some idea of the shape of the quantitative results. Table I, which compares random samples of inmates in five different institutions, confirms that inmates are relatively unhappy in prison.[1] Of more interest is the fact that two institutions differ significantly from the rest: One (Adult A) is rated relatively low; the other (Adult B) does comparatively well.

---

[1] One measure of discontent is the fact that our "low" category includes only three scale intervals; cutting the scale higher would have skewed the distribution.

TABLE I. DISTRIBUTION OF SELF-ANCHORING RATINGS WITHIN CORRECTIONAL
INSTITUTIONS (RANDOM SAMPLES)

Prisons		Self-anchoring ratings[a]			
		High (Scores 7–10)	Medium (3–6)	Low (0–2)	Total
Adult					
1.	A				
	(N = 54)	13%	35%	52%	100%
2.	B				
	(N = 57)	30	56	14	100
3.	C				
	(N = 56)	27	43	30	100
Youth					
1.	A				
	(N = 49)	23	38	39	100
2.	B				
	(N = 39)	27	43	30	100

[a] Differences significant at .01 level of confidence.

Table II breaks the data down by ethnicity and expands on the point about differential inmate reactions. It shows us that while in some prisons white inmates are unhappier than blacks, in other prisons there is a difference in favor of whites. We infer that inmates who come from different cultural backgrounds respond differentially to different prison environments.

TABLE II. PROPORTION OF BLACK AND WHITE INMATES IN SMALL RANDOM
SAMPLES WHO RATE INSTITUTIONAL CLIMATES FAVORABLY OR UNFAVORABLY

Setting/ethnicity			Institutional self-anchoring ratings			
			Low	Medium	High	Total
Adult A[a]	White	(N = 27)	40.7%	55.6%	3.7%	100%
	Black	(N = 19)	57.9	15.8	26.3	100
Adult B[b]	White	(N = 16)	6.3	43.7	50	100
	Black	(N = 33)	12.1	63.7	24.2	100
Adult C[b]	White	(N = 15)	13.3	53.3	33.4	100
	Black	(N = 29)	37.9	44.9	17.2	100
Youth A[b]	White	(N = 15)	46.8	40	13.2	100
	Black	(N = 25)	40	32	28	100
Youth B[b]	White	(N = 9)	22.2	11.1	66.7	100
	Black	(N = 21)	38.1	57.1	4.8	100

[a] Differences significant beyond .01 level.
[b] Differences significant beyond .001 level.

While these tables illustrate the point that inmate suffering is not uniformly distributed, they obviously cry out for further interpretation. And we cannot say much more about the differences until we have analyzed the subjective data that go with the scales. But we can at least provide some idea about the shape our findings will probably take. This can be done by relaying the results of an impressionistic look at our first group of scales, which we administered at Youth Prison B.

When the returns came in, we selected the four highest, lowest, and most "middly" scale values from the group, and examined the anchoring responses. It was found (Table III) that the inmates in the discontented group were single-mindedly concerned about authority issues, and about their relationship with officers. No comparable portrait emerges for the other inmates. This is not to suggest, of course, that the situation would be the same for other institutions. Instead, we are likely to find *some* themes (tied to inmate needs and institutional offerings) which differentiate the contented from the discontented inmates.

What would one mean by *theme*? It might help to consider one inmate from our Discontent Four group. In reading this youth's interview, we find that he stresses that he is not being treated as a "man," meaning a person who ought to exercise autonomy. He also talks of feelings of impotence and resentment:

> W: You might call it Kiddyland. This is more strict, whereas you know—
> it's not really like a prison, you dig it, because if it was like a prison, we
> would have more privileges and we would be treated like men. You know,
> they treat us like kids. Have an officer wherever you go. You can't even
> think.

> W: To me it would make a person more bitter, you know. Every two
> minutes you hear "shut up," "step off," "lock in," "don't step out until I
> say so," "lock your gate." You know, you can't even think no more. The
> way you tuck your shirttail in and all this. I mean, you can't do nothing in
> this place.

He also harps on what he sees as arbitrariness in custodial decisions, meaning that guards can enforce views that reflect their own whims rather than attending to inmate needs or norms. The youth feels placed in the position of having to perform acts which to him serve no purpose:

> W: No, you don't have no choice, you dig it? Now, there's a sergeant,
> right, he might want everybody to have his shirttail in, you might be in

TABLE III. PRINCIPAL FEATURE OF BEST AND WORST INSTITUTION AS PERCEIVED BY CONTENTED AND DISCONTENTED COXSACKIE INMATES

	Discontented inmates (Average SA ranking = 0)	Inmates assigning medium rank (Average SA ranking = 5)	Contented inmates (Average SA ranking = 8)
Perceived principal feature of best institution	1. Inmate participation in officer selection 2. Custodial officers "from your own environment, who would understand inmates." 3. Officers "who give us respect." 4. Freedom of movement and "minimum regulations."	1. Understanding guards. 2. Commissary and material facilities. 3. Furlough or work-release. 4. Fellow inmates "from your own environment," who are "adult," "quiet."	1. Programs that facilitate self-improvement. 2. Fellow inmates who are "my brothers." 3. Work-release 4. Home visits or furloughs.
Number of mentions of congenial officers	4	1	0
Perceived principal feature of worst institution	1. "Creep officers" running a "military" setting. 2. Officers who "treat you like a kid." 3. "No respect" from officers. 4. Officers who are "always with you."	1. No human contacts, or activities. 2. No commissary, possessions, or recreational facilities. 3. Constant lock-in and inactivity. 4. Restricted freedom and poor food.	1. Constant lock-in. 2. No congenial fellow inmates ("couldn't see my brothers"). 3. Authoritarian officers. 4. A population of black inmates doing "big time."
Number of mentions of authoritarian officers	4	0	1

the laundry and you press your shirt, and you might like the way it looks out, you dig it? Now, it's clean and everything, you dig it, you're not going around dirty or nothing and you just like your shirt out and he tells everybody to put it in because that's the way he wants it. I mean, you can't force a prisoner—you can't force a personal view on everybody else. I mean, if you just neat and clean, you dig it, and not, you know, doing nothing to anybody else I can't see why you can't exercise your own thing that you like.

W: And every time you ask them, "get some hot water" oh, they think you're fuckin' slick. Man, just because they heard that New York City is where all these pimps and everything are from they figure everybody from there is slick or something, you dig it? So, they got their own little ideas how dudes come up here, that you're a slick guy or you a wise guy.

One mitigating aspect to this youth's perception of the prison is that he sees tangible improvements in the educational program, though he views these programs as inapplicable to himself, personally:

W: Like the school program has been changed and it's a little better now. And they're changing, you know, the shops. They're improving them. Before, you dig it, the school didn't have no college courses when I first came here, you know, they only had, what you called, regents. That's all they went up to was regents. Now, they you know—they keep adding stuff, you know. You can't say, you know, it stops right here because tomorrow they might have something else.

W: The education did improve, you dig it. They got more school and learning labs and all that, college courses in the evening. But again, for me, the college courses are zero because I dropped a bomb.

This inmate also talks about himself, and of problems he has controlling his resentments and feelings of rage. As he sees it, he would engage in a wholesale retaliatory massacre of custodial staff if he were not concerned about his release date. As it stands, he must cope with narrowly suppressed feelings of unexpressed rage:

W: Like if I had 25 and the mother fucker told me to step off and shut off and all this shit, I'd just punch him in his mouth. I mean, what could I lose.

W: This is myself, you know. Nobody going to tell me to shut up. They better not give me 25 years. They'd never hear the end of it. They'd have to give me the chair or some fucking thing. I mean, this place gives you a lot of frustration.

W: Well, all you got to do is think about if you want to go home. If you
want to go home, you going to do this; if you don't you're not going to do
it. See, I was fucking up and an officer told me to shut up and I said, "fuck
you, you can suck my dick," and all this. And after awhile I said, "I want
to go home," so I just shut up, all right. I know that you wouldn't tell me to
shut on the street, I know that you wouldn't tell me to shut up on the street
because it would be an absolutely different atmosphere, you dig it?
Between me and him. I know, especially where I come from, New York, if
me and him got some static in the street, ain't nobody going to help him.
Not in New York. Because they'll get killed too. But being that he tells me
to shut up, "I'll shut up, you bigot," you know. Dudes will laugh, you
know, "It ain't nothing big." Go ahead and laugh, it ain't nothing big.

W: You know what you do? You lay down and you go to sleep and you
think about beating that officer's ass. Just sleep on it. Just like, you're
sleeping on it and in this dream you're breaking his fucking neck, you
know, you just got him right here and he can't go nowhere and you got
him alone and you just banging his head into a wall.

When we look at a "contented" inmate, we find, in effect, that the
"real world" that is described does not differ as much as we may
suppose. What does differ is what the man positively and negatively
values. Our inmate thus makes clear to us that the aspect of prison our
first inmate conceded was probably good (the educational program) is
the most salient feature of the place, as far as he is concerned:

M: Well, I think it's a good educational facility for one. You know, if you
want to get a better education, you know, you can get it in here, you
know, then if you want to get it other places.

M: It has good trades. I like the trades I have. When I came in here I had
a ninth grade education. I have my high school diploma now. I took
sociology in college and have three college credits now. As far as that goes,
that's about all that benefited myself, you know, that was something that I
didn't have when I was out there. I'm taking music up now. Before when I
first came in we didn't have a music class. I spoke with the music
instructor at the time, and he told me that they would have to get new
equipment and things like this. So now they have it set up. That's another
achievement now. They have the whole room remodeled and everything,
and they have a session now. We got a JC organization here which is for
the inmate population.

The youth also talks of the guards, and he sees guards having
problems with inmates. But he attributes much of the blame for the
situation to the uncooperativeness of some youths—presumably, of

men like our first inmate:

> M: A lot of times someone is asked to do something and they'll say they don't want to do it just to put on, more or less, an act, you know, and it will go on and on until they see that you're not getting anywhere and they do it eventually anyways.

> M: You just say so much and then after that, you know, they tell you what to do, and what not. If they don't like what you say, they just, you know, do their own thing and this is a conflict between the officers and the inmates right there. Inmates, they don't, you know, try to more or less adjust to the standard of the institution you know, and they like to fight against, you know . . . I can only speak for myself as an individual, you know, I can't put myself in anybody else's place. But I can only say that when I'm asked to do something I try to do it instead of giving them a hassle.

> M: I mean you're all in there for doing one crime or another. So they feel that, you know, if one inmate does something, then the next one is going to fall right along with him. So, if I saw another inmate doing something that I didn't think was right, you know, I wouldn't very well be able to go over there and tell him, you know, "you're not doing the right thing." . . . I don't get too involved with his personal feelings, you know. If he has a conflict with somebody, you know, let him take it out in his own way.

As far as our respondent is concerned, his concern for his own development gives him a sense of "real" values, and protects him against becoming involved with what he sees as trivialities:

> M: I got to get down on the books, you know, and find myself while I'm in here, you know, because, you know, in my own mind, you know, I try not to look at it as just, you know, doing time, you know, but I look at it as trying to get myself ready for the unknown. So, when I get out I'll be able to say I'm here, right, and I'll find out what I left when I was here before. So now that I know where I left, I can do something about it.

> M: Is it an easier place, it all depends on how the individual makes it; I try to make it this way, you know. I try to mind my business, you know. I try not to get involved, you know.

What of a "moderate" inmate? In assessments of a multidimensional environment, intermediate scale values can be an average of positive and negative feelings. They can also represent a dispassionate reaction to the overall climate.

Our "moderate" inmate falls into the "composite rating" group. On the one hand, he feels warmly about academic programs and about his relationship to training staff. He sees himself benefited, and is grateful:

> R: They have a good academic program here. I noticed that when I first came here they didn't have any night college. Now they got night college, you know, and I've been going. I got 18 credits and I think it's pretty good, you know. Basically, they got a good vocational program, too.

> R: One of the teachers here, he went out of his way to help me, try to get me into college, you know—when I go to the board, you know. And they done a lot for me, you know. But they don't try to push a rap on you, you know, like "I can tell you what to do, so you got to do what I say." That's why I like a lot of them.

On the other hand, he feels that the custodial staff is heavy-handed, and that the regime they maintain is suffocating:

> R: I don't like the way it's run. They don't give you a chance to show yourself, or anything here. People who run the programs, they're all right. The guards, I don't like the way they run the place, you know. There's nothing you can do about it either; you just, you know, take it in your stride.

> R: Whatever they want to do, they do. When they want you to talk, you talk. When they want you to be quiet, you're quiet, you know. They tell you when you smoke, when you sleep, when you get up, everything, you know. It's like that in most of the jails I'd say, but in the other ones you get more freedom, you know. Like, in here you can't even walk from one corridor to another, you know, without one of them asking you where your pass is. In other jails like, there are people here I've talked with that were in other jails and they said it was more liberal. Like you can go here and there. People aren't harassing you all the time, telling you to shut up, do this. In here it's always like that.

He sees himself affected by this environment, but not to the point of paralysis. For one, he has worked out a *modus vivendi* with staff; he is also more or less resigned or, at least, self-controlled.

> R: After you're here awhile you can get to know them and they don't harass you no more. I know a lot of the guards here and they don't bother me. They know me and say, "George, get up," or something like that, and that's it. I respect them because I know them and stuff, and they respect me too. It's all right for me now, you know. But for a while there, you know, it was a pain.

> R: I don't do nothing, you know. I just do it. If you don't do it, all they are going to do is lock you up, you know. Sometimes they say someting and then I say, "Just forget it," and I do whatever they tell me to do. Cause there's a lot of trouble and static if you don't do it.

What these men see, and what they differentially prize or reject, are attributes, dimensions, properties or features of the same environment. In this case, the attributes are autonomy and opportunities for learning, but other connotations sneak in.

To map various differential concerns, we must have a more multidimensional portrait. And if we want to quantify this portrait, we must define as many separable prison attributes as we can, reduce them to items, and contain them in an instrument. We have tried to explore this possibility by constructing what we call our "Prison Profile Inventory."

THE PPI

The PPI instrument consists of 56 forced-choice paired comparisons. Each of the two alternatives that make up a comparison set is considered a sample from one of the eight sampling domains which we assume might be a distinct environmental dimension; these dimensions are:

Privacy: Concern about social and physical overstimulation; preference for isolation, peace and quiet, absence of environmental irritants such as noise and crowding.

Safety: Concern about one's physical safety; preference for social and physical settings that provide protection and that minimize the chances of being attacked.

Structure: Concern about environmental stability and predictability; preference for consistency, clear-cut rules, orderly and scheduled events and impingements.

Support: Concern about tangible assistance and rewards; need for services and preference for dependent relationships.

Feedback: Concern about being loved, appreciated, and approved of; a desire for intimate relationships that provide emotional sustenance and empathy.

Social stimulation: Concern with congeniality and preference for settings which provide opportunity for social interaction, companionship, and gregariousness.

Activity: Concern about understimulation; a need for maximizing the opportunity to be occupied and to fill time; need for distraction.

Freedom: Concern about circumscription of one's autonomy; need for minimal restriction and maximum opportunity to govern one's own conduct.

In the questionnaire, each dimension (in the form of an item selected from the dimension's item pool) is paired twice with each of the other dimensions. The outcome of this item comparison scheme is an instrument yielding 8 dimension scores based on 14 summative items. We assume that each item is monotonically related to the dimension it represents and we obtain a total score for each dimension between 0 and 14 by adding the individual item scores for each dimension.

We have viewed the first version of our instrument as an experimental form, which we hoped would be adequate for research use. In testimony to this hope we administered the instrument to 632 inmates from eight independent samples, some random and some "special."

Reliability coefficients were computed by means of parallel tests and estimated by Kuder-Richardson 20 for our random inmate samples ($N = 473$). We constructed parallel tests for each dimension by randomly assigning each of the two items from Dimension A paired with items from Dimension B to separate tests. The result was two parallel tests composed of seven items each per dimension. The total scores for each dimension test pair were correlated and adjusted by the Spearman Brown formula.

Table IV presents the raw and adjusted correlation coefficients for the parallel tests on each dimension and a measure of internal consistency, the Kuder-Richardson 20 estimates. You will note that for most dimensions, the reliabilities reach a level that allows interpretation of the questionnaire results for research purposes.

On the basis of item-total correlations we rescued well over half our items for a second go-around with a revised instrument. We have also refined our "interpersonal" dimensions (support, feedback, and

TABLE IV. QUESTIONNAIRE RELIABILITY FOR GENERAL POPULATION SAMPLE
($N = 473$)

Dimension	Parallel tests correlation coefficient	Spearman Brown	KR 20
Privacy	.3777	.5483	.4865
Safety	.5238	.6875	.6141
Structure	.3164	.4807	3688
Support	.0034	.0067	.1451
Feedback	.1632	.2806	.3146
Social stimulation	.2327	.3775	.2806
Activity	.3012	.4630	.4084
Freedom	.3500	.5185	.4654

social stimulation), which proved less than perfect in the original version. We hope for enough homogeneity in our item clusters to make the instrument ultimately employable as an aid in classification.

DO INMATE GROUPS DIFFER IN THEIR ENVIRONMENTAL PREFERENCES AND AVERSIONS?

Tables V through IX list the items that best discriminate among our samples of inmates. These items refer to themes that denote differential concerns. In other words, they deal with aspects of the prison environment that seem more important (or less important) to one group of inmates than to another.

Table V compares the forced choice preferences of younger and older inmates from intake and prison populations. We note that the younger inmates are more concerned than the older inmates about their personal relationship with staff; they seem more dependent on staff. They prize guards who are friendly (Item 5), gregarious (Item 16), or protective (Item 1); they are more appreciative of privileges (Item 18) or guidance (Item 13); they are upset about guards who "won't help people" (Item 37), and about situations where "no one cares" (Item 39).

Younger inmates place more weight than older inmates on filling time. They prize housing that "lets people rap" (Item 19) and are irritated about slack time (Item 41), lack of recreation (Item 45), or being locked up (Item 47). The last item relates to a third concern of younger inmates, which is the issue of feeling safe. This is highlighted by the emphasis on protective guards (Item 1) and on "a place where you can be safe" (Item 64); there is also the disproportionate worry about having to be "scared of people" (Item 46), about "inmates who are dangerous" (Item 51), and about inmate bullies (Item 55).

Older inmates—compared to younger inmates—show a more substantial need for structure and stability. They prize guards who are consistent (Item 5) or who are understanding (Item 16); they are irritated with guards who are inconsistent (Item 37); they prize "fair and firm discipline" (Item 25). They reject "no rules at all" (Item 34), "a prison with no rules" (Item 71), and "not knowing things" (Item 46).

Older inmates seem more concerned about their privacy and peace of mind, and about irritants and disturbances. We see this in the composite emphasis on "housing that keeps out noise" (Item 19), "a place you can be alone" (Item XX) "inmates who let me work" (Item

TABLE V. ITEMS THAT DISCRIMINATE BETWEEN ADULT INMATE AND YOUTH
INMATE RANDOM SAMPLES (IN RANK ORDER)

Item set	Youthful inmates ($N = 234$)	Older inmates ($N = 229$)
	Proportions of sample selecting each alternative	
5. Guards who are consistent	17%	48%[a]
Guards who are friendly	83[a]	52
19. Housing that keeps out noise	39	59[a]
Housing that lets people rap	61[a]	41
37. Guards who are inconsistent (−)	16	36[a]
Guards who won't help people (−)	84[a]	64
41. Talk of a riot (−)	58	76[a]
Time on my hands (−)	42[a]	24
39. Tension in the air (−)	48	65[a]
No one who cares (−)	52[a]	35
18. Knowing I can get privileges	25[a]	10
Knowing my people still love me	75	90[a]
34. No rules at all (−)	52	67[b]
A lot of noise (−)	48[b]	33
1. Guards who leave me alone	46	60[b]
Guards who protect me	54[b]	40
25. Packages and money from home	68[b]	54
Fair and firm discipline	32	46[b]
xx. A place you can be alone	36	49[b]
A place you can be safe	64[b]	51
45. A prison with no recreation (−)	42[b]	29
A prison with no rules (−)	58	71[b]
46. Not knowing things (−)	67	80[b]
Being scared of people (−)	33[b]	20
47. Being locked up (−)	45[b]	33
Having nothing to do (−)	55	67[b]
51. Inmates who are dangerous (−)	67[b]	55
Inmates who are rats	33	45[b]
55. An inmate bully (−)	63[b]	51
A disloyal woman (−)	37	49[b]
16. Guards who understand people	87	98[a]
Guards who enjoy a good laugh	13[a]	2
13. Teachers who get me to study	71[b]	60
Staff who are warm	29	40[b]
17. Inmates who let me work	79	89[b]
Inmates who do me favors	21[b]	11

[a] Difference significant beyond the .001 level of confidence.
[b] Difference significant beyond the .01 level of confidence.

17), and "guards who leave me alone" (Item 1); we see it in the displeasure these inmates feel in "talk of a riot" (Item 41) and "tension in the air" (Item 39). Not surprisingly, older inmates show more concern than younger inmates about the stability of their family bonds (Item 18, "knowing my people still love me" and Item 55, "a disloyal woman").

Male and female responses are compared in Table VI. Male inmates are more interested than female inmates in keeping active and occupied. We see this in Item 2, "housing in which I keep busy"; Item 6, "chances to keep busy"; Item 47, "having nothing to do"; Item 20, "a very busy day"; and Item 17, "inmates who let me work." Men seem also more concerned than women with privacy (Item 28, "housing in which there is noise"; Item 53, "inmates who disturb me").

The principal concern of female inmates is with friendship (Item 2, "housing in which I have friends") and warmth (Item 20, "a very

TABLE VI. ITEMS THAT DISCRIMINATE BETWEEN MALE AND FEMALE INMATE
SAMPLES (IN RANK ORDER)

Item set	Proportions of sample selecting each alternative	
	Male random sample ($N = 473$)	Female sample ($N = 32$)
2. Housing where I have friends	23%	59%[a]
Housing in which I keep busy	77[a]	41
6. Housing in which no one can harm me	23	58[a]
Chances to keep busy	77[a]	42
32. Not knowing what staff expects (−)	71[b]	45
Too much time to think (−)	29	55[b]
47. Being locked up (−)	39	65[b]
Having nothing to do (−)	61[b]	35
28. Housing in which there is noise (−)	37[c]	16
Housing with no room for activities (−)	63	84[c]
44. Guards who are always around (−)	20	41[b]
Guards who won't help me (−)	80[b]	59
53. Inmates who disturb me (−)	75[c]	55
Inmates who are selfish (−)	25	45[c]
20. A very busy day	60[c]	41
A very close friend	40	59[c]
17. Inmates who let me work	84[c]	69
Inmates who do me favors	16	31[c]

[a] Difference significant beyond the .001 level of confidence.
[b] Difference significant beyond the .01 level of confidence.
[c] Difference significant beyond the .05 level of confidence.

TABLE VII. ITEMS THAT DISCRIMINATE BETWEEN "WEAK COMPANY" INMATES
AND RANDOM YOUTH INMATE SAMPLE (IN RANK ORDER)

	Item set	Random sample (N = 243)	"Weak company" inmates (N = 19)
		Proportion of sample selecting each alternative	
3.	Rules that tell me what to expect	84%[a]	32%
	As few rules as possible	16	68[a]
24.	Being occupied	90[a]	42
	Being alone	10	58[a]
23.	Knowing that staff likes me	11	47[a]
	Knowing what the parole board wants	89[a]	53
2.	Housing where I have friends	19	53[b]
	Housing where I keep busy	81[b]	47
xx.	A place you can be alone	36	63[c]
	A place you can be safe	64[c]	37
40.	Unfair punishment (−)	47	74[c]
	No schools or training (−)	53[c]	26
44.	Guards who are always around (−)	16	37[c]
	Guards who won't help me (−)	83[c]	63

[a] Difference significant beyond .001 level of confidence.
[b] Difference significant beyond .01 level of confidence.
[c] Difference significant beyond .05 level of confidence.

close friend"). The female inmates also seem troubled by unwanted thoughts and feelings (Item 32), particularly when confined (Item 47). They are more prone than men to seek or expect aid and assistance from staff (Item 44) or peers (Items 53 and 17).

Tables VII and VIII compare random and special samples of younger inmates. Table VIII centers on men in a youth prison tier which is informally known as the "weak company." These youths show concern about their personal relationship with staff members, and particularly seem to worry about staff authority, power, and discipline (Items 3, 40, and 44). The ambivalence these inmates show about staff also characterizes their stance toward peers; while they disproportionately prize solitude (Items 24, XX), they express a need for inmate friends (Item 2).

The average young inmate seems more concerned than the "weak" inmate about participation in activities and programs. He stresses the desirability of keeping busy (Items 24, 2) and the value of schooling or training (Item 40). The random group also seems generally oriented toward "making it" in prison, as well as in getting out of prison as early as possible (Item 3).

The special sample in Table VIII derives from settings that are described by staff as "special environments." The assignments vary substantially (shops, farm, janitorial, reduced privileges) and include variations in pattern of supervision and in inmate routine.

The subenvironment sample shows special concern about freedom, supervision, and staff intrusiveness. This theme comprises two-thirds of the items on the list, i.e., Items 25, 31, 27, 49, 37, and 44. Like the "weak" inmates, the subenvironment sample also shows ambivalence toward peer presence and seems to desire friendship (Item 20) as well as privacy (Items 29 and 26).

Compared to the subenvironment sample, the random group admits to being more soft or dependent and more vulnerable or afraid. The first of these dimensions consists of a willingness to seek help from other persons (Items 25, 37, 44, and 4) and a desire for warmth or affection (Items 29 and 49). Concern about danger is suggested in Items 27, 51, and 52.

TABLE VIII. ITEMS THAT DISCRIMINATE BETWEEN SUBENVIRONMENT INMATES AND RANDOM YOUTH INMATE SAMPLE (IN RANK ORDER)

	Proportion of sample selecting each alternative	
Item set	Youth random sample ($N = 243$)	Subenvironment sample ($N = 22$)
20. A very busy day	61%[a]	27%
A very close friend	39	73[a]
25. Packages and money from home	68[a]	36
Fair and firm discipline	32	64[a]
29. Inmates who give me no privacy (−)	63	91[b]
Inmates who don't care about me (−)	37[a]	9
31. Restricted movement (−)	47	73[b]
No chance for recreation (−)	53[b]	27
27. Guards who don't watch for trouble (−)	68[b]	45
Guards who give me orders (−)	32	55[b]
49. A lot of rules (−)	32	55[b]
Lots of cold people (−)	68[b]	45
26. Open doors in the evening	89[a]	68
Staying in my cell	11	32[a]
37. Guards who are inconsistent (−)	16	36[b]
Guards who won't help people (−)	84[b]	64
44. Guards who are always around (−)	16	36[b]
Guards who won't help me (−)	84[b]	64

[a] Difference significant beyond the .01 level of confidence.
[b] Difference significant beyond the .05 level of confidence.

TABLE IX. ITEMS THAT DISCRIMINATE BETWEEN "INVALIDS" AND ADULT MALE INMATES (IN RANK ORDER)

	Proportions of sample selecting each alternative	
Item set	"Invalid" sample (N = 24)	Adult random sample (N = 229)
50. Guards who are unfriendly (−)	67% [a]	15%
Guards who ask for trouble (−)	33	85 [a]
24. Being occupied	43	87 [a]
Being alone	57 [a]	13
47. Being locked up (−)	75 [a]	33
Having nothing to do (−)	25	67 [a]
49. A lot of rules (−)	75 [a]	35
Lots of cold people (−)	25	65 [a]
2. Housing where I have friends	65 [a]	28
Housing where I keep busy	35	72 [a]
54. Inmates who pick fights (−)	58	91 [a]
Inmates who won't rap (−)	42 [a]	9
18. Knowing I can get privileges	42 [a]	10
Knowing my people still love me	58	90 [a]
26. Open doors in the evening	50	82 [a]
Staying in my cell	50 [a]	18
28. Housing in which there is noise (−)	71 [b]	40
Housing with no room for activities (−)	29	60 [b]
23. Knowing that staff likes me	46 [a]	15
Knowing what the parole board wants	54	85 [a]
17. Inmates who let we work	60	89 [a]
Inmates who do me favors	40 [a]	11
30. Programs that don't help me get out (−)	79 [a]	40
News about family troubles (−)	21	60 [a]
11. Regular news from home	70	98 [a]
Inmates who protect me	30 [a]	2
4. Inmates who help me pass time	48	75 [c]
Inmates who listen to my problems	52 [c]	25
34. No rules at all (−)	39	67 [c]
A lot of noise (−)	61 [c]	33
44. Guards who are always around (−)	50 [b]	23
Guards who won't help me (−)	50	77 [b]
3. Rules that tell me what to expect	58	83 [b]
As few rules as possible	42 [b]	17
16. Guards who understand people	74	98 [a]
Guards who enjoy a good laugh	26 [a]	2
53. Inmates who disturb me	52	74 [c]
Inmates who are selfish	48 [c]	26

[a] Difference significant beyond the .001 level of confidence.
[b] Difference significant beyond the .01 level of confidence.
[c] Difference significant beyond the .05 level of confidence.

Table IX lists responses of the random sample of older inmates and of a relatively inactive group of long-term residents in a prison "invalid" tier. The "invalids," as compared to the "randoms," show strong concern for staff goodwill and friendliness (Items 50, 23, and 16) and for privacy (Items 24, 26, 28, 34, and 44). They are worried about restriction (Items 47, 49, and 3) and they want sociable, reliable, and congenial peers (Items, 54, 17, 2, 11, and 4). The random sample is predictably more interested in being active and occupied (Items 24, 47, 2, 28, 17, and 4). It shows worry about the volatility of prison environment (Items 50, 54, 34, 3, and 53) and about relationships with the outside (Items 18, 30, and 11).

One must emphasize that these trends feature relative differences, and that they highlight differential aspects of environmental preferences and aversions. The dominant concerns of our groups must in each case be in part relatively congruent. The validity of the distinctions we draw hinges on the magnitude of differences we find. Validity is further enhanced by the degree to which relative emphases are represented in clusters of consistent items.

ENVIRONMENTAL PREFERENCE PROFILES

How do the item differences we have described relate to the scores our groups would have received if we had used our dimensional profiles to describe them? Tables X through XIII answer the question by providing mean dimension scores for all our groups.

TABLE X. ENVIRONMENTAL PREFERENCE PROFILE FOR YOUNGER AND OLDER INMATES

Dimension	Mean dimension scores for	
	Youthful inmate random sample ($N = 234$)	Older inmate random sample ($N = 229$)
Privacy	5.78	6.30[a]
Safety	7.00	6.52
Structure	7.96	8.88[b]
Support	7.11[b]	6.54
Feedback	6.59	6.81
Social stimulation	6.75	6.45
Activity	8.11	7.95
Freedom	6.59	6.75

[a] Difference significant beyond .02 level of confidence.
[b] Difference significant beyond .001 level of confidence.

TABLE XI. ENVIRONMENTAL PREFERENCE PROFILES FOR MALE AND FEMALE
INMATES

| | Mean dimension scores for | |
Dimension	Male random sample (N = 473)	Female inmates sample (N = 32)
Privacy	6.04	6.04
Safety	6.77	5.90
Structure	8.40	7.97
Support	6.84	7.04
Feedback	6.70	7.12
Social stimulation	6.67	7.00
Activity	8.03	7.52
Freedom	6.67	7.52

Table X lists scores for younger and older inmates. It shows significant differences on three dimensions. The responses of older inmates are consistent with our item clusters, in that they show concern with privacy and structure. Our third cluster (family bonds) is not represented in the profile.

The younger inmates have a high score on the support dimension, which has not met our criterion of reliability. The difference suggests that if we draw on the support item pool we might construct a new (related) dimension that described younger inmates. It is possible that such a dimension might center on staff dependence, as suggested by the item clusters.

We hypothesize one other concern for younger inmates in reviewing item differences. This concern—safety—is not highlighted by the profile scores, though the difference approximates significance.

Table XI shows the profiles of male and female inmates. These two profiles are statistically indiscriminable, though trends suggest that a better instrument might show differences favoring structure, safety, and activity for males and freedom for females. Other differences suggested by our item clusters (privacy, feedback, and social stimulation) do not materialize.

Table XII compares the special samples of younger inmates to the main young inmate sample. The profiles prove discriminating. The "weak company" is high in its concern with privacy, social stimulation, and freedom, and low in its emphasis on structure. The picture for the subenvironment sample is somewhat similar, with relative highs on privacy and freedom. The subenvironment inmates also

Table XII. Environmental Preference Profiles of Younger Inmates in the Population and in Special Samples

Dimension	Young random sample (N = 243)	"Weak company" sample (N = 19)	Subenvironment sample (N = 22)
Privacy	5.78	7.11[a]	6.73[b]
Safety	7.00	6.39	5.68[b]
Structure	7.96	6.26[c]	8.00
Support	7.11	6.50	6.90
Feedback	6.59	7.00	6.64
Social stimulation	6.79	7.79[b]	6.68
Activity	8.11	7.11	7.64
Freedom	6.59	8.11[a]	7.80[b]

[a] Significant difference beyond .01 level.
[b] Significant difference beyond .05 level.
[c] Significant difference beyond .001 level.

show a relative de-emphasis of safety. Among other differences in the table, the activity difference between the "weak" sample and random inmates is close to significance. This picture does not coincide completely with item differences, and suggests that some aspects of staff–inmate and inmate–inmate relationships may not be captured by the profiles. But the dimensional differences appear in our item clusters.

Table XIII. Environmental Preference Profiles of Older Inmates in the Population and in Special Samples

Dimension	Older random sample (N = 229)	Invalid company (N = 24)	Self-segregation protection (N = 13)
Privacy	6.30	7.45[a]	6.82
Safety	6.52	6.52	9.27[b]
Structure	8.88	7.59[a]	8.75
Support	6.54	6.82	5.81
Feedback	6.81	7.00	7.20
Social stimulation	6.45	7.69[a]	7.09
Activity	7.95	6.56[c]	6.50[a]
Freedom	6.75	6.95	5.36[a]

[a] Difference significant beyond .05 level.
[b] Difference significant beyond .001 level.
[c] Difference significant beyond .01 level.

Table XIII compares the older inmate sample to the invalid company and to a group of inmates who are in protection (self-requested segregation) status.

The invalid company shows highs on privacy and social stimulation, and relative lows on structure and activity. This picture is similar to that of item differences, if we allow for the absence of dimensions (such as outside support and staff congeniality) that are not available in the profile.

The protection company shows a high on the safety dimension, and lows on activity and freedom. The two subsamples are similar in their relative lack of concern for activity, but different in other respects.

In one institution—the one we described as "Adult B"—we gathered background information about inmates who responded to our questionnaire. In assessing these data, we may recall that in self-ratings, Adult B stood out as relatively positively valued. We may also recall that white inmates seemed more favorably disposed toward this prison than did black inmates.

A few tables help to summarize the differences we find in this institution, in terms of climate dimensions which seem important to

TABLE XIV. ACTIVITY, FREEDOM, AND SUPPORT SCORES
BROKEN DOWN BY ETHNICITY OF THE INMATE

Profile dimension	Ethnicity of inmate		
	Black	White	
Activity	(N = 37)	(N = 25)	N = 62
Low	22%	12%	
Medium	56	36	
High	22	52[a]	
	100	100	
Freedom	(N = 34)	(N = 24)	N = 58
Low	15	54[b]	
Medium	44	21	
High	41	25	
	100	100	
Support	(N = 34)	(N = 26)	N = 60
Low	24	54[a]	
Medium	38	19	
High	38	27	
	100	100	

[a] Difference significant at .05 level.
[b] Difference significant at .01 level.

TABLE XV. ITEMS THAT DIFFERENTIATE BETWEEN BLACK AND WHITE
INMATES IN THE ADULT B SAMPLE

Item set	Ethnicity of respondents	
	Black (N = 37)	White (N = 27)
31. Restricted movement (−)	70%[a]	37%
No chance for recreation (−)	30	63[a]
26. Open doors in the evening	89[b]	63
Staying in my cell	11	37[b]
20. A very busy day	43	74[b]
A very close friend	57[b]	26
45. A prison with no recreation (−)	32[b]	7
A prison with no rules (−)	68	93[b]
55. An inmate bully (−)	30	56[c]
A disloyal woman (−)	70[c]	44

[a] Difference significant beyond .02 level.
[b] Difference significant beyond .05 level.
[c] Difference n.s.

the inmate. To help us, we have broken down the dimensional scores into "high," "middle," and "low" groups that are as roughly equal as we could manage.

Table XIV shows differences between black and white inmates. It tells us that white inmates are more concerned with activity, but that they tend to have relatively little need for freedom (from staff control) or for tangible supports. Table XV lists some of the items that enter into differences in the freedom and activity dimensions. In Tables XVI and XVII we see that inmates with less time left to serve seem concerned with structure and feedback, while long-term residents place value on freedom and privacy. And Table XVIII suggests that younger inmates are relatively uninterested in activity—at least, in this setting.

DIFFERENTIAL SURVIVAL

In prisons, some inmate preferences and aversions are more easily accommodated than others. Most prisons offer structure, activity, and social stimulation; few provide privacy, freedom, and feedback. Safety is hard to come by; support takes initiative.

TABLE XVI. STRUCTURE, PRIVACY, FEEDBACK, AND FREEDOM
OF LONG-TERM AND SHORT-TERM INMATES

Dimension	Time until conditional release date		
	Less than 5 years	5 years or more	
Structure	(N = 34)	(N = 38)	N = 72
Low	12%	37%	
Medium	26	29	
High	62^a	34	
	100	100	
Privacy	(N = 36)	(N = 36)	N = 72
Low	50	28	
Medium	36	36	
High	14	36^a	
	100	100	
Feedback	(N = 35)	(N = 38)	N = 73
Low	23	32	
Medium	34	55	
High	43^a	13	
	100	100	
Freedom	(N = 34)	(N = 36)	N = 70
Low	41	25	
Medium	35	28	
High	24	47^b	
	100	100	

^{a} Significant at .05 level.
^{b} Difference n.s.

TABLE XVII. ITEM DIFFERENCES BETWEEN SHORT-TERM AND LONG-TERM INMATES

Item set	Time remaining before parole is possible	
	Less than 5 years (N = 37)	More than 5 years (N = 39)
49. A lot of rules (−)	28%	62%^{a}
Lots of cold people (−)	72^a	38
32. Not knowing what staff expects (−)	92^a	67
Too much time to think (−)	8	33^a
53. Inmates who disturb me (−)	68	90^b
Inmates who are selfish (−)	32^b	10

^{a} Difference significant at .01 level.
^{b} Difference significant at .05 level.

TABLE XVIII. ACTIVITY SCORES FOR YOUNGER AND OLDER
INMATES

Dimension	Age		
	Under 30	Over 30	
Activity	(N = 40)	(N = 25)	N = 65
Low	27%[a]	0%	
Medium	45	56	
High	28	44	
	100	100	

[a] Difference significant at .01 level.

But prisons differ much more from each other than meets the outsider's eye. And within prison, there are settings that maximize or minimize scarce attributes. The most crowded prison has assignments in which inmates work alone; there are shops that are more supervised, or more paternalistically staffed, than others; in some tiers, congeniality is infectious; in others, men seek refuge.

The unique portrait of prisons, or of work and living assignments, takes shape through the complaints of its detractors or the testimonials of its partisans, as well as through the more neutral comments of more dispassionate men. This holds for the New York prison (Adult B) from which our last tables derive.

A guard, for instance, describes what he sees as a relative absence of structure in the institution:

H: They might do something today one way, whereas tomorrow it might be changed to do it another way—you know, depending on how it best works out. There is no actual set way to do a lot of things here. They have—well, we have gotten—it is a lot looser than it used to be and it is—I think your younger inmate is more apt to get along here better than your older one, who just wants to do time or something like that because they feel like—I have had older inmates tell me that, you know, they would rather march or they would rather—if they have got to go to the mess hall they would rather go as a company in an orderly manner because they want to go in there and eat in peace and quiet. . . . It is a lot looser here and it is actually like when I work relief—I call the officer and see how he runs his shop, if there is any changes from the last time that I worked the job, because they do vary from time to time. Like I might work a job this week and work the same job next week but something new has changed, or they don't do something that they did before.

Several inmates talk to us—each from his perspective—about the same lack of structure:

> 21: Right, you're really not aware of what is expected of you. Other institutions, as soon as you get there they give you a set of rules to let you know where you stand. After I came out of reception, the first day I got a keep lock because I didn't know what was going on. . . . Well, see that is one of the major things that deals in rules. And it's not so much the officers, because I could find a way to get around. It's just the rules. If they could give everybody a set of rules what is expected of them, understand, while they're staying here, that would be so much better.

> I: Well, the slacker the place is the harder the place is to do time. It is funny to say that, but it is true.

> —: Why do you say that? Could you run that down for me?

> I: Because there ain't no respect no place, you see. When you got to go by a line, you know the line is there. You know the difference between right and wrong, and actually I do know the difference, but I am trying to say that if I wanted to go I would just go, but when the rules were there you couldn't go. There is a difference. This time that they give you—all this time that they give you in the yard—they are supposed to change the yard now until 10 o'clock at night. Many of the kids go out there play cards and all that, and they feel that it is a good thing. I don't feel that it is a good thing, because the day is not—what I am trying to say is that the kids that come in here today are happy here and they really are, and it doesn't mean nothing to them. Of course their bits are so small. If they get a 15- or 20-year bit it is different. See I was like that when I first came in here. I had a 5-year bit, and I used to just run wild. There was no sense in minding them, so I figured I only have got 5 years and I will do it and go home. But now that I have got a 20-year bit and I have got 9 years in there is a big difference. Nobody cares. They just fool around.

> EE: In other words, let a guy know what he can do and what he can't do. This is a big problem here. . . . I would say the rules as far as uniformity—basically—they give you handbooks when you come in and they say these are the rules, and now there is probably maybe 100 rules that they are not telling you about out of the 600 rules that they are telling you about. Now in other words you do it and they tell you that you are not supposed to do it, but how were you supposed to know it? I have been here 3 years and nobody has ever told me, "This is the set of rules that you have to go by." The only way you learn is by experience, and experience is not always the best teacher.

How does the institution do on privacy? Again, several inmates agree:

> Z: You can just be sitting there and you know you're not alone. Where I'm at I've got 25 guys on the gallery I'm on. So I've got like guys laying

there, guys defecating, guys coughing, and it's close quarters. I feel that if a guy is locked up somewhere he should at least have his privacy so he's away from all the other noise and distraction. I find that very—you got guys that don't take showers, and you're around them.

Q: Now myself, at night in the cells I like a little quiet. I have a tape player, I like to listen to my music and I enjoy reading. Now you got guys listening to the basketball game on the radio, and they're not listening, they're running their mouths. Or they're listening to some music on the tapes and radio, they're not listening, they're singing. Now this is very distracting when you're trying to read or you are trying to do something else. And sometimes in fact I might be working on my legal work or something. And you sit there trying to do legal work with some clown moaning or humming or singing in falsetto, it can drive you up a tree. And especially when it's unnecessary, it's just nonsense. I mean, they ring a quiet down there, because they ring it for the purpose of giving people a time to do things. . . . It's annoying when you're trying to read to hear the clack clack clack of a typewriter. But now these are guys doing leatherwork, pounding. And that can really get on your nerves. So I asked this guy about it, "What's the scoop on the leatherwork?" He says, "Them guys are not supposed to be pounding after the 7 o'clock bell." I says, "It's a funny thing, them guys are locking right near this front, and you can't hear them." He says, "I hear them, I tell them to shut up." I said, "Come on, who are you trying to kid?" I find they play excessively—horseplay once in a while fine, that's all right. There's nobody going to walk around with a long face all the time, that's ridiculous. But there's more to life than just horseplay. Even though we're inside the walls it doesn't change. A man has got pride, just because he's in here doesn't change that. There's no nails on that wall out there, we didn't hang our pride on the wall.

24: You have a lot of guys that are doing long time and then you bring a whole lot of kids, two and three up there, you know kids today. And you mix them together. And if you compare them there is nothing in common. A guy who is doing a life bit and then another kid doing 3 years. And you don't know what is going to happen. . . . Well, the galleries are not segregated and the companies are not segregated, so you might have a guy doing a life bit. And then the next day you might have two guys locking next to each other and they are both doing 3 years. And as soon as the radio comes on he is trying to get something going. And this one guy is trying to get something out of the law book and the other guy is listening to the radio. And this irritates.

By the same token, the institution emerges as one that ranks highly on staff support, and does extremely well in providing meaningful activity for those who want it:

Q: They have a trade here, they have a body shop here. Industrial body shop, which this is actually the only type of work that I have ever found that I really enjoy doing. It's a form of creating. Well, maybe I'm wrong in saying creating. It's working with my hands, which I like to do and it's taking something, a wreck, and making something usable out of it. Now in all the years I've been in jail, and all the jobs I had, I can honestly say the only—I'm honestly enjoying myself in the job I have how. It's a type of job where the man gives me credit for knowing what I know, he assigns me a job and leaves me alone. This is the type atmosphere that I like even in the street. . . . They have a good school program here if somebody wants to take advantage of it. I finished my high school education here. And as I said they've got good vocational training. You've got to go get it, it's not going to come to you. A man's got to have some gumption. You can't just lean back doing nothing and expect that it's going to just happen. It's not like that, I don't care where it is.

S: I asked to transfer here to get into the fab shop because they have new materials that they use on these cabinets that they have come out with since I have been in prison. I want to find out the new ways they have of doing them so that I can learn how to do them. So I want to benefit myself. See, everything I learn is a benefit to myself. . . . I don't feel any different than I would be if I were out there. I am sure there is little things that bother you because you are inside the wall but normal living—I don't see no problem with this here. . . . There isn't any officer here or any employee that wouldn't do anything that they could to help me if I had any problems. So like the fellows found out that I was going to the board next month—my release board—they said, "We will do anything to help you. If you have any problems, don't hesitate to ask us. If we don't have the answer we will get the answer."

J: When I got back and I seen the assignment board and they asked me what I wanted to do, and I told them, "I want to go back to the shop that I was in," and he says, "There is some opening there," and he tells me what they have got, and he runs them down, and I say, "I don't want that," and he says, "All you want is the school." And he said, "All you want to do for the next 70 days is then to hang out," and I said, "Yeah, that is what I want to do." And he says, "Okay," and he put me down for school, and so he gave me what I asked for and wanted. Someplace else, like I ask for one thing and they put me into something else. I had no choice.

—:   Well, has your impression of B always been the same or was it different?

J: Yeah—to me this is the best joint in the state.

I am not suggesting that views of a prison always converge neatly. Some testimonials are very subjective. They tell us more about the perceiver than they tell us about his environment. Some men walk in fear, or are steeped in rage. They feel unsafe in protection, or seek cues to restrictions in permissiveness. Some men don't resonate to opportunities or impingements that seem obvious to others. Our high support-activity prison contains inmates who say nothing of vocational or educational programs. Their interests, and their perspectives, rest elsewhere. Our summaries are averages, not consensus. They allow for obsessions, skewed views, disinterest, and apathy.

A man's preferences, his aversions, condition his emphases. One man's meat is another's stress. Diminished structure can signify painful ambiguity for one man and relaxation of tension for another. One person's social stimulation is another's lack of privacy; it may be a third's impaired safety. And safety is best secured by threatening an aggressor's prized freedom.

In Institution B we hear inmates complain of others. Older men talk of the hordes of the wild young who callously abuse freedom, destroy privacy, and show weak stomach for activity. The young, in turn, feel socially displaced and callously managed. Men hearken nostalgically to the certitudes of an upstate fortress that represents medieval repression to others. Some miss the games of youth prison, which others recollect as chaos.

These differences are a source of problems and opportunities. They are problems, in that they attenuate our success in matching men with settings. Well-matched geese live with ill-matched ganders, who contaminate the congeniality of goose climates. Our opportunities lie in purifying classification, once we know how inmates react to the environments we have available.

There are less obvious opportunities in using or creating subenvironments. Large, multifaceted prisons can accommodate settings that enhance some features of climate at some others' expense. We have havens of privacy in beehives of activity. We have quiet retreats, congenial clubs, supportive wombs, supervised and undersupervised settings. Our task is to get inmates in need of specialized climates into enclaves we have, and to create others that can accommodate vulnerable inmates now floundering in prison yards.

The task presents some difficulties and some challenges. It introduces unfamiliar criteria of classification; it requires staffing flexibility that boggles the civil service mind; it means creating program options for settings we now view as residual.

But the logic and the strategy are not new; nor are they unfamiliar. Classification seeks "best fit." Institutions assign inmates (such as those in search of safety) to sanctuaries. The task we have is to make the survival problem more salient, to enhance our concern for it and to learn more about what inmates need and what prisons can offer them.

REFERENCES

Cantril, H. *The patterns of human concerns.* New Brunswick: Rutgers University Press, 1965.

Clemmer, D. *The prison community.* Boston: Christopher Publishing Company, 1940.

Goffman, E. On the characteristics of total institutions: The inmate world. In D. Cressey (Ed.), *Studies in institutional organization and change.* New York: Holt, Rinehart & Winston, 1961.

Sykes, G. *The society of captives.* New York: Atheneum, 1966.

Toch, H. *Men in crisis: Human breakdowns in prison.* Chicago: Aldine, 1975.

Ward, D. A., and Kassebaum, G. G. *Women's prison: Sex and social structure.* Chicago: Aldine, 1965.

Zimbardo, P. Pathology of punishment. *Trans-Action*, 1972, *9*, 4–8.

8

Judgments about Crime and the Criminal

A MODEL AND A METHOD FOR INVESTIGATING PAROLE DECISIONS

JOHN S. CARROLL AND JOHN W. PAYNE

"An eye for an eye" is the historical precursor to the principle "Let the punishment fit the crime." However widespread this view of justice, modern law prescribes that the punishment for a crime, or more generally the response to a crime, be based on the nature of the offender as well as on the nature of the crime. The means of achieving this goal has both negative and positive components. Negatively, there are proscriptions against dealing with offenders solely on the basis of their crime. For example, judges are enjoined from using a "fixed and mechanical approach," such as imposing the same sentence for a given offense (Heinz, Heinz, Senderowitz, & Vance, 1976, pp. 22–23). Positively, the use of *discretion* is considered an essential element in the administration of justice (e.g., Davis, 1971). Thus, the criminal justice system necessarily works through the application of individual human judgment to unique cases.

JOHN S. CARROLL • Carnegie-Mellon University, Pittsburgh, Pennsylvania. JOHN W. PAYNE • University of Chicago, Chicago, Illinois. Support for this research was provided by National Science Foundation Grant SOC75-18061 to the authors. We gratefully acknowledge the cooperation of the Pennsylvania Board of Probation and Parole and its expert decision-makers at all levels. Their candor and genuine interest have been marvelous, and we only wish that the validity of the information available to them about a case was as strong as their desire to make the best possible decisions in a difficult situation.

The purpose of this chapter is to examine how the lay public and the criminal justice professional perceive and respond to crime and the criminal. We will argue that the same basic processes occur in both layperson and expert, although the expert may know more and have a different set of priorities. We propose a model for understanding these processes, incorporating theories from social psychology. Some preliminary evidence for this model will be presented, using both real parole decisions by experts and simulated parole decisions by experts and laypeople. We will also focus on the techniques used to collect this evidence, which allow intensive scrutiny of the judgment process without interfering with the decision-maker.

Crime is clearly one of the most urgent problems facing our society. City residents consider it first on a list of social issues involving their community (Gallup, 1975a). Statistics show crime rates to have recently increased more in suburbs and rural areas than in cities (*Time*, 1975), making the problem far broader than the "city as jungle" image of crime. Nationwide, an average of one household out of every four was hit by a crime at least once in the last year (Gallup, 1975b). Law and order is a central political issue, and probably more permanent than our current economic woes or the corruption issue of the post-Watergate years.

People's perceptions and responses to crime are important for three reasons. First, they represent the way crime actually affects us at a psychological level—the feelings and behaviors elicited in response to a crime or a criminal. Second, as previously expressed, the criminal justice system bases its responses on individual perceptions and discretion (cf. Shaver, Gilbert, & Williams, 1975, for a discussion of the potential for studying discretion from a social psychological perspective). Third, these perceptions and responses are important to the causes and cures of crime. Sociological theorists speak of deviant behavior (e.g., crime) as a product of a labeling process (Becker, 1963; Lemert, 1967; Kitsuse, 1969). People who receive the label of "criminal" or "delinquent" will be more likely to have criminal careers because of the way others treat them and their resultant self-images. People who are incarcerated even for "crimes" which are hardly criminal (e.g., truancy, possession of marijuana) become prisonized— less able to respond normally in the outside society, at the same time as they become criminalized—more imbued with new skills and self-definitions from the criminal subculture of the institution. Finally, when the "criminal" emerges into society, he or she is shunned and systematically cut off from the means to achieve social goals. The person then turns to crime as a means of achieving economic goals, a self-definition, and getting back at society for what has occurred. While we certainly do not claim that labeling *causes* crime, we strongly feel that our society's way of dealing with those who are "tainted" makes it that much harder for them to create decent lives.

PUBLIC PERCEPTION OF CRIME

According to public polls, people believe that high crime rates are due to leniency in the laws and law enforcement, and to the use of drugs (Gallup, 1972, 1973). Over half the public believe society to be more to blame for crime than is the individual (Gallup, 1970). Yet the uniform response to the problem of crime is to demand that society deal with the individual offender more surely and with increased penalties (Gallup, 1972). Reed and Reed (1973) found people to have an image of the criminal as a psychologically unstable and socially undesirable person—evil, mean, and dangerous. The preferred means of responding to criminals is not treatment but punishment and removal from society, as well as avoidance of anyone with a criminal background. In short, the criminal is viewed as opportunistic but unmalleable. Society is to blame for crime because society has not made the penalty high enough nor removed criminals from our midst. This overly simplistic view of crime is reflected in public culture. For example, Dominick (1973) concluded from his survey of television dramas that "a TV criminal is a function, not a person. He exists solely as a criminal; his character is seldom developed any further" (p. 249).

The person who commits a criminal act is seen as *responsible* for the act, and further, the possessor of a *criminal* disposition. The concepts of responsibility and criminality are central to popular ideas of crime causation. But causation in this case is not physical causation in the sense of doing the act, but *responsibility* for the act in the moral sense of guilt or blame (Pepitone, in press). While people in general perceive the crime-doer as knowing and intending the consequences of the criminal act, and therefore responsible, as well as permanently possessing character traits of criminality, individuals vary greatly in their perceptions of crime. Miller (1973) attaches an ideological basis to these differences. The ideology of the conservative political right proposes that the bulk of serious crime is committed by people who lack moral conscience and self-control and are encouraged by radical or liberal values supporting illegal behavior and by the leniency of authority. Crime control and moral retribution demand severe punishment for criminals. The ideology of the left proposes that social conditions of inequality and discrimination lead victimized people into acts which are criminal, and further punish the crimes committed by the poor while ignoring the crimes of the rich. Their response to crime is to divert people out of the brutalizing prison system, work to change society, and rehabilitate the individual person.

PERCEPTION OF CRIME BY CRIMINAL JUSTICE PROFESSIONALS

DISCRETION AND EXPERTISE

One of the first things to recognize in examining the criminal justice system is that it operates primarily as an expression of the public's attitude toward crime. The criminal justice system is not a monolithic institution, regardless of its size and complexity. The policeman deciding to arrest, the judge setting bail, the jury evaluating guilt, and the parole board evaluating the inmate are all instances of individual human judgment. Laws and administrative rules place only broad constraints on individual discretion. For example, mandating harsher sentences for a crime makes conviction for that crime more difficult. When England authorized the death penalty for thefts valued over 39 shillings, juries would frequently return conviction for theft of 39 shillings when the actual value was as high as 1,000 pounds (Page, 1937). Although 59% of people in the United States believe in the death penalty (Harris, 1973a), only 39% would always vote guilty as jurors in a trial in which guilt had been proven for an offense carrying a mandatory death penalty (Harris, 1973b). People exercise or are expected to exercise individual judgment subject to due process. This holds true not only for jurors, who are certainly not expert, but for experts as well. As previously mentioned, it is an abuse of judicial discretion for judges to employ a "fixed and mechanical approach," e.g., by imposing the same sentence for a given offense. They *must* use their best judgment in individually evaluating each case.

If discretion is simply the opportunity for experts to use their special skills, knowledge, and training to best advantage in unique situations, why are we concerned with this issue? The answer is that studies of experts in a wide variety of fields have shown the popular concept of "expertise" to be substantially a myth. The expert may be better informed than the layperson, but essentially the expert operates with knowledge and skills, misinformation and bias, common to us all. For example, expert clinical psychologists and psychiatrists are generally worse at predicting patient progress than an actuarial formula (Goldberg, 1968). They utilize the same beliefs about people that the lay public has in their judgments, such as "illusory correlation" (Chapman & Chapman, 1969) and sex-role stereotypes (Broverman, Broverman, Clarkson, Rosencrantz, & Vogel, 1970). Government policy-makers are no better (Janis, 1972; Slovic, Fischhoff, & Lichtenstein, 1976). Even professional researchers fall prey to the same mistakes as do the lay public of reasoning incorrectly from small samples or failing to use the information about the population in judging a sample (Tversky & Kahneman, 1974).

Studies of decision-making within the criminal justice system also reveal the common human aspect of the experts. There is a large amount of variability in how different individual experts respond to the same or similar cases, for example, judges (Frankel, 1973) and parole boards (Kingsnorth, 1969; Wilkins, Gottfredson, Robison, & Sadowsky, 1973). Further, neither experts nor laypersons do well at predicting future behavior. Hakeem (1961) found that both experts and laypersons did worse than chance at predicting whether parole releasees would be returning as violators (also Gottfredson reported in Grant, 1962).

What, then, are the major components of crimes and criminals as perceived by criminal justice professionals? In legal terms, a crime has two aspects: *actus reus*, the physical act, and *mens rea*, the state of mind or intent of the person. Aside from the factual evidence about the crime, a person is accountable or legally responsible for an act only if the act was accompanied by a criminal state of mind. This determination is one of the most complex imaginable, whether addressed by psychiatrist or juror. Consider as well the legal concept of dangerousness (Von Hirsch, 1972), by which an offender can be imprisoned for lengthy periods because he or she is perceived as a potential threat to society. These judgments are highly subjective, and are based primarily upon common sense rather than expertise (Kastenmeier & Eglit, 1973; Genego, Goldberger, & Jackson, 1975).

PUNISHMENT, RISK, AND CHANGE

A broad range of judgments in the criminal justice system can be considered to represent two goals: punishing the offender and reducing the risk of future crime. For example, in studies of the use of information in evaluating applicants for parole, Hoffman (1973) found that two case factors seemed of primary importance: (a) severity of offense, relating to a concern with accountability, sanctioning, or the serving of a sufficient minimum term, and (b) parole prognosis, relating to a concern with public safety or risk of new offenses. Kastenmeier and Eglit (1973) claim that parole board members examine an offender's past history on the basis of two premises:

> One is that the board is a moral arbiter, considering a man's past and the offense which he has committed as elements in the decision as to the duration of his present confinement. The second is that the past is indicative of the future. (p. 507)

Experts within the criminal justice system also differ as to the specific attitudes and goals they have about crime and criminals, and the type of policies they advocate. Four basic orientations can be identified within the criminal justice system: (a) punishment or retribution—the offender is responsible for an act which deserves punishment; (b) deterrence—people are kept from committing crimes by fear of punishment for criminal acts; (c) social defense—crime is prevented by removing from society a person who is deemed dangerous; and (d) rehabilitation—treatment and training programs change the offender's behavior and thus reduce crime (Gerber & McAnany, 1972). Essentially, these four orientations represent combinations of the two previously discussed goals of punishment and risk reduction, with the inclusion of one extra component—whether it is believed that criminal behavior can be changed or not. The punishment orientation is concerned with punishment or just deserts with no implication of change. The deterrence orientation uses punishment or threat to reduce crime by influencing potential criminals' evaluation of their future. The social defense model is primarily concerned with risk reduction by isolating the dangerous, while the rehabilitation orientation is concerned with risk reduction by changing the criminal into a noncriminal.

Scientific theories of crime causation can also be seen to involve basic positions on issues which are closely tied to the previous discussion. These theories typically focus either on the biological and psychological abnormalities of the individual offender or on factors in the environment or social milieu of the person which promote criminal activity (e.g., Johnson, 1974). Reasonable and consistent implications of one theory of crime causation is to blame the individual and to view changing the individual as arduous or impossible. Punishment or social defense models are reacting appropriately to these assumptions. However, the other theory of crime causation blames the environment, sees the individual as malleable, and advocates deterrence, rehabilitation, and system reforms.

ATTRIBUTION THEORY APPROACH

The above discussions of the perception of crime and criminals by layperson and expert should begin to seem parallel. Although the expert can draw on *more* knowledge and experience, as well as a normative set of values in his training (e.g., priorities set up by his organization such as isolating "dangerous" persons from society), we would argue that the basic process of judgment is the same as that of the layperson. It is a principle of psychology that behavior is not simply judged by its objective components. Rather, what is perceived is always an interpretation on the part of the observer, a set of inferences which partly ignore, and partly go beyond, whatever "act" was performed. The law recognizes that the objective crime, the broken law, is only part of the judgment. There is also a state of mind, which must be assessed in judging the person legally responsible for the act. More generally, the concern with fitting the punishment to the person as well as to the crime is at the heart of the indeterminate sentencing paradigm and calls for discretionary judgments by decision-makers.

In the past 15 years, social psychologists have developed a theoretical framework which could be used to address this issue. This approach, *attribution theory*, is concerned with how people interpret information about their own behavior and the behavior of others in making judgments about the causes of events, and how these judgments are used and thus affect the person's behavior. Attribution theory does not attempt to specify the "real" cause of behavior, but rather how a person will infer or attribute cause and what will happen once he does. In the seminal work by Heider (1958), the theory is based on the principle that people attempt to determine the causes of events in order to predict and control their social world. We propose that judgments about people who commit crimes, including the parole decision, are at least in part attribution judgments: To what extent was this person responsible for the act, and to what extent does this reflect a disposition to act in such a manner, i.e., criminality?

A person commits a criminal act. In attribution theory terms, judgments made about the crime and the criminal will involve inferences of why the crime occurred—what caused the event. We have noted that, in general, the criminal is considered the causal agent of the criminal act; he or she is responsible and dispositionally implicated. Attribution theory has long recognized the general tendency for observers or evaluators to attribute causality to the people in a situation more than is objectively warranted (Jones & Nisbett, 1971).

As demonstrated by Zimbardo and his colleagues (Haney, Banks, & Zimbardo, 1973), common assumptions that behavior within a prison is due to the inner nature of prison inmates and guards conflicts with the demonstrably powerful causation exerted by the structured environment of a prison.

The differences of opinion represented in ideological, professional, and scientific schools of thought about crime causation and societal response can easily be seen as different attributional tendencies in evaluating crime. The primary issue is whether the crime is attributed to the *person*, as in conservative ideologies, biological and psychological theories of crime causation, and punishment and social defense orientations within the criminal justice system, or attributed to the *environment*, as in liberal ideologies, sociological theories, and rehabilitation (and to some degree deterrence) orientations. This is a fundamental distinction in attribution theory (Heider, 1958). The second issue in evaluating a criminal act is whether the offender is seen as a permanent source of criminal activities (whether or not he is the cause) or as subject to change strategies. Here we focus on how expectancies or predictions are developed. This issue underlies the conflict between rehabilitation and punishment/isolation orientations in the criminal justice system (remember, part of the system is called corrections!). The third issue is how responsibility, in the sense of blameworthiness and *mens rea*, is attributed in the criminal act. Shaw and Sulzer (1964) describe how responsibility can be treated as a series of levels, including sheer physical causality without motivation, and a level at which the person foresaw the consequences of the act and intended them to occur. Essentially, the levels represent how much the person had immediate control over the events. This issue is best labeled intentionality.

The three issues discussed above are directly represented in Weiner's (1974) attribution framework. Internal–external locus of causality, stability, and intentionality are conceived as three independent dimensions representing the core aspects of attributional judgments. Attribution research has shown that these dimensions have separable consequences for the responses made by people to events. Locus of causality and intentionality (the two are as yet confounded) affect general evaluation—praise and punishment, while stability affects future expectations. Studies have shown that events attributed to internal factors are experienced with more pride or shame than events seen as externally caused (Weiner, 1974) and also result in more extreme evaluation by others (Rosenbaum, 1972). Many studies have found rewards and punishments to be assigned on the basis of perceived effort (e.g., Weiner & Kukla, 1970), an internal and intentional factor. Piliavin, Rodin, & Piliavin (1969) showed that a person is helped more when his distress is seen as externally caused (illness) than internally caused (drunkenness, also a failure of effort and usually seen as intentional). Expectancies for future events depend on the stability of the attributed causes (Feather & Simon, 1971; Frieze & Weiner, 1971; Valle & Frieze, 1976). Events attributed to stable causes are seen as more diagnostic of future events than those attributed to unstable causes.

In the case of criminal behavior, we would now propose the following: (a) To the extent that the criminal act is attributed to the person (internal), the person will be perceived as more responsible, more criminal, will be punished more severely, and generally evoke more negative affect in others. In the context of parole decisions, this represents the severity or punishment dimension. This will be further increased by indications of intentionality on the part of the offender. (b) To the extent that the criminal act is attributed to stable factors, the person will be seen as more criminally disposed and more likely to commit future crimes. This is the prognosis or risk dimension in parole decisions. In terms of specific responses to a criminal act, attributing the cause of the criminal act to dispositional factors (e.g., aggressiveness, criminality) which are internal and stable would lead to high judgments of both punishment and risk. Attributions to task difficulty (e.g., his friends, financial difficulty, discrimination) which is external and stable would lead to low punishment but high risk judgments. Presumably the evaluator then adjusts his specific response, such as prison term, by the value he or she places on the punishment and risk aspects of that response. Figure 1 schematically represents this proposal. Specific case information consisting of what is known about the crime and the offender is combined with general knowledge possessed by the evaluator to produce a causal attribution, which mediates specific responses. The precise role of intentionality is not yet theoretically clear, but we presume that internal–intentional attributions would lead to the most negative affect, and that intentionality cues would be particularly important in evaluating responsibility.

Although this position is reasonable and parsimonious in theory, a demonstration is clearly needed. An experiment was designed and carried out using college students (with the assistance of Carol Shapiro) which manipulated the attributional dimensions and examined the resulting judgments. A similar experiment with a few alterations was then carried out using criminal justice professionals. These will be reported in turn.

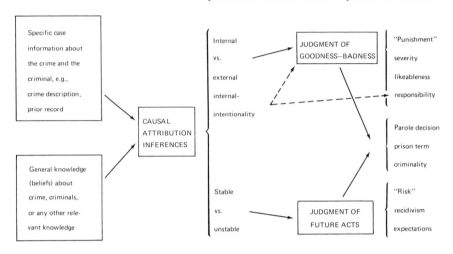

Fig. 1. Attributional analysis of perceptions of crime and criminals.

STUDY 1. ATTRIBUTIONS AND JUDGMENTS ABOUT CRIME AND CRIMINALS BY COLLEGE STUDENTS

The basic plan of this experiment was to present subjects with brief descriptions of a crime and brief information suggesting one attributional cause from the combination of internal versus external, stable versus unstable, and intentional versus unintentional dimensional dichotomies, a 2 × 2 × 2 arrangement of eight possible causes. In order to maintain realism, generality, and subject interest, and to conserve the number of subjects needed, it was decided that each subject would judge a sequence consisting of the eight causes each paired with a different crime description (necessitating eight crime descriptions). They were told that the crimes had actually occurred last year, and that personal details had been removed and names changed. Every subject therefore saw every crime and every cause, but the particular pairings of crime–cause combinations and order of presentation were systematically varied for each of the 64 college student subjects. The eight causes constructed to fit the attribution dimensions are shown in Table I. The set of crimes, which was chosen to represent a wide variety of crime types, is given in Table II.

For example, one combination of crime and cause was the following:

Mr. Green is a 25-year-old male convicted of second-degree murder. He was in a bar having a drink and talking to the victim when they began to argue, push and punch each other. He pulled out a gun and shot the victim several times; the victim was pronounced dead on arrival at the hospital. Mr. Green surrendered himself to police called by the bartender.

He has no previous record of convictions.

Interviews indicated that he had thought about this situation for some time and had developed several plans.

All stimuli contained the phrase "He has no previous record of convictions." The purpose of this phrase was to keep people from inferring a criminal career solely from the crime description, thus overriding the cause manipulation.

Contrast the above crime and cause (internal, stable, intentional) with a different cause:

Mr. Green is a 25-year-old male convicted of second-degree murder. He was in a bar having a drink and talking to the victim when they began to

Table I. Cause Manipulations

	Stable	Unstable
	Intentional	
Internal	Interviews indicated that he had thought about this situation for some time and had developed several plans.	Interviews indicated that he had made a momentary decision to do it and had deliberately ignored the consequences.
External	Interviews indicated that he had been under constant intense pressure from his elderly mother and his family to do things for them, make more money, and give up his free time.	Interviews indicated that his wife had told him without warning that she had decided to divorce him.
	Unintentional	
Internal	Interviews indicated that he has an aggressive nature and exhibits many hostile feelings toward society in general. He has difficulty following social rules.	Interviews indicated that he was in a depressed mood, had been drinking, and was overcome by impulse.
External	Interviews indicated that he could not find a good job because his skill had been replaced by mechanization. The circumstances around the crime had been acting on him for some time.	Interviews indicated that he had been temporarily laid off work due to economic situations. At the time of the act, circumstances seemed to come together to make it happen.

TABLE II. CRIME DESCRIPTIONS

Person Crimes

Mr. Smith is a 28-year-old male convicted of attempted armed robbery. He walked up to a bank teller and handed her a note instructing her to give him all the cash on hand. He warned her that he had a gun. He was stopped by policemen outside the bank, who were responding to a silent alarm, and surrendered quietly.

Mr. Green is a 25-year-old male convicted of second-degree murder. He was in a bar having a drink and talking to the victim when they began to argue, push and punch each other. He pulled out a gun and shot the victim several times; the victim was pronounced dead on arrival at the hospital. Mr. Green surrendered himself to police called by the bartender.

Mr. Jamison is a 23 year-old male convicted of forcible rape. Victim was accosted at night on a dark street near her home. He threatened her with a knife and then sexually assaulted her. Her cries for help were heard by a policeman who made the arrest.

Mr. Jones is a 27-year-old male convicted of assault and battery. He became very loud and insulted several patrons in a restaurant. When a waiter tried to make him leave, he hit the waiter and broke his nose. The restaurant owner called the police and they arrested him.

Property Crimes

Mr. Roberts is a 22-year-old male convicted of possession of an illegal substance with intent to sell. He attempted to sell $30 worth of heroin to another person at a party. An off-duty policeman at the party overheard the conversation and arrested him before any exchange was made.

Mr. Barry is a 25-year-old male convicted of larceny. In a large department store, he put on a $350 leather coat and left without paying. A sales clerk and security guard apprehended him on the street.

Mr. Edwards is a 30-year-old male convicted of forgery. He stole three company checks from work, made them out to a fake company at a post office box address, and forged an official signature. He then picked up the checks and deposited them into a personal account. The checks were noticed in the company records and he was arrested.

Mr. Johnson is a 26-year-old male convicted of larceny and breaking and entry. After driving up to a dark suburban house and checking that no one was home, he broke in through a back door and took jewelry and $160 in cash. He was apprehended by a policeman in a cruising patrol car.

---

argue, push and punch each other. He pulled out a gun and shot the victim several times; the victim was pronounced dead on arrival at the hospital. Mr. Green surrendered himself to police called by the bartender.

·   He has no previous record of convictions.

Interviews indicated that he could not find a good job because his skill had been replaced by mechanization. The circumstances around the crime had been acting on him for some time.

This cause (external, stable, unintentional) should give a very different attributional "picture" of the offender. Instead of a scheming desperado, he is a victim of blind social forces.

MEASURES AND PREDICTIONS

Each crime–cause stimulus was followed by two pages of questions about the crime and the offender. All questions except two were responded to on an 11-point rating scale. Prison term was rated on a 23-choice scale of years and "what caused the crime" was open-ended. Not all these questions had specific predictions, but were included to potentially increase our understanding of the perception of crimes and criminals. In this discussion we will treat only the questions with specific predictions and manipulation checks. The central predictions involve the cause manipulations. Specific predictions involving eight variables were the following: (a) Internal causes (vs. external causes) would lead to increased judgment of crime severity, responsibility, criminality, prison term, purpose of prison is punishment, and lower judgments of liking. (b) Stable causes (vs. unstable causes) would lead to increased judgments of criminality, prison term, purpose of prison is removal from society, and likelihood of recidivism. (c) Internal-stable causes would lead to increased judgments of criminality, and (d) internal–intentional causes would lead to increased judgments of responsibility, and possibly exacerbate the other judgments affected by internal causes.

RESULTS

Since there was a large number of tests performed on a large number of variables, the possibility of finding several significant results purely by chance was clearly present. Accordingly, effects that were predicted were considered to be supported by results significant at $p < .05$ or better, but unpredicted effects were deemed to require discussion only if significant at $p < .01$ or better. Table III summarizes all significant F tests among eight predicted variables and the manipulation checks, for the cause manipulations and for the crimes variable.

Among the predicted variables, every specific prediction was confirmed, and only four effects were found that had not been predicted. For example, averaging across the eight crimes, crimes with internal causes were given an average prison term of 7.8 years, crimes with external causes were given an average of 4.4 years. Crimes with stable causes were given an average term of 7.1 years as compared to 5.1 years for unstable causes. The effects of these dimensions were additive, such that the internal–stable causal information led to an average 9.1-year sentence against 3.6 years for external–unstable causes. Of the predicted variables, only responsibility and criminality

TABLE III. SIGNIFICANT RESULTS: STUDENTS

	Internal-external[a]	Stable-unstable[a]	Intentional-unintentional[a]	I-E × S-U[a]	I-E × I-U[a]	S-U × I-U[a]	I-E × S-U × I-U[a]	Crime[b]
Severity	4.69[c]							53.12[d]
Responsibility	47.53[d]	32.56[d]	8.52[e,f]	19.96[d]	4.82			6.45[d]
Criminality	64.38[d]	32.39[d]		22.64[d]				12.84[d]
Prison term	20.90[d]	7.11						35.79[d]
In prison to punish	11.23[e]							8.84[d]
In prison to remove	40.28[d]	9.75[e]				5.46		12.16[d]
Recidivism risk	48.94[d]	35.69[d]				6.98		4.63[d]
Likableness	36.96[d]	5.69						7.34[d]
Manipulation checks								
Internal-external	109.40[d]	125.01[d]				6.91		3.14[e]
Stable-unstable	22.11[d]			5.26			6.34	
Internal intentionality	18.60[d]	50.48[d]	4.09	8.24[e]	12.68[d]			22.76[d]

[a] df = 1,49.
[b] df = 7,49.
[c] Unmarked Fs are p < .05.
[d] p < .001.
[e] p < .01.
[f] Underlined cells are predicted.

judgments exhibited interactions which presented the following patterns: internal–stable causes led to high responsibility and high criminality judgments, and internal–intentional causes also led to high responsibility. External causes showed little differences on stability or intentionality.

An examination of the manipulation checks[1] revealed results basically supportive of the internal–external and stable–unstable manipulations, but not as clearly of the intentional–unintentional manipulation. Summarizing, the internal–external dimension was appropriately and strongly manipulated by the internal versus external causes. The stability dimension was strongly manipulated by the stable versus unstable causes, but internal–stable causes were rated particularly stable. The (internal) intentionality dimension was correctly manipulated by internal, intentional, and internal–intentional causes, but incorrectly manipulated by the stable versus unstable causes, and internal–stable causes were also seen as more intentional. The problem with the intentionality manipulation may account for the dual nature of responsibility judgments, such that the unexpected effects of internal–stable causes could be due to their inappropriately high intentionality value. In addition, comparisons of the effect of causes to the effect of crime descriptions on the manipulation checks showed that the crime descriptions carried little information about internal–external or stable–unstable dimensions, but were as important as the causes in determining intentionality. Thus, the intentionality manipulations were made more difficult by their competition with crime descriptions.

In summary, the clear pattern of results supporting all predictions demonstrated that college students use information suggestive of causal attributions to evaluate crimes and offenders in ways predicted by attribution theory. Attributions to causes internal to the offender led to generally more negative affect—higher ratings of severity, responsibility, punishment, and prison term. Attributions to stable, long-term causes led to higher expectations for recidivism, higher ratings of criminality, removal from society, prison term, and responsibility. Internal–stable causes led to higher ratings of criminality and responsibility than did external or unstable causes and internal–intentional causes led to higher ratings of responsibility than did

---

[1] The question checking intentionality was clearly used only in terms of the offender, and is thus best considered as a check on internal–intentionality. Open-ended attributions about "What caused the crime?" were coded dichotomously on each of the three dimensions. These data basically supported the rating scale responses.

external or unintentional causes. These results are highly consistent with the proposed theory that internal–external attributional judgments are important for general evaluative/punishment issues, while stable–unstable attributional judgments are important for predictions of recidivism risk. Criminality was seen as an internal and stable attribution, while responsibility may have been seen in two fashions—internal and intentional (which was predicted), or internal and stable, the latter of which could have been due to overly high intentionality cues in these causes. Judgments of recidivism risk and removal from society, hypothesized to be affected only by the stability dimension, were even more strongly influenced by the internal–external dimension, such that more internal causes led to higher ratings of risk and removal. This may indicate that people are very prone to focus on the offender as the source of future crimes, or it may indicate a defect in the theory. Prison term was assigned on the basis of both punishment and risk factors, and thus was an additive sum of internal–external judgments and stable–unstable judgments. Finally, the apparent difficulty in manipulating intentionality leaves open the way in which these cues affect judgment.

STUDY 2. ATTRIBUTIONS AND JUDGMENTS ABOUT CRIME AND CRIMINALS BY CRIMINAL JUSTICE EXPERTS

The basic plan of the previous experiment was retained in order to make them as comparable as possible. Minor wording changes were made in two of the cause manipulations in an attempt to clarify their attributional implications. However, no subsequent differences in responses could be traced to these changes. More importantly, experts were told that the cause manipulations were excerpts from interviews, selected because of the kind of material they contained, rather than a summary of the interview. This was done because the statements were simply not credible enough as summaries for experts.

Questionnaires were initially sent by mail to all 44 persons in an expert parole decision-making capacity in the Pennsylvania State Board of Probation and Parole. These consisted of 5 board members, 5 regional directors, 10 district office supervisors, 15 parole case specialists, and 9 institutional parole representatives. Thirty were received back, of which several were discarded because of unanswered items, and several others were discarded because the design (see below) required an equal number of subjects in each of eight conditions and their condition was overrepresented. This left 21 usable responses, 3 short of an even distribution across conditions. An additional 3 expert subjects were obtained who were assistant district office supervisors for a total of 24 expert subjects.

The design of this study was changed to reflect a different emphasis. Interest arose in whether the cause manipulations worked on all crimes equally, or whether there was an interaction (particularly the intentionality manipulations). Thus the experiment was redesigned using a repeated measurement latin square offering tests of the cause manipulations, the crime descriptions, and the cause × crime interaction.

MEASURES AND PREDICTIONS

Each crime–cause stimulus was again followed by two pages of questions. A few minor changes were made in the questionnaire which turned out not to affect the results discussed in this chapter. The specific predictions were the same as in the previous experiment, although it was felt that interactions were likely to arise, reflecting the varying attributional cues present in different crime descriptions. No attempt was made to predict these interactions.

RESULTS

Results are shown in Table IV. The manipulation checks revealed a similar pattern to that of the students—appropriate results on the internal versus external and stable versus unstable dimensions, but difficulty with intentionality. Internal causes were more internal, but also more intentional; internal–stable causes were particularly stable and intentional, as were internal–intentional causes. The following predictions were confirmed: (a) Internal causes led to higher ratings of severity, responsibility, criminality, and lower ratings of likableness; (b) stable causes led to higher ratings of recidivism; (c) internal–stable causes led to higher ratings of criminality; and (d) internal–intentional causes led to higher ratings of responsibility. There were five unpredicted significant effects at $p < .01$ or less. As in Study 1, the experts also rated internal causes as more likely than external causes to produce recidivism. The major difference between experts and students was that in this study the key variable of prison term failed to obtain significant cause effects.

The lack of results with prison term arose, we believe, from an active discounting of the cause manipulations for this variable. Many of the experts made comments and some refused to do the task for the

TABLE IV. SIGNIFICANT RESULTS: EXPERTS

	Internal-external[a]	Stable-unstable[a]	Intentional-unintentional[a]	I-E × S-U[a]	I-E × I-U[a]	S-U × I-U[a]	I-E × S-U × I-U[a]	Crime[b]	Cause × crime[c]
Severity	8.76[d,e]			8.76[d]	6.75	10.25[d]		56.46[f]	3.29[f]
Responsibility	8.88[d]			11.76[f]	4.32	8.22[d]		5.10[f]	2.10[d]
Criminality	15.30[f]	—		7.30[d]				7.79[f]	
Prison term		—						11.31[f]	
In prison to punish								4.78[f]	2.12[d]
In prison to remove				4.07				8.86[f]	
Recidivism risk	6.31[g]	4.85		7.11				4.54[f]	
Likableness	3.93							5.22[f]	
Manipulation checks									
Internal-external	5.43			7.18[d]	6.27			2.81[d]	2.02[d]
Stable-unstable		26.42[f]						5.08[f]	
Internal intentionality	9.95[d]	34.93[f]	—	5.55	4.27			9.85[f]	

[a] df = 1,112.
[b] df = 7,112.
[c] df = 42,112.
[d] p < .01.
[e] Underlined cells are predicted.
[f] p < .001.
[g] Unmarked Fs are p < .05.

reason that they felt uncomfortable making decisions based on so little information (even though realistically it is often comparable to what experts actually *use*, Wilkins *et al.*, 1973). The experts had been told these were real cases, and we feel that the judgment of prison term for real cases based on so little information made them very cautious and uncomfortable, and strongly reduced their reliance on the cause manipulations. Further, they knew the cause manipulations to be excerpted interviews and hence less important, while the students, to whom the interviews must have seemed more impressive, did not. The experts presumably censored their "speculations" about the manipulations when dealing with the actual prison term.

The experts' judgments showed an added degree of complexity in three significant crime–cause interactions (such tests were not available in the design used for students) on the variables of severity, responsibility, and stability. The interactions had two interesting features: The causes seemed to generate larger differences for some crimes than others; and the same cause sometimes influenced judgments in different directions for different crimes. For example, the murder was seen as most severe, the offender most responsible, and the cause most stable when paired with the aggressive personality. The murder was seen as least severe, the person least responsible, and the cause least stable when due to the permanent unemployment cause. However, the heroin sale was seen as most severe, and the person most responsible, when permanent unemployment or the aggressive personality was the cause. Thus, unemployment was a mitigating factor for murder, but an exacerbating factor for heroin sale, possibly because the unemployment became reinterpreted as part of a different scenario or schema (cf. Kelley, 1973) involving hard drugs.

Multiple Regression Reanalysis

Because of the difficulty in manipulating the intentionality dimension, the data from each experiment were reanalyzed using multiple regression techniques. Subjects' ratings of internal versus external, stable versus unstable, and intentional versus unintentional cause were used to predict severity ratings, and then these four variables were used to predict the other seven variables. Table V reports those β-coefficients with significant predictive power in a multiple regression equation for both students and experts.

The results for the students were very similar to the previous findings in Table III. It did become clear that intentionality affected

TABLE V. SIGNIFICANT β-COEFFICIENTS FROM MULTIPLE REGRESSIONS: STUDENTS AND EXPERTS

	Students[a]				Experts[b]			
	S[c]	I-E	S-U	I-U	S	I-E	S-U	I-U
Severity	[d]	—	.16[e,f]			—	.25[e]	
Responsibility	.25[e]	.22[e]		.38[e]	.45[e]	.15		.27[e]
Criminality	.48[e]	.20[e]	.22[e]	.26[e]	.48[e]	—	.18[g,h]	.32[e]
Prison term	.46[e]	.11[g]	.08		.41[e]	—	—	
In prison to punish	.19[e]	—		.16[e]	.27[e]	—		.14
In prison to remove	.40[e]	.11[g]	.14[e]	.11[g]	.41[e]		.15	
Recidivism risk	.09	.15[e]	.24[e]	.15			.29[e]	.26[e]
Likableness	−.30	−.22[e]		−.12[g]	−.16		−.15	

[a] df for each t test is 507, except severity is 508.
[b] df for each t test is 187, except severity is 188.
[c] S = severity; I-E = internal vs. external; S-U = stable vs. unstable; I-U = intentional vs. unintentional.
[d] Severity was not used to predict severity.
[e] $p < .001$.
[f] Unmarked βs are $p < .05$.
[g] $p < .01$.
[h] Underlined cells are predicted, cf. Tables III and IV.

the same judgments as did internality, however these two variables correlated only $r = .10$ with each other, indicating they were not simply sharing their predictive power. Intentionality was indeed most important for judgments of responsibility. Internal causes were again considered more indicative of recidivism and the need to remove the offender from society. Hence, there was a deviation from theory in that recidivism or expectations were influenced by the internal–external dimension as well as the stability dimension (these dimensions correlated $r = .06$ and thus were independent in the ratings). Stability judgments did show higher relationships with these predicted dependent variables than did internal–external judgments.

The experts' judgments revealed a pattern very similar to the larger-sized β-coefficients of the students, and moderately supportive of attribution theory. There seemed to be an increased importance placed on intentionality and a decreased importance on internal–external judgments (these two dimensions correlated only $r = .07$). Stability and severity had nearly identical relationships to the dependent variables as in the students' judgments. These results strongly present the necessity of detailing the role of intentionality attributions in theory and in practice.

Very early in this discussion we proposed that prison term would be judged from crime severity and recidivism risk. We used the ratings of severity and recidivism risk to predict prison term for each group of subjects. For students, we indeed found significant β-coefficients for severity (.46) and recidivism risk (.17). For experts, however, only severity was significant (.44). Hence, experts may have shown less effect for the cause manipulations because they did not use risk judgments in assessing prison term. Parole authorities do vary from place to place in the importance they give to severity, risk, and institutional behavior (Cosgrove, 1976). However, this could simply be detecting the uncertainty and unwillingness of the experts in dealing with the sketchy information, leading them to rest their judgments of prison term on the clearest information present—severity.

Comparisons of Students and Experts

Several features of the data presented thus far address the issue of whether or not students and experts differ in their judgments, and if so, how. For example, in Table III students' judgments on the eight important variables exhibited 15 significant main effects and 5 significant interactions. In contrast, in Table IV the experts' judgments revealed only 6 main effects but 9 interactions. In general, many judgments by students that were additive functions of the internal-external and stable-unstable dimensions appeared to be interactive for experts. Taking judgments of prison term as a case in point, students gave mean ratings of 9.1 years for internal-stable crimes, 6.6 years for internal-unstable, 5.2 years for external-stable, and 3.6 years for external-unstable, which the analysis portrays as two significant main effects. Corresponding mean ratings for experts were 5.9 years, 3.1 years, 3.7 years, and 4.0 years. Although this example was a nonsignificant trend, the pattern was consistent across several variables and showed internal-stable crimes differing from all others. Thus, there is some indication that experts combine information about internality and stability in a way different from that of students.

Additional analyses were also done to compare the students and experts more directly. The mean ratings of the eight causes by students, averaged over all judgments, and the mean ratings by experts were correlated. For the three attribution manipulation checks, the correlations were .81 (I-E), .87 (S-U), and .94 (I-U). Thus, the manipulations of attributional cues were highly similar interpreted by expert and student. A similar examination of the other variables across the causes revealed high agreement on responsibility (.79), criminality (.97), likableness (.80), and recidivism risk (.77); moderate agreement on the purpose of prison as removal from society (.62); but low agreement on severity (.34), and prison term (.41), and prison as punishment (−.16).

One possible interpretation of these data is that experts and students agree on the attributional content of the cause manipulations, and agree on the responses for more attributional judgments (e.g., responsibility, criminality), but the two groups disagree on the nonattributional information in the cause manipulations (e.g., severity) and subsequently differ when making less attributional judgments (e.g., prison term). Specifically, average judgments on the severity of the eight causes showed good agreement for six causes, although experts generally rated everything more severely by about .3 scale units. However, on two causes the experts were between 1 and 2 scale units higher than the students: the aggressive personality and the divorce. The aggressive personality was rated by experts as 9.2 on the 11-point scale, over a full scale unit from the next cause, which in turn was less than a scale unit from the least severe cause. Whether this person was seen as more brutal in the actual crime, or a specific danger to society in more of an attributional sense, is unknown, but this stimulus really tipped off the experts to something. The divorce cause was interesting also, moving from seventh place for students to second for experts. Students presumably treated this as a reason to excuse certain behaviors, but experts treated this as a negative factor, perhaps now reflecting a pattern of interpersonal difficulties or lack of family support.

We also compared the judgments of students and experts on the ratings of crimes, averaged over the cause manipulations. There was very high agreement on severity ($r = .86$), criminality ($r = .90$), prison term ($r = .95$), and purpose of prison to remove from society ($r = .93$); moderate agreement on purpose of prison to punish ($r = .76$), internal−external judgments ($r = .62$), and intentionality ($r = .79$); and lower agreement on responsibility ($r = .41$), likableness ($r = .53$), recidivism risk ($r = .41$), and stable−unstable judgments ($r = .46$). A partial summary would be that there was agreement on the seriousness of a crime and its punishability, but not on the relative risk represented by the people who commit given offenses. For example, students rated the murderer as third most likely to commit another crime, but the experts rated him as the least likely. This could be taken as an example where the experts simply knew more than the students about murderers being statistically good risks.

These differences between students and experts highlight the distinction between laboratory and field research. Attribution theory specifies only a few features of the information about an offender, and our task and design require students to make judgments calling upon only general knowledge and simple reasoning. Most laboratory tasks make similar demands upon subjects who are considered objective to the extent they are "naive." In contrast, field research is more concerned with the details of what people know about real settings; our expert decision-makers made more and more complex inferences from our simple crime reports because they knew more about the task. Thus, our attribution framework was only partly successful in capturing the complex and detailed knowledge of crime patterns and offender types possessed by the experts. In order to explore these judgments more inductively, without being tied to the testing of a specific theory, we decided to explore the usefulness of "process-tracing techniques" which have been developed by cognitive psychologists interested in human information processing in complex tasks.

PROCESS-TRACING TECHNIQUES

Cognitive psychologists are concerned with the *process* by which a person gathers and evaluates information to make a judgment. This means that *how* the person treats the information, the way in which he processes it, is of interest in addition to *what* judgment is finally made. Process-tracing techniques have been developed to allow ongoing observations during the temporal course of a judgment, thus providing an intensive set of data from which to examine the process. Attribution theorists are very concerned with the process of making an attribution, the complex sequence of inferences and subjudgments that occur, yet attribution research typically examines only the final judgment made to a structured set of information such as those in Studies 1 and 2. We believe that process-tracing techniques, used in concert with other procedures, offer an enriched set of observations from which to derive and test theories. In this section we will describe the techniques used in our studies, and then present the studies.

VERBAL PROTOCOLS

A prime example of a process-tracing technique is the collection of verbal protocols, a running record of everything a subject says while instructed to "think aloud" during the task. Verbal protocols can be used as a source of data against which to test a model, or as a data base from which to derive models of the underlying processes (Newell & Simon, 1972; Payne, 1976).

The collection of verbal reports is an old idea in psychology. Introspection, the trained observation of the contents of consciousness under experimental conditions, at one time was *the* method of investigation in psychology. However, in the early part of the 20th century, the introspective method was strongly criticized as lacking objectivity and was abandoned by most American psychologists.

Unfortunately, as mentioned by Hayes (1968), the apparent parallel between verbal protocol analysis and introspection has undoubtedly discouraged some modern researchers from adopting the verbal protocol technique of process tracing. It is important, therefore, that the distinctions between verbal protocol analysis and introspection be made clear. One important distinction is that subjects under the process-tracing strategy are naive about the theoretical constructs of interest to the researcher. In contrast, highly trained subjects (sometimes the researcher himself) were used to generate the introspective data. Second, a subject giving verbal protocol data is *not* asked to theorize about his behavior. Instead the subject is asked "only to report the information and intentions that are within his current sphere of conscious awareness. All theorizing about the causes and consequences of the subject's knowledge state is carried out and validated by the experimenters, not by the subject" (Newell & Simon, 1972, p. 184). A third distinction is the emphasis within verbal protocol analysis on the processes of thought, as contrasted to the introspectionist emphasis on the content of thought. As a result, process-tracing data are collected during the actual performance of the task of interest, rather than through later questionnaires or interviews. Verbal reports elicited during the task performance, particularly when there is correlated objective evidence of what the subject is doing, may provide valuable information which would otherwise be lacking. In contrast, later descriptions leave much more opportunity for the subject to mix current knowledge with past knowledge, making reliable inferences difficult.

MONITORING INFORMATION ACQUISITION

Another process-tracing technique which may prove useful in understanding parole decision-making is the monitoring of information search, where subjects must view or select information sequentially. A sophisticated version of this technique is eye-movement recording (e.g., Just & Carpenter, 1976; Russo & Rosen, 1975). The data collected provide information about what the subjects are viewing, in what order, and of what duration.

Because of technical difficulties, eye-movement recording has been restricted to the study of decision tasks involving rather simple stimuli. Decision tasks involving the evaluation of more complex stimuli, such as information regarding a parole applicant, have had to be investigated using a related technique. Basically, subjects are presented with decision tasks where they have to explicitly search for information about the stimulus or stimuli to be evaluated. This technique has been used in attribution research (e.g., Frieze, 1976) and has proven valuable in decision-making research, especially when combined with the collection of verbal protocols (Payne, 1976). A related information selection procedure was used by Wilkins *et al.* (1973) in an earlier study of parole decision-making.

In the next section of this chapter, we will present a preliminary report of research designed, in part, to investigate the efficacy of the process-tracing techniques of verbal protocol analysis and explicit information search for identifying attributional processes involved in parole decision-making.

STUDY 3. AN INFORMATION SEARCH AND PROTOCOL STUDY OF SIMULATED PAROLE DECISIONS BY COLLEGE STUDENTS

A major result of an earlier study of parole decision-making by Wilkins *et al.* (1973) was that different parole decision-makers go about their task in different ways. In particular, different people were found to use different items of information, even in arriving at the same conclusion. This finding of individual differences is consistent with the findings from a large number of studies concerned with judgment in a wide variety of decision situations (cf. Slovic & Lichtenstein, 1971). Wilkins *et al.* concluded: "Decision-makers may be of several 'types,' and possibly differences among them, as they relate to information search strategies, are of importance in relation to the planning of computer-assisted decision analysis." However, as Gottfredson, Wilkins, Hoffman, and Singer (1973) have noted in the summary report on their parole decision-making project, while "the information search strategies of decision-makers, as well as the goals they seek are important," they are "but little understood at the present time" (p. 43).

The present study sought to replicate the findings of Wilkins *et al.* and to extend the research on how decision-makers process parole information by combining the information search methodology with the process-tracing technique of verbal protocols. The multimethod procedure allowed us to determine if attribution theory might help to explicate the reasons which may underly differing "styles" of decision behavior. In particular, our expectation was that decision-makers would search the information relevant to their own hypothesis about the cause of a crime.

Each of 20 college student subjects made judgments about two parole cases. Half the subjects judged each case first. Each case consisted of 24 pieces of information organized by category, e.g., crime imprisoned for, age, number of prior arrests, and alcohol use. These 24 categories had been the most often used in the study by Wilkins *et al.* (1973). The information in each category for each case was available on one slide in a random access slide projector. Subjects had to request a specific category by number from a list, at which time the information in that category was shown on a screen. It has been argued that the random access slide projector simulates the use of a computer information retrieval system (Gottfredson *et al.*, 1973). Table VI presents the 24 categories.

The 20 subjects were randomly assigned to two groups: (a) Parole Judgments and Protocol—these subjects were presented with the two cases sequentially. They were told to consider the first case as practice. Before beginning the first case, they were instructed as to the nature of parole decisions (minimum and maximum sentences, supervision, role of parole authority) and the nature of each category was explained. They were told they were free to look at as much or as little information as they wanted to or felt was necessary in order to decide whether the parole applicant should be paroled, and if not, when the applicant should again be considered. No time constraints were placed on the subject. Finally, this group of subjects was requested to "think aloud" during the task by reading each slide out loud, verbalizing conclusions, decisions, considerations, and intuitions, trying to label their feeling, and avoiding long silences. (b) Parole Judgments—these subjects were given the exact instructions as the previous group, but were not asked to "think aloud"; no protocols were taken.

The purpose of having both groups was to allow a comparison of the judgmental processes under verbal protocol and no verbal protocol instructions. Giving verbal protocols is often perceived, especially at first, as strange and even distracting. It is important to establish

TABLE VI. 24 ITEMS OF INFORMATION AVAILABLE, BY MEAN RANK ORDER OF SEARCH

Rank	Item	Rank	Item
1	Crime imprisoned for	13	Release plan job prospects
2	Age	14	Changes in attitude noted
3	Type of prior conviction	15	Early home environment
4	Education level and adjustment	16	Prior parole and probation revocations
5	Time served to present hearing		
6	Number of prior arrests	17	Susceptibility to influence
7	Recent employment history	18	Release plan living arrangements
8	Prediction of future criminal acts	19	Alcohol use
9	Time to mandatory release	20	Drug use
10	Financial resources	21	Cooperation with police
11	Number and type of disciplinary problems	22	Academic progress in prison
		23	IQ score
12	Living arrangements before prison	24	Homosexuality

whether protocol procedures interfere with the natural judgment process, by comparing judgments made under both sets of instructions.

MEASURES

The search data for each subject were organized in terms of the amount of information searched and the order in which the information was searched, as well as the total time taken to reach a decision. Ratings made by each subject at the end of the task included parole judgments, seriousness of offense, and likelihood of recidivism. Protocols were examined from transcripts made of the tape-recorded statements in the group with protocol instructions. For both groups, the first case was considered to be practice and will not be discussed.

Consistent with the procedure suggested by Newell and Simon (1972), the protocols were broken up into short phrases. The phrases were labeled, for example, A1, A2, . . . , A125, for the 125 phrases of subject A. Each phrase is a naive assessment of what constitutes a single task assertion or reference by the subject. Newell and Simon (1972) have argued that breaking verbal protocols into small phrases "goes a long way towards isolating a series of unambiguous 'measurements' of what information the subject had at particular times" (p. 166). Because of space limitations in this chapter it is impossible to reproduce the complete protocol for each of the 10 subjects or to provide a detailed analysis of each of the protocols. The complete protocols for the 10 subjects may be obtained from the authors. Instead, we will present excerpts from the protocols of a few of the subjects together with some informal analyses. The primary purposes are to provide the reader with a feel for the kind of information provided by verbal protocol data, and to provide examples of the insights that kind of data may give to the reasons underlying the differing "styles" of parole decision-making found in this study.

RESULTS

Comparisons between the Protocol and No Protocol groups revealed no differences significant at .10 or less. Although we cannot prove the existence of no differences, these results suggest that the collection of verbal protocols did not affect the judgment process, as measured by number of items searched, time taken, or final judgments. An examination of the order of search provides further evidence. The correlation across the mean rank order of search of the 24 categories between the two groups was $r = .84$, which strongly supports the argument that protocols did not alter the way subjects performed the parole judgment task.

Consistent with previous research utilizing an information search procedure (Wilkins et al., 1973; Siegel, Sullivan & Greene, 1974), judgments were made on the basis of only a subset of the available information. Across both groups, subjects searched from 5 to 22 pieces of information. This large amount of variability across subjects and the use of only a limited amount of information is consistent with a large number of studies concerned with human judgment.

There was obviously some consistency across subjects in their search of the available information. In particular, information about the actual crime committed was sought first by 15 of the 20 subjects. For the remaining 5 subjects, crime was the second item of information examined. However, there were also substantial differences among all 20 subjects in terms of the order in which the information was searched. A measure of concordance among the rankings of the 20 subjects was calculated according to Kendall (1948). The coefficient of concordance W ranges from 0 to 1. As W increases from 0 to 1, there is a greater degree of agreement in the rankings by the subjects. For the 20 subjects, $W = .339$. This finding of substantial individual differences in the order in which information was searched is again consistent with the results obtained by Wilkins et al. (1973), who found that there could be several "types" of decision-makers. An analysis of the verbal protocol data suggests some possible ways in which decision-makers might differ.

Protocols

The informal analysis of the 10 protocols was intended to provide evidence for the applicability of attribution theory to parole decisions. Excerpts from several protocols will be shown to illustrate how subjects appear to make attributions as an integral part of the parole decision. For example, consider subject C, whose protocol on the second case consisted of 117 statements, numbered C133 to C249 (C1 to C132 are the statements on the practice case). The order of use of information categories for this subject is given in Table VII.

The first few statements made by the subject refer to information about the crime committed. Statements in quotation marks refer to the subject reading information from a slide.

TABLE VII. ITEMS OF INFORMATION SEARCHED BY SUBJECTS C AND G

Subject C	Subject G
Crime	Crime
Number of prior arrests	Type of prior convictions
Early home environment	Age
Educational level and adjustment	Time served
Age	Prior parole and probation revocations
Susceptibility to influence	Cooperation with police
Financial resources	Number and type of disciplinary problems
Alcohol use	Alcohol use
Drug use	Financial resources
Living arrangements before prison	Drug use
Release plan job prospects	Living arrangements before prison
Time served	Recent employment history
Release plan living arrangements	Academic progress in prison
Prediction of future criminal acts	Changes in attitude noted
Number and type of disciplinary problems	Release plan living arrangements
Cooperation with police	Release plan job prospects
Changes in attitude noted	Prediction of future criminal acts
Time remaining to mandatory release	Educational level and adjustment
	Susceptibility to influence
	IQ score
	Time remaining to mandatory release
	Homosexuality

C137:   I guess we ought to look at the crime.
C138:   Crime imprisoned for, number 6.
C139:   Look at that first.
C140:   "Arrested during an armed robbery at a supermarket."

Initially subject C's behavior is consistent with the large majority of the subjects in looking at crime information first. The next statements made by the subject begin to give some insight into the decision process.

C141:   Well, there we go with the money idea again.
C142:   Uh, let's look at his past.
C143:   Had any prior arrests, number 14.
C144:   "Has never been arrested prior to present offense."

Statements C143 and C144 may reflect a search for information about how stable the behavior is. The next few statements provide clear support for the hypothesis that the decision-makers will seek to make attributional judgments when faced with a parole decision task:

C145:   Uh, I'm trying to look for the same reason as before,
C146:   a reason for the offense, for the crime.

This seems to be an explicit statement of an attribution goal. The following pattern of search would support that interpretation:

C147:   Let's look at early home environment, number 8.
C148:   "First of three children raised by an intact family in an urban environment. Father worked while mother remained at home."

C155:   So, it doesn't really fit in that the person would need the money.

C159:   Let's try educational level and adjustment, number 9.
C160:   "Subject is a high school graduate, 2 years of college, considered an average student."
C161:   All right, 2 years of college.
C162:   I guess that . . .
C163:   I don't know if the person dropped out or is still in college.
C164:   Let's look at age, number 2.
C165:   See if that'll give us a clue.
C166:   "38 years old."
C167:   I guess he dropped out.

These last few statements are very interesting. The subject looked at educational level apparently guided by the working hypothesis that the reason for the crime was the applicant's need for money. The educational level of the applicant did not seem consistent with the hypothesis so then the subject apparently formulated a mitigating consideration, i.e., the person had "dropped out," and looked for information, age, to confirm that hypothesis. Additional support for the idea that the subject was seeking information in reference to the causal explanation, need for money, may be seen in the next few statements.

C172:   Uh, still trying to find a reason.
C173:   Let's try financial resources, number 10.
C174:   "Subject has a bank account of $200."
C175:   Not too much.
C176:   All right. Let's look at alcohol use, number 3.
C177:   "limited history of alcohol use."
C178:   That doesn't say if he was an alcoholic or he just drank socially,
C179:   you can't really tell from that.
C180:   Let's try drug use, number 7.
C181:   "No history of drug use."
C182:   So I guess I wouldn't—he wouldn't need the money for either of those two reasons.

It appears clear that this subject was searching through the information available about the parole applicant guided by the desire to find a causal explanation for the crime. The use of the verbal protocol procedure appears to have been useful in this case in explicating the reasons underlying one particular pattern of parole information search.

Additional support for the idea that information search may be guided by the desire to make causal attributions can be found in the protocols of other subjects. For example, consider the following brief excerpt from the protocol of subject B. The subject had just examined the applicant's IQ score and found that the applicant was above average in intelligence.

B127:   So he's above average in intelligence,
B128:   can't quite figure out why he's uh, why he is doing what he is doing.
B129:   Is he sus. . .susceptible to influence, number 21.
B130:   "There's no susceptibility to influence cited."

Another example is provided by subject H. Once again the first item of information searched was crime. The next two items of information searched were types of prior convictions and recent employment history. An insight into this subject's early pattern of information search is given by the following excerpt:

> H67:   Um, again I'm looking for some sort of motive.
> H68:   He doesn't have trouble getting a job.
> H68:   His employers like him,

As a final example consider the behavior of subject I. The subject found out early that the crime committed was armed robbery of a supermarket. This apparently led to a tentative causal hypothesis that the parole applicant had needed money. This tentative hypothesis was used to guide the search for additional information. Support for this idea is provided by the following excerpt from subject I as he starts to look at the third item of information searched.

> I82:   but I'll have to see how much money he has and stuff,
> I83:   so can I see number 10?
> I84:   "Financial resources. Subject has a bank account of $200."
> I85:   Seems to be in some kind of uh, financial problems.
> I86:   So I'm going to try to find out what they are.
> I87:   So can I see number 7?
> I88:   "Drug use. There is no history of drug use."

After looking at some additional information, the subject seems to feel that his causal attribution has been confirmed.

> I99:   Well, judging that he probably just got out of school about 12 years
>   ago or something,
> I100:   and he's only had one crime,
> I101:   I'd say that he ran into some kind of financial problems
> I102:   and he resorted to crime to get money.

The final protocol to be discussed is from subject G. The various items of information searched by subject G are listed in the order of search in Table VII. The subject's search behavior appears to be somewhat different from the search behavior of subject C (see Table VII). In particular, the first seven items of information searched by subject G are primarily concerned with the applicant's criminal record. Perhaps this information is being used to generate a judgment of severity of the applicant's past behavior. Or, perhaps, the subject is just trying to form an impression about the stability of the applicant's criminal behavior. In any event, it later becomes clear that this subject also seeks to make causal attributions during the parole decision process, although there appears to be a difference between subject G and subject C in terms of when in the parole decision process the search for a causal explanation takes place.

G88: Um, number 15.
H89: "Number and type of disciplinary problems. Subject has been in one fight, otherwise a clear conduct record."
G90: Let's try to find motives.
G91: Number 3.
G92: "Alcohol use. There is a limited history of alcohol use."
G93: Number 10.
G94: "Financial resources. Subject has a bank account of $200."
G95: Uh, that could be a motive.

DISCUSSION

The protocol data provide evidence that subjects do seek to make attributions when judging a parole applicant. Furthermore, it appears that a search for a causal explanation of the crime committed may occur very early in the parole decision process. For example, the selection of the third item of information, early home environment, by subject C would seem to be a clear instance of information search behavior being guided by an attribution goal. More generally, this study supports attribution theory as a useful theoretical framework for the study of the parole decision process.

In addition to providing evidence of attribution processes in parole decision-making, the present study supports the view that the process-tracing technique of verbal protocol collection can be a useful compliment to the previously used process-tracing method of recording a decision-maker's explicit information search behavior.

In terms of the information search data, the present results offer some support for the findings of Wilkins et al. (1973). The judgments about parole were apparently made on the basis of only a subset of the available information. There was also substantial variation between the subjects in the amount of information searched, and in the order in which items of information were searched. While this result concerning individual differences does seem consistent with earlier findings, there were also indications of substantial commonality of behavior across the subjects. The types of common behavior ranged from a consistent preference for information about the crime to be selected very early in the decision process, to an apparent general goal of the subjects in this study to seek for information relevant to an attribution judgment. It seems likely that one source of observed individual differences in information search behavior may be in the order in which certain subjudgments are made in the parole decision process. More specifically, the parole decision-maker may be seen as evoking certain subgoals in pursuit of the general goal of making a parole decision. The order in which these subgoals are evoked, and consequently the order in which information is searched, may be related to certain general attitudes or priorities the decision-maker might have regarding the purposes of prison and parole. Evidence for differences among experts in terms of the specific attitudes and goals they have about crime and criminals was discussed earlier. Future research is planned which will examine the possible relationship between parole experts' basic orientations toward crime and punishment and their decision behavior as revealed through such process-tracing techniques as explicit information search and the collection of verbal protocols.

STUDY 4. A PROTOCOL STUDY OF REAL PAROLE DECISIONS BY EXPERTS

This study was a very preliminary attempt to collect data on the parole decision processes of actual parole experts. The data collection methodology used was a version of the verbal protocol technique discussed in the previous study. We were concerned that the verbal protocol procedure which had proved valuable in investigating the decision behavior of student subjects might not prove useful when expert parole decision-makers were asked to "think aloud" while reviewing actual parole case files. The purpose of this study was simply to determine if the verbal protocol procedure would yield useful information when applied in a natural field setting. In addition, if the protocol technique proved useful, additional evidence reflecting on the validity of our theoretical framework for studying parole decision processes might be obtained.

The subjects in this study consisted of expert parole decision-makers at three separate levels of the Pennsylvania system: (a) Two parole case specialists, who work at separate state correctional Institutions, and whose job is to prepare summarizations and recommendations of each case prior to parole interviews. Each case specialist examined three different real cases actually up for parole and made actual summarizations and recommendations. While doing this they were tape-recorded after being told to verbalize their thoughts, feelings, judgments, questions, intentions, conclusions, etc. (b)Two interviewers, who were district office supervisors in the districts where the above case specialists worked. These interviewers each examined the three cases summarized by the corresponding case specialist and recorded their impressions, although we could not record actual interviews with the offenders. (c) One parole board member, who examined all six cases from both interviewers, and made the usual judgments. Excerpts from two of these subjects will be presented as illustrative examples.

RESULTS

A complete transcript of the verbal reports given by each subject was made. The protocols were then broken up into short phrases. Again, each phrase is a naive assessment of what constitutes a single task assertion or reference by the subject. Complete copies of the protocols with personal data and identifiers removed are available from the authors.

A Case Specialist

The following excerpt from the protocol of case specialist subject A, on case B, provides an example of the type of verbal report data obtained from the subjects in this study:

AB1: All right, well, the first thing I usually do is see if what he's here on.
AB2: Since it's a, you know, this guy's been convicted of burglary.
AB3: Plead guilty to it.

It is clear that this expert parole decision-maker, like the student subjects in Study 3, initially focuses on information about the crime for which the applicant was committed. The next excerpt indicates that this expert very quickly reached an initial judgment about the severity of the offense committed.

AB10: Now this is not too bad.
AB11: He broke a window and entered a food market.
AB12: He left a credit card box uh, left with the credit card box containing uh, 37,—oh, a cardboard box containing 37 cartons of associated cigarettes
AB13: totaling so much money.
AB14; So, he stole a bunch of cigarettes.
AB15: And, he did this with uh—one other person.
AB16: So, that's really not too bad.

The expert continued to seek information about the crime actually committed. In particular, the expert decided to look at the report of the presentence investigation to make sure that the offense for which the applicant was committed reflected what the applicant actually did.

    AB17:   Now, in his case I also have a presentence investigation
    AB18:   which I consider one of the better documents,
    AB19:   if it's done right.
    AB20:   And uh, let's see, I'll see if this one was done on the same charge.
    AB21:   Yep, it was.

It is obvious throughout the protcols of case specialists that a large amount of time is spent establishing the facts–verifying statements, examining conflicting information, backing up personal statements by people including the offender, and so forth. Then the valid information is considered and summarized, and recommendations are made. For example, at this point the subject decides he has sufficient information about the crime committed. It is interesting to note that the subject apparently on the basis of his severity judgment decides that only a limited amount of information search is needed. Also notice in the next excerpt that the subject explicitly mentions a goal concerned with making an attribution judgment for more serious crimes.

    AB34:   I really don't have to delve too much into—
    AB35:   into what he actually did.
    AB36:   But on more serious crimes,
    AB37:   I like to get a better picture of what he actually did in terms of uh.
    AB38:   That might indicate psychological motivations for the crime.

The next brief excerpt suggests that the subject was concerned with making a judgment about how stable the behavior of the applicant was.

    AB55:   So well, I wanna look at prior records.
    AB56:   To see if the present offense is along with other types of behavior.

After searching for information about previous behavior using such sources as "rap sheets" and the report of the presentence investigation, the subject finds that "both reports indicate that he hasn't been in trouble since '64 til '75."

Having established the basic facts of the case, the subject continues immediately,

AB107:   So then, I start reading social history on him.
AB108:   I look for things like supports

AB114:   Uh,—how skilled he is,
AB115:   his intelligence level,
AB116:   his potential, that way.
AB117:   Uh—and the things goin' aginst him
AB118:   Drug abuse
AB119:   Alcohol abuse
AB120:   Uh, pscho—extreme psychological problems
AB121:   uh, family problems
AB122:   interpersonal kin—
AB123:   uh, behavior problems.

This list of problems turns out to be an agenda for examining the information in the case, a set of possible causes for the offender's behavior. The subject begins with family relationships.

AB149:   Sometimes, uh—the parents are overprotective
AB150:   and they've always covered him for everything he's ever done.
AB152:   And if that's indicated here,
AB153:   That would certainly be a, you know, somethin' that I would look at
AB154:   as—as a reason for the way he is now
AB155:   and also somethin' that would you know—add—detract from him bein' able to make it when he hits the street.
AB156:   Nothing like that is indicated here.

He continues after consideration of several other possibilities, and finds in "an evaluation summary" that "he indicated he was intoxicated at the time of the crime," which could indicate that during the years he was not arrested he might have been "in and out of trouble . . . [and] awful lucky that he didn't get caught." Later, more information turns up about this issue,

AB412:   he—he also indicated to the counselor
AB413:   that when he found himself out of work
AB414:   that he started hitting the bottle.
AB415;   Which is, you know, that's his, you know, reason for—for doin' it.
AB416:   For goin' to the alcohol.
AB417:   as to why—why there would be some alcohol abuse.

He later notes that the parole applicant had been involved in the Alcoholics Anonymous program in the institution.

Some of the clearest statements from the case come from our recording of one end of a phone conversation in which the case specialist discussed this case with another member of the "support team" which makes a recommendation from the institution's viewpoint. These excerpts show that the alcohol problem has become focal and interest has shifted to why the alcohol problem exists, in a manner similar to "causal chains" in attribution theory (Brickman, Ryan, & Wortman, 1975).

AB1128:	Uh—the guy—the difficulties that the guy had in the past
AB1129:	—the records would show that it was due to alcoholism, you know.
AB1130:	Uh—and since he's been here uh,
AB1131:	he has been participating in the AA.
AB1133:	He hasn't been any trouble.
AB1143:	I think the area that we're gonna be concerned with,
AB1144:	or the parole agent should be concerned with this man
AB1146:	is that—of his alcoholic problems.
AB1153:	The guy has the ability to be stable out there.
AB1210:	OK, you know, what he did was so—was done so impulsively, man.
AB1211:	He was out—
AB1212:	he had been drinking with this cat—
AB1213:	and uh,—they were drunk . . .
AB1224:	and they needed cigarettes.
AB1215:	And he went into this place
AB1216:	and he got the cigarettes.
AB1217:	They didn't even go in it.
AB1227:	The alcohol is probably uh—an escape
AB1228:	to dealin' with uh—uh—depressions or whatever.
AB1231:	you know, with superior intelligence—
AB1232:	and he's not usin' it.
AB1233:	And that's this man's case.
AB1234:	So—I would seek—I would seek therapy
AB1235:	also in the areas of trying to wh—get him to realize you know, his capabilities.

In general, the verbal report provided by this expert parole decision-maker was encouraging. It was clear that the protocol technique could be useful as a data collection method for the study of expert parole decision-making in field settings. Furthermore, the verbal protocol of this expert contained instances of behavior which were consistent with the theoretical concepts presented in this paper.

An Interviewer

Interviewers are relieved from the more tedious task of establishing the validity of facts. Instead of tapping multiple sources for any information as the case specialists do, they treat the information as a valid base from which to draw inferences. For example, the following excerpts illustrate the rapid examination of summary statements provided to the interviewer by a case specialist. This is from case C, and interviewer C, using summaries prepared by case specialist A. It is interesting that this subject starts off reviewing the pieces of information in the case file in an order similar to the mean order of our student subjects from Study 3 (Table VI).

CC1: Ah, ok, this summarization sheet says 22-year-old single male.
CC2: Young,
CC3: perhaps an immature kind of individual
CC4: ah, charge?

CC8: Let me see here, official version,
CC9; resident did assault girl age 11,
CC10: attempt to rape her.

The third item of information searched by this expert was prior arrest records.

CC14: Prior arrest records
CC15: seven juvenile arrests
CC16: four convictions
CC17: has a juvenile history of solicitation

CC22: recidivistic of the offenses.

Note that even this early the subject has set up a hypothesis about the offender's immaturity and has made an early observation of parole prognosis. Later, he continues on a related issue.

CC180: This guy is having problems,
CC181: Sexual problems, apparently,
CC182: at least he's gotten into several sexual offenses.
CC183: The classification summary at some point says that—
CC184: ah—er, OK—he never knew his father,
CC185: his mother died when he was 6 years old,
CC186: and he and his siblings lived with an aunt,

CC187:   where he lived until the present offense.
CC188:   Now whether he is mixed up
CC189:   or has problems
CC190:   because of the aunt that he lived with,
CC191:   I don't know,
CC192:   but—ah—I think that would be something I'd get into a little discussion with him
CC193:   or in terms of what his relationship is with the aunt,
CC194:   and see whether or not there was anything that might—that,
CC195:   ah—in their relationship
CC196:   that might have brought him to being a what, sex offender.

The attributional impressions of this offender lead to a dismal prediction of future behavior.

CC320:   I guess this guy really, deep down inside, I'm just guessing, would have the potential to—ah—actually be one of these—ah—ah—people you read about in the newspapers,
CC321:   sex murderer doing in some young girl or boy.

In a different case, this same interviewer notes early a history of assaultive behaviors and drug abuse. He states, "We've got to consider that—ah—very seriously,—since our main argument for the John Q. Public is that we're going to protect society from these kind of people," which clearly reflects the priorities surrounding the risk judgment. Shortly after, he begins to examine the causes of behavior, as the excerpts reveal.

CA171:   apparently he might be a very frustrated kind of individual.

CA190:   or, can't seem to handle stress,
CA191:   or, ah—, I don't know really what his problem is.

CA221:   Maybe he's copying his father's habits.

CA225:   His parental home has always been characterized by incompatibility and strife.

CA283:   The man maybe doesn't know how to deal with stress or frustration,
CA284:   so he's either escaping by using drugs
CA285:   or—ah feels that perhaps by throttling somebody
CA286:   or beating the hell out of somebody,
CA287:   he's going to—ah—ah—work off the problems he has in terms of dealing with the frustration.

CA299:   he wants to take on the staff here at the institution
CA300:   and assault people.

DISCUSSION

As illustrated by the previous excerpts from two expert parole decision-makers, the collection of protocols appeared to provide useful information at a level of detail difficult to achieve otherwise. The primary purpose of this study has thus been met: Verbal protocol techniques show promise as a means of observing actual parole decision-makers in a field setting. To ensure that the decision-makers did not alter their decision behavior as a result of the verbal prototols, subjects in this study were asked to comment on the protocol procedure, to express whether the protocols had interfered in any way with their decision-making, and how confident they were that the decision would have been the same without the protocols. The subjects uniformly felt that the procedure had taken longer but in no way had changed how they handled the cases or the ultimate outcomes. Confidence judgments were expressed in the following fashion by subjects: "very confident," "about 100% sure," "probably make the same decision," "a high degree of confidence," "I'm sure."

ANALYSIS OF CODED PROTOCOLS

Given the usefulness of this technique, the second purpose of this study was to gather additional evidence about the attribution process in parole decisions. Accordingly, an informal analysis of the protocols was carried out based on a preliminary coding scheme. Our goals in coding the protocols were, first, to establish what proportion of statements indicative of the processing of case information consisted of attributional inferences. Second, we wanted to generate evidence of when certain subjudgments were made during the decision process, such as attributions, severity, and risk. This was done by dividing each protocol into quarters and examining what type of subjudgments occurred in the first, second, third, and last quarter. Third, we sought to identify what types of attributions were made about crime and criminals, and to see if the occurrence of certain types could differentiate cases that were paroled from those denied parole. Finally, we attempted to examine similarities and differences in the role of attributions in the decision process across cases, decision-makers, and levels in the parole system.

Coding Procedure

We focused on statements made by subjects which went beyond the information available, e.g., evaluations, hypotheses, inferences, judgments, and recommendations. Thus, we explicitly left out a large number of statements (about 80%) made by subjects, including their verbalizations of what they were reading (information search), their comments on the organization of the task (for example, a lengthy discourse on how explicit dangerousness ratings are made by a case specialist), and anecdotal remarks about other cases which had no apparent connection with the immediate case. Some verbalizations in these latter two categories were probably elicited by the intermittent consciousness of an audience engendered by the protocol procedure.

The broad categories in the coding scheme were determined principally by the structure of the parole decision and by our theoretical concerns, and these were:

A. Severity judgments—severity of the offense, the offender's record, or recommended punishment, e.g., "now this is not too bad" and "rather in view of the serious nature of offenses, serious pattern of criminal offenses."

B. Risk judgments—statements about returning to a pattern of behavior, fear of specific acts, undifferentiated risk of further criminal behavior, statements about returning to crime-conducive circumstances, or statements about confidence in risk assessment, e.g., "the potential is certainly there for this client to possibly fall back into his past pattern" and "potential to ah—actually be one of these—ah—ah—people you read about in the newspapers, sex murderer."

C. Institutional behavior evaluations—severity of misconducts, program participation, or conduct, e.g., "it's kind of a serious misconduct" and "adjustment in the institution has been inadequate."

D. Parole recommendations—final decision or provisional leanings, e.g., "I would concur with the parole staff's recommendation that this individual be refused parole" and "although my thinking right now tends to be toward paroling to a prerelease center."

E. Supervision recommendations—treatment proposals, restrictions, goals, or the role of the parole agent, e.g., "continued ah—involvement in ah—psychotherapy" and "I think the agent, again, needs to keep himself in tune with this."

F. Information seeking—requests for information in interview, other requests for information, or believability and other evaluations of information, e.g., "in talking with this client I would want to find out some of his explanations for the offenses which he's been involved in" and "I find that hard to accept."

G. Attributions—about the current offense or potential offenses, a pattern of behavior, a change in behavior, or a perceived problem, e.g., "it's also noted that the client has had a past alcohol problem which is one of the reasons why he became involved in the present offense" and "he's able to deal with frustration which he couldn't deal with before." Attributions were further classified into five types:

1. Internal and stable—personality disposition or long-term need, e.g., "quite inadequate socially."
2. Internal and unstable—impulse, temporary need, or mood, e.g., "that was just a foolish thing."
3. Internal and intentional—reason, motive, or plan, e.g., "wants to deal with the frustration by drinking or something."
4. External—e.g., "probably because of the low pay."
5. External acting with internal—e.g., "in a different group of people, you know, [he could] become prosocially oriented."

Two coders initially coded roughly half the protocols each, and overlapped on one protocol as a check for reliability. The overall reliability on this protocol was 73% agreement for the seven categories. Over three-quarters of the disagreements were instances in which one coder coded a statement the other missed. Very few "true" disagreements were found. However, there was only 51% agreement on the five subtypes of attributions. Accordingly all previous attribution codings were reexamined after discussions attempting to clarify the subtypes and to make the attribution category more rigorous.

RESULTS AND DISCUSSION

Table VIII presents the number of statements of each category for each of four quarters of the protocols, summed over all 18 protocols (6 cases for each of 3 levels of decision-maker). Attributions were the single largest category, representing 22% of all coded statements. Thus, decision-makers spent considerable effort making attributions, because of both their importance and their difficulty. In contrast, severity judgments, clearly an important factor, were far fewest in the protocols, presumably because the judgments were straightforward and required little effort.

Looking at the protocols by quarter, later quarters became progressively denser in codable statements, since information acquisition was heaviest at the beginning and gradually declined. Severity and risk judgments were made both very early and, expecially for risk, very late. Institutional adjustment evaluations were highest in the second quarter, but remained an important consideration subsequently. Parole and treatment decisions primarily occupied the final quarter. Questions dominated the first quarter and rose slowly

TABLE VIII. TOTAL NUMBER OF STATEMENTS BY TYPE AND POSITION IN PROTOCOL

	Statement type	Position in protocol (quarter)				
		First	Second	Third	Fourth	Total
A.	Severity	8	6	9	10	33
B.	Risk	15	13	22	46	96
C.	Institutional adjustment	10	32	25	28	95
D.	Parole decision	5	13	18	41	77
E.	Treatment	5	16	33	92	146
F.	Questions	26	43	41	52	162
G.	Attributions	6	43	66	58	173
	Total	75	166	214	327	782

throughout. Attributions took place around the third quarter. Attributions differed significantly in their position in the protocols from severity and risk combined judgments ($\chi^2 = 25.6$, $df = 3$, $p < .001$), and from parole and treatment combined judgments ($\chi^2 = 22.5$, $df = 3$, $p < .001$). The framework of Figure 1, showing attributions preceding severity and risk judgments which in turn precede parole (and presumably treatment) decisions, was upheld, except that severity and risk judgments occurred *both* after *and* before attributions.

Table IX provides interesting information about the impact of attributions on the decision process. The five attribution subtypes were collapsed into internal attributions (subtypes 1, 2, and 3) and external attributions (subtypes 4 and 5). The percentage of internal

TABLE IX. INTERNAL ATTRIBUTIONS AS PERCENTAGE OF TOTAL BY
CASE AND DECISION-MAKER

Case	Decision-maker			
	Case specialist[a]	Interviewer[b]	Board member	Total
1	100 (2)[c]	72 (14)	50 (2)	72 (18)
2[d]	50 (12)	62 (16)	(0)	61 (28)
3	100 (21)	42 (12)	(0)	79 (33)
4	68 (28)	100 (6)	100 (1)	74 (35)
5[d]	62 (34)	66 (9)	50 (4)	60 (47)
6	43 (7)	100 (5)	(0)	67 (12)
Total	69 (104)	68 (62)	57 (7)	68 (173)

[a] Two case specialists each did half the cases: 1–3 or 4–6.
[b] Two interviewers each did half the cases: 1–3 or 4–6.
[c] Numbers in parentheses are the total number of attributions in that protocol.
[d] These cases were granted parole.

TABLE X. ATTRIBUTIONS AS PERCENTAGE OF TOTAL CODED STATEMENTS AND
ATTRIBUTION TYPES, EACH BY CASE AND DECISION-MAKER

| Case | Decision-maker | | | Total |
	Case specialist[a]	Interviewer[b]	Board member	
1	6 (33)[c]	23 (60)	11 (19)	16 (112)
	1-0-1-0-0	10-0-0-0-4	1-0-0-0-1	12-0-1-0-5
2[d]	32 (38)	24 (67)	0 (19)	23 (124)
	3-0-3-3-3	8-0-2-2-4	0-0-0-0-0	11-0-5-5-7
3	25 (85)	14 (83)	0 (25)	17 (193)
	13-2-6-0-0	4-0-1-2-5	0-0-0-0-0	17-2-7-2-5
4	23 (125)	21 (28)	3 (31)	19 (184)
	8-1-10-8-1	5-1-0-0-0	0-0-1-0-0	13-2-11-8-1
5[d]	49 (70)	50 (18)	24 (17)	45 (105)
	11-2-8-7-6	5-0-0-3-1	2-0-0-1-1	18-2-8-11-8
6	15 (46)	13 (14)	0 (4)	19 (64)
	1-0-2-2-2	5-0-0-0-0	0-0-0-0-0	6-0-2-2-2
Total	26 (397)	23 (270)	6 (115)	22 (782)
	37-5-30-20-12	37-1-3-7-14	3-0-1-1-2	77-6-34-28-28

[a] Two case specialists each did half the cases: 1-3 or 4-6.
[b] Two interviewers each did half the cases: 1-3 or 4-6.
[c] Numbers in parentheses are the total number of coded statements in that protocol. The second line of each cell gives the number of each of the five attribution types in order: internal-stable, internal-unstable, internal-intentional, external, and external/internal combination.
[d] These cases were granted parole.

attributions for each protocol appears in Table IX along with the number of attributions made in the protocol. Decision-makers appeared to give consistently two-thirds internal attributions, regardless of level. However, they differed greatly by case, and the two cases which received favorable parole decisions consistently received the most external and fewest internal attributions, supportive of our theory and the findings of Studies 1 and 2 in this chapter. Collapsing these cases into paroled or not paroled, the relationship was significant ($\chi^2 = 4.2$, $df = 1$, $p < .05$).

Table X shows the percentage of attributions made as compared to the total number of coded statements. The total number of coded statements appeared to be a good indicator of the amount of work generated by the case. There was complete agreement across decision-makers for each case. For example, cases 1-3 were examined by one case specialist, one interviewer, and the board member. Case 3 was the richest case, with case 2 far behind, and case 1 slightly behind, uniformly across the three decision-makers. A similar pattern existed for cases 4-6, with a different case specialist, and a different interviewer. This agreement vanishes if protocol length rather than number of coded statements is used to indicate what the decision-makers were doing. We also see that the number of coded statements dropped greatly with later decision-makers, who undoubtedly profited by being able to read the prior judgments, and that individuals varied in the sheer number of their codable statements (the interviewer for cases 1–3 made over three times as many codable statements as did the interviewer for cases 4–6, although the case specialist and board member differed three to two the opposite way).

The percentage of codable statements that were attributions also showed good agreement across decision-makers. Complete agreement existed for the decision-makers on cases 4–6, but very little for those on cases 1–3. Someone might speculate about the differences these decision "teams" would experience. There were more attributions made about the cases that were granted parole than about those that were denied parole ($\chi^2 = 21.2$, $df = 1$, $p < .001$). Decision-makers were relatively consistent in what percentage of statements were attributions, but the board member made barely any attributions at all (it should be noted that he read the attributions of other decision-makers, but these were not coded as his attributions).

Table X also shows the individual types of attributions made on each protocol: internal–stable, internal–unstable, internal–intentional, external, and external/internal combinations. One way of examining this data has been discussed in Table IX. A second interesting feature is that internal-intentional attributions were quite common at the case specialist level (29%), but virtually nonexistent thereafter (5% and 0%, $\chi^2 = 14.1$, $df = 1$, $p < .001$). No ready explanation is available for this finding. Finally, there was a uniformly high level of internal-stable attributions throughout, fully 45% of the total. Hence, personality traits and intentions formed the bulk of attributions about crime and criminals, however the relative ratio of attribution types was important for how the case was perceived, as previously discussed.

SUMMARY

The four studies presented here are not a definitive answer to the questions of how people respond to crimes and criminals, how attributions influence these responses, or how parole decisions are made. However, a reasonably clear picture has emerged demonstrating the usefulness of the attribution framework in furthering our understanding of real and simulated decisions by laypersons and experts. Our work represents a beginning for both theory and method.

The theory appears to fit students better than experts, due probably to the large amount of specific information that experts derive from each case. As we learn more of what the experts know, we can see more clearly how they apply that knowledge to specific cases. The nonexperimental procedures of monitoring information search and taking verbal protocols are promising ways to build a detailed picture of the expert, a necessary precursor for hypothesis-testing in a rigorous fashion. Further work will continue the very large task of filling in this picture.

REFERENCES

Becker, H. *Outsiders*. New York: Free Press, 1963.

Brickman, P., Ryan, K., & Wortman, C. Causal chains: Attribution of responsibility as a function of immediate and prior causes. *Journal of Personality and Social Psychology*, 1975, *32*, 1060-1067.

Broverman, J. K., Broverman, D. M., Clarkson, F. E., Rosencrantz, P. S., & Vogel, S. R. Sex-role stereotypes and clinical judgments of mental health. *Journal of Consulting and Clinical Psychology*, 1970, *34*, 1-7.

Chapman, L. J., & Chapman, J. P. Illusory correlation as an obstacle to the use of valid psychodiagnostic signs. *Journal of Abnormal Psychology*, 1969, *74*, 271-280.

Cosgrove, C. A. Classification for parole decision policy. In J. Payne (Chmn.), *Parole: Legal, policymaking, and psychological issues.* Symposium presented at the American Psychological Association meeting, Washington, D.C., September 1976.

Davis, K. C. *Discretionary justice: A preliminary inquiry.* Urbana: University of Illinois Press, 1971.

Dominick, J. Crime and law enforcement on prime-time television. *Public Opinion Quarterly*, 1973, *37*, 241-250.

Feather, N. T., & Simon, J. G. Causal attributions for success and failure in relation to expectations of success based upon selective or manipulative control. *Journal of Personality and Social Psychology*, 1971, *37*, 527-541.

Frankel, M. E. *Criminal sentences*. New York: Hill and Wang, 1973.

Frieze, I. H. Causal attributions and information seeking to explain success and failure. *Journal of Research in Personailty*, 1976, *10*, 293-305.

Frieze, I., & Weiner, B. Cue utilization and attributional judgments for success and failure. *Journal of Personality*, 1971, *39*, 591-606.

Gallup, G. *Society more to blame for crime than individuals.* Gallup Poll, October, 1970.

Gallup, G. *Growing fear of crime could become number one issue in November election.* Gallup Poll, April 23, 1972.

Gallup, G. *Public blames drugs, courts for high crime rate in U.S.* Gallup Poll, January 15, 1973.

Gallup, G. *Crime named more often than economic problems as top city problem.* Gallup Poll, July 27, 1975. (a)

Gallup, G. *One household in four hit by crime in last 12 months.* Gallup Poll, July 29, 1975. (b)

Genego, W. J., Goldberger, P. D., & Jackson, V. C. Parole release decision-making and the sentencing process. *Yale Law Journal*, 1975, *84*(4), 810-902.

Gerber, R. J., & McAnany, P. D. (Eds.). *Contemporary punishment.* Notre Dame: University of Notre Dame Press, 1972.

Goldberg, L. R. Simple models or simple processes? Some research on clinical judgments. *American Psychologist,* 1968, *23,* 483–496.

Gottfredson, D. M., Wilkins, L. T., Hoffman, P. B., & Singer, S. *The utilization of experience in parole decision-making: A progress report.* National Council of Crime and Delinquency Research Center, Davis, California, 1973.

Grant, J. D. It's time to start counting. *Crime and Delinquency,* 1962, *8,* 259–262.

Hakeem, M. Prediction of parole outcomes from summaries of case histories. *Journal of Criminology, Criminal Law, and Police Science,* 1961, *52,* 145–150.

Haney, C., Banks, C., & Zimbardo, P. Interpersonal dynamics in a simulated prison. *International Journal of Criminology and Penology,* 1973, *1,* 69–97.

Harris, L. *Majority of Americans now favor capital punishment.* Harris Survey, June 11, 1973. (a)

Harris, L. *Though public favors death penalty, most would use it sparingly.* Harris Survey, June 14, 1973. (b)

Hayes, J. R. Strategies in judgmental research. In B. Kleinmuntz (Ed.), *The formal representation of judgment.* New York: Wiley, 1968.

Heider, F. *The psychology of interpersonal relations.* New York: Wiley, 1958.

Heinz, A. M., Heinz, J. P., Senderowitz, S. J., & Vance, M. A. Sentencing by parole board: An evaluation. *Journal of Criminal Law and Criminology,* 1976, *67,* 1–31.

Hoffman, P. B. *Paroling policy feedback.* Supplemental report eight, National Council on Crime and Delinquency Research Center, Davis, California, 1973.

Janis, I. L. *Victims of groupthink.* Boston: Houghton Mifflin, 1972.

Johnson, E. H. *Crime, correction, and society* (3rd ed.). Homewood, Illinois: Dorsey, 1974.

Jones, E. E., & Nisbett, R. E. *The actor and the observer: Divergent perceptions of the causes of behavior.* Morristown, New Jersey: General Learning Press, 1971.

Just, M. A., & Carpenter, P. A. Eye fixations and cognitive processes. *Cognitive Psychology,* 1976, *8,* 441–480.

Kastenmeier, R., & Eglit, H. Parole release decision-making: Rehabilitation, expertise, and the demise of mythology. *American University Law Review,* 1973, *22,* 477–525.

Kelley, H. H. The processes of causal attribution. *American Psychologist,* 1973, *28,* 107–128.

Kingsnorth, R. Decision-making in a parole bureaucracy. *Journal of Research in Crime and Delinquency,* 1969, *6,* 210–218.

Kendall, M. G. *Rank correlation methods.* London: Griffin, 1948.

Kitsuse, J. T. Societal reactions to deviant behavior: Problems of theory and method. *Social Problems,* 1969, *9,* 248.

Lemert, E. M. *Human deviance, social problems, and social control.* Englewood Cliffs, New Jersey: Prentice-Hall, 1967.

Miller, W. Ideology and criminal justice policy: Some current issues. *Journal of Criminal Law and Criminology,* 1973, *64,* 141–162.

Newell, A., & Simon, H. A. *Human problem solving.* Englewood Cliffs, New Jersey: Prentice-Hall, 1972.

Page, L. *Crime and the community.* London: Faber and Faber, Ltd., 1937.

Payne, J. W. Task complexity and contingent processing in decision making: An information search and protocol analysis. *Organizational Behavior and Human Performance,* 1976, *16,* 366–387.

Pepitone, A. Social psychological perspectives on crime and punishment. *Journal of Social Issues,* in press.

Piliavin, I., Rodin, J., & Piliavin, J. Good samaritanism: An underground phenomenon? *Journal of Personality and Social Psychology*, 1969, *13*, 289–299.

Reed, J., & Reed, R. Status, images, and consequence: Once a criminal always a criminal. *Sociology and Social Research*, 1973, *57*, 460–471.

Rosenbaum, R. M. *Antecedents and consequences of three dimensions of causal attributions.* Unpublished doctoral dissertation, University of California, Los Angeles, 1972.

Russo, J. E., & Rosen, L. D. An eye fixation analysis of multi-alternative choice. *Memory and Cognition*, 1975, *3*, 267–276.

Shaver, K. G., Gilbert, M. A., & Williams, M. C. Social psychology, criminal justice, and the principle of discretion: A selective review. *Personality and Social Psychology Bulletin*, 1975, *1*, 471–484.

Shaw, M. E., & Sulzer, J. L. An empirical test of Heider's levels in attribution of responsibility. *Journal of Abnormal and Social Psychology*, 1964, *69*, 39–46.

Siegel, L. J., Sullivan, D. C., & Greene, J. R. Decision games applied to police decision making—an exploratory study of information usage. *Journal of Criminal Justice*, 1974, *2*, 131–146.

Slovic, P., & Lichtenstein, S. Comparison of Bayesian and regression approaches to the study of information processing in judgment. *Organizational Behavior and Human Performance*, 1971, *6*, 649–744.

Slovic, P., Fischhoff, B., & Lichtenstein, S. Cognitive processes and societal risk taking. In J. S. Carroll & J. W. Payne (Eds.) *Cognition and social behavior.* Hillsdale, New Jersey: Lawrence Erlbaum Assoc., 1976.

Time. The crime wave. June 30, 1975.

Tversky, A., & Kahneman, D. Judgment under uncertainty: Heuristics and biases. *Science*, 1974, *185*, 1124–1131.

Valle, V. A., & Frieze, I. H. Stability of causal attributions as mediator in changing expectations for success. *Journal of Personality and Social Psychology*, 1976, *33*, 579–587.

Von Hirsch, A. Prediction of criminal conduct and preventive confinement of convicted persons. *Buffalo Law Review*, 1972, *21*, 717–758.

Weiner, B. Achievement motivation as conceptualized by an attribution theorist. In B. Weiner (Ed.), *Achievement motivation and attribution theory.* Morristown, New Jersey: General Learning Press, 1974.

Weiner, B., & Kukla, A. An attributional analysis of achievement motivation. *Journal of Personality and Social Psychology*, 1970, *15*, 1–20.

Wilkins, L. T., Gottfredson, D. M., Robison, J. P., & Sadowsky. A. *Information selection and use in parole decision making.* Supplemental report five, National Council on Crime and Delinquency Research Center, Davis, California, 1973.

9

Social Accountability

PREFACE TO AN INTEGRATED THEORY OF CRIMINAL AND MENTAL HEALTH SANCTIONS

JOHN MONAHAN

When the definitive legal history of the 20th century is written, the 1960s may well be remembered as a time when the spotlight of judicial attention turned to the rights of those accused of crime. The 1970s, it now appears, may be recorded as the time when that spotlight moved toward the rights of those accused of mental illness. With the 1975 United States Supreme Court decision on the "right to treatment" (*O'Connor* v. *Donaldson*), the mental hospital has begun to overtake the prison as the focus of contemporary legal scholarship.

This chapter will consider criminal law and "mental health law" as two variations on a common theme, that theme being the power of the state to sanction acts or people believed to threaten it. We shall compare and contrast these two forms of state sanctioning in terms of their outcomes, their procedures, and their justifications, with the goal of preparing the way for the development of a set of common principles underlying both imprisonment and hospitalization. The articulation of such an integrated set of principles, it will be argued, would greatly improve our ability to deal with a variety of problems currently addressed by one system or the other.

Some of the more prominent characteristics of criminal and mental health law are listed in Table I. "Mental health law" refers to all forms of involuntary commitment, whether following an insanity plea

JOHN MONAHAN • University of California at Irvine, Irvine, California.

TABLE I. CONTRASTS BETWEEN CRIMINAL AND MENTAL HEALTH LAW

		Criminal law	Mental health law
1.	Product dispensed	punishment	treatment
2.	Societal judgment	condemnation	compassion
3.	Disposition	prison	hospital
4.	Decision-makers	peers	experts
5.	Procedure	due process	discretion
6.	Temporal referent	past behavior	future behavior
7.	Basis for decision	moral culpability	professional diagnosis
8.	Philosophical assumptions	free will	determinism
9.	Attribution of responsibility	personal	heredity or environment
10.	Justifications	(a) rehabilitation	(a) rehabilitation
		(b) special deterrence	(b) special deterrence
		(c) general deterrence	
		(d) retribution	

or a determination that the individual is a "sexual psychopath," or upon a civil finding that a person, by reason of mental illness, alcoholism, or other drug abuse, can be confined for treatment against his or her will.

The criminal law dispenses a harsh product, punishment, in a place called a prison, along with society's official condemnation. Mental health law, on the other hand, presents a more benign visage. It offers the prospect of treatment in a hospital, combined with the compassion of society toward one of its less fortunate members.

In the criminal law, decisions are arrived at through a process of peer review, and decision rules are set out in a detailed catalog of due process rights. The focus is on the adjudication of moral culpability or desert for past acts (Morris, 1974). In mental health law, on the other hand, experts in human behavior at least partially replace one's randomly chosen peers as the jury, and their professional discretion is frequently weighted more heavily than what they view as legalistic constraints upon their expertise. The focus here is on the prediction of future behavior by diagnostic acumen.

Criminal law is rooted in a conception of human beings as the masters of their fate, the possessors of free will and free choice. "Historically," Pound wrote almost 50 years ago, "our substantive criminal law is based on a theory of punishing the vicious will. It postulated a free agent confronted with a choice between doing right and doing wrong and choosing freely to do wrong" (1927, xxxvi). More recently, the 1972 *Brawner* decision reaffirmed that "our jurisprudence . . . while not oblivious to deterministic components, ultimately rests on a premise of freedom of will." Responsibility under the criminal law lies with the offender himself. Mental health law, on the other hand, operates on explicitly deterministic and positivistic principles. "Responsibility," or, better yet, "causation" of behavior is to be found in unknown and perhaps even unknowable blends of genetic and environmental influence.[1]

---

[1] It might be noted in this connection that the criminal law does not necessarily take a philosophical position on actual existence of free will. The criminal law, Justice Cardozo said, "assumes the freedom of the will as a *working hypothesis* in the solution of its problems" (*Steward Machine Co.* v. *Davis*, 1937, p. 590). Herbert Packer wrote that "neither philosophic concepts nor psychological realities are actually at issue in the criminal law. The idea of free will in relation to conduct is not, in the legal system, a statement of fact, but rather a value preference having very little to do with the metaphysics of determinism and free will. . . . Very simply, the law treats man's conduct as autonomous and willed, not because it is, but because it is desirable to proceed as if it were" (1968, p. 74).

A recently completed study (Monahan & Hood, 1976) is relevant in this regard. Individuals randomly selected from California jury rolls were presented with a case description of a violent crime. They were also provided with a description of the offender's past history. In one condition, the history mentioned that the offender had in the past received treatment in a hospital for psychological disorder. In another condition, the history mentioned that the offender had previously been convicted of crime and spent time in a prison. The results showed that those offenders whose violent act was placed in the context of psychological disorder were perceived by the jurors as having significantly less "free will," being significantly less morally responsible and blameworthy, and significantly less deserving of punishment than offenders whose act was placed in the context of criminality.

These initial assumptions laid the groundwork for differing sets of justifications for the imposition of sanctions in each system. The four frequently cited justifications for imposing the criminal sanction are *rehabilitation*, helping the unfortunate offender improve the quality of his or her life; *special deterrence*, protecting society by keeping the given offender out of circulation for a while, and making him or her think twice about breaking the law in the future; *general deterrence*, protecting society by using the offender as an example so that others will take note and thereby hold firm against temptation; and *retribution*, exacting a price against an offender for having trespassed against us.

Mental health law shares only the first two of these justifications. It attempts to rehabilitate those believed to be disordered, for their own benefit, and it attempts to change them for the benefit of society, so that they will no longer flout its laws or norms. This latter attempt at change consititutes a form of special deterrence. Since the psychologically disordered are not believed to possess the powers of choice and personal responsibility, however, at least not to the extent that other citizens possess them, it is assumed that they would not learn from the example of one of their fellows. Hence, general deterrence is never mentioned as a justification for commitment. Likewise, it would be both senseless and cruel to exact retribution from those who were determined to behave as they did by their genes or their environment. "If man has an unfettered free will to elect between several possible courses of action, the fact that one chooses a prohibited action then becomes sufficient justification to punish him. Without this free will, however, punishment would be unfair and ineffective. This reasoning was especially evident in the classicists' vigorous efforts to abolish the punishment of insane persons under the criminal law" (Kittrie, 1971, p. 23).

It may be that these contrasts between criminal and mental health law are somewhat overdrawn. There are, for example, elements of due process in mental health law and a considerable amount of discretion in applying the criminal sanction. Mental health treatment is sometimes offered in the penal system, and punishment, such as aversive conditioning, is on occasion claimed to be valid under mental health law. But the emphases, the thrusts, of criminal and mental health law are as indicated in Table I.

The vast amount of psychological, sociological, and legal research on the differences between criminal and mental health law could reasonably be summarized by three very general observations.

The first observation is that there is a substantial overlap in the behavioral correlates of criminal and mental health sanctions (Stone, 1975). Despite all the differing labels, procedures, and justifications, it is entirely possible that the two sanctions would be indistinguishable to the individuals upon whom they are imposed (Monahan, 1974). While there is little question that a stay in prison, given the current abominable condition of our correctional institutions, provides ample punishment under the criminal law, it is at best arguable how this punishment differs from the treatment provided in most mental hospitals (Rosenhan, 1973).

One can, of course, find numerous differences between incarceration as a prisoner and commitment as a mental patient. What is unclear, however, is where the balance of benevolence lies. Law and order advocates are forever disparaging the mental health sanction as being too "soft" on offenders. They charge that the frequently indeterminate nature of commitment in a mental hospital allows dangerous people to be released sooner than they would be if the criminal sanction had been invoked. They resent the absence of official social condemnation in the decision to hospitalize, and see a loss of the deterrent and retributive value of imprisonment. Time spent in a hospital is seen as "easy time," whiling away the hours in conversation with bleeding-heart and naive mental health professionals.

Radical groups, on the other hand, paint a very different picture of the differences between imprisonment and hospitalization. They charge that the indeterminate nature of commitment allows society to isolate the offender in a hospital for much longer than he or she would spend in a prison for the same act (American Friends Service Committee, 1971). They hold that far from being free of social condemnation, those involuntarily sent to a mental hospital are doubly stigmatized, "both bad and mad." These radical critics of commitment see it as a much more invidious institution than imprisonment. Mental health professionals are portrayed not as naive do-gooders, but rather as would-be totalitarians, forcing conformist treatments on individuals drugged into submission, individuals who would have the right to refuse such treatments if they were in a prison (Mitford, 1974).

It would take us too far afield to adjudicate these competing claims that mental patients are better or worse off than prisoners. For the present purpose, we can settle for a draw and conclude that there is a substantial degree of overlap between the two sanctions, so much so that we may consider them behaviorally synonymous.

The second observation that could reasonably be made on the basis of the literature in criminal and mental health law is that, while there are substantial similarities between the outcomes of the two systems, there are drastic differences in the decision-rules or procedures that are used to invoke them. Principles of legality which derive from centuries of Anglo-American jurisprudence have coalesced to form a corpus of due process rights to guide the decisions necessary for imprisonment. No such tradition has developed in mental health law. While the last few years have seen a veritable surge of judicial interest in this area, to the point where the U.S. Supreme Court is beginning to involve itself in the commitment process (*O'Connor* v. *Donaldson*, 1975), there is still a vast gap between the legal rights and recourses available under the criminal sanction and under mental health law. Kittrie lists the earmarks of due process in mental health law as time to prepare one's case, an opportunity to be heard, trial by one's peers, and the assistance of counsel (1971, p. 83). Most states have very far to go to meet even these minimal procedural safeguards.

The question arises as to *why* criminal law and mental health law use such widely divergent procedural routes to reach what must be considered very similar behavioral destinations. The answer here is our third observation, namely, that the differing assumptions and justifications underlying the two systems allow the inconsistency in their decision-rules to be reconciled.

If one assumes that people have the capacity for freely choosing to commit crime, then it follows that people also have the capacity to make choices in their own defense, such as cooperating with counsel and making appropriate strategy moves to demonstrate innocence and avoid or lessen sanctioning. Rational people are supposed to understand the rules of the legal game and play accordingly and in their own best interests.

But if one assumes, on the other hand, even as a "working

hypothesis" or "value preference," that people have been determined by their nature or their nurture to act in programmed ways, then it makes less sense to emphasize legal procedures and rules, since they probably wouldn't understand them anyway, and even if they did, they would respond out of their pathological needs rather than in their own rational self-defense. Since mental health sanctions do not ostensibly involve making an example out of the person in order to deter others, and since compassion rather than retribution is what's being offered, why worry about complex rules or intricate procedures? The law, after all, is only trying to help.

If these observations on the differences between criminal and mental health sanctions are accepted—that the outcomes are largely the same, the procedures widely divergent, and that this state of affairs derives from the differing assumptions and justifications of the two systems—then the question still remains as to why this state of affairs is undesirable. While the two systems may be inconsistent in their approach to serving society, is not the pursuit of consistency for its own sake merely the hobgoblin of little minds—to paraphrase Ralph Waldo Emerson? While having two systems to produce the same result may offend our sense of efficiency or appear aesthetically unpleasing, are these sufficient reasons to consider revamping our entire structure of state sanctioning? If we attempt to integrate them, might we not be jumping out of two frying pans and into one fire?

But, there are, I believe, important disadvantages, heavy social costs, involved in maintaining two separate systems of sanctioning, costs that go beyond the merely academic pursuit of parsimony. These costs occur in at least three areas.

For one thing, having two separate systems of sanctioning promotes profound unfairness and inequity. The issue of which is "worse," imprisonment or commitment, has already been considered and ruled a toss-up. But there is no such toss-up when it comes to the manifest fairness of the decision-rules by which these sanctions are invoked. While the situation in regard to the rights of the committed has improved markedly in recent years, and the horror stories such as those so poignantly depicted by Thomas Szasz (1963) are becoming fewer and farther between, the procedural inequities between the two systems are still substantial. Nor are they ever likely to be completely remedied as long as dual and overlapping systems of sanctioning remain in effect. The assumptions and justifications of mental health law are simply not conducive to the emphasis on due process and peer review that characterizes the imposition of the criminal sanction.

Secondly, maintaining two separate systems of social sanctioning wastes scarce judicial and mental health resources in usually useless triage functions. Enormous time and energy are expended in deciding which system to invoke.

Consider the case of Sirhan Sirhan, for example. With scores of witnesses to the event, there was very little doubt that he killed Senator Kennedy. Yet the state of California spent nearly $1 million on a trial where the chief issue was whether Sirhan killed Kennedy of his own free will, and should therefore suffer the criminal sanction, or whether factors in his past compelled him to pull the trigger on that tragic Los Angeles evening. The defense, seeing the mental health sanction as the preferred goal, produced a psychologist who testified that "by killing Kennedy, [Sirhan] kills his father and takes his father's place as heir to the mother," and a psychiatrist who more colloquially testified that "you might say he went berserk." The prosecution countered with their own psychiatrist who held that "though mentally ill, [Sirhan] is nonetheless responsible under the law." And so it went. The prosecutor translated the defense experts' statements for newsmen as, "If you hate a guy a little bit and kill him, it's murder; if you hate a guy a lot and kill him, you're sick." After the trial, one juror said, "I think the jury took the testimony of the psychiatrist and psychologist into consideration fairly, but the feeling was that they contradicted each other, and even themselves from time to time" (Dix, 1971, p. 313).

Without undue cynicism, it is possible to ask whether anyone really cares what Sirhan's mental state was at the time of the killing. Is anyone interested in whether he fell off a horse several years before, as the defense alleged, or whether he had a "pathological" hatred of pro-Israelis like Senator Kennedy? Was it really worth all that time and all that money to haggle over whether Sirhan should be sent to a prison or to a mental hospital?

Finally, maintaining two separate systems of sanctioning has the distinct disadvantage of impairing the resolution of substantive issues in either realm. Difficult cases and thorny issues for one system can be avoided by simply declaring them "off limits" and asserting that they are within the jurisdiction of the other system. Preventive detention is a case in point. Many lawyers pride their libertarian souls on their opposition to preventive or pretrial detention for criminal offenders. They confidently cite the voluminous and accurate literature on the inability to predict violence (Monahan, 1975, 1976; Geis & Monahan, 1976). But many see no problem in involuntarily committing persons diagnosed as dangerously mentally ill, despite the fact that this is just as clearly preventive detention, and that accuracy in predicting violence is just as poor in the case of the allegedly mentally ill. Their response when this seeming inconsistency in their positions is pointed out to them is usually a shrug of the shoulders and some mutterings to the effect that "I only deal with the criminal law." That, it would seem, is precisely the problem. We have compartmentalized our thinking to the point that basic substantive issues, such as preventive detention, are only partially dealt with. Those parts which do not fit neatly into our cognitive templates of "criminal" or "mental health" are fobbed off as somebody else's business. We play a game of intellectual hot potato with those who challenge our notions of how people should act. Proponents of both the criminal and the mental health sanctions are equally involved here. Thomas Szasz (1963) manages to make the mental health system a paragon of libertarian freedom by dumping all the difficult cases on the doorstep of the nearest prison. Herbert Packer (1968), in his efforts to limit the criminal sanction, did so in part by transferring all of Szasz's problem cases back to the hospital admitting room.

So here we have it: two parallel systems of social accountability, both delivering involuntary total institutionalization, but via different routes and with different purposes; two systems which involve dissimilar levels of protection for the individuals in their grasp, which can be highly inefficient in their division of labor, and which can serve to camouflage and thereby impede the resolution of critical policy issues.

Numerous reformist solutions to these difficulties have been proposed, most systematically by Nicholas Kittrie (1971). Kittrie argues for a "Bill of Rights for the Therapeutic State," *therapeutic state* being his term for the expanding role of the mental health sanction. The general thrust of these reformist solutions is to infuse legal protections—such as rights to trial, to counsel, and to treatment—into mental health law, so that the gap between criminal and mental health law in terms of procedural rights will be narrowed. Proposals such as these have a great deal to offer in the short run, and should be vigorously pursued. They are already achieving some notable measure of success.[2]

But this author believes that a more comprehensive resolution of the problems raised above will require a bolder strategy than simply

[2] This is not to say that providing due process criminal rights to involuntarily committed persons will resolve their problems. "Surely no one familiar with the American criminal justice system would suggest that it deals effectively with either the problem of crime or of correction. There is, therefore, no reason to hope, at initio, that imposing one terrible system on another will be productive" (Stone, 1975, p. 3).

peppering mental health law with due process protections. Perhaps we should consider whether two parallel systems of social sanctioning are actually one too many, and whether it would be possible to coalesce criminal and mental health law into one philosophically and procedurally integrated system—one system which could avoid currently rampant inequities, which could obviate the necessity for dissipating our energies in meaningless triage rituals, and which would be *forced* to deal with difficult issues, for the simple reason that there would then be no place else to dump them.

It is impossible to provide the blueprint, or even an artist's rendering, for such an integrated system. But let me present some developing notions of what an integrated system would look like, and of what it would not resemble.

There are at least six idealized cases that an integrated system of social sanctioning would have to address. They are outlined in Table II, as they are currently processed by criminal or mental health law. The last two columns list the two most frequently cited philosophical reasons for sanctioning of any sort, namely, that it serves utilitarian purposes, that there is some social benefit to sanctioning (Wootton, 1959), or that it involves moral culpability, that the community would find the offender blameworthy or deserving of sanction (Morris, 1974).

Consider case 1, the individual who murders on a contract basis. Here the criminal law is dealing with an act which has already occurred. If the defendant committed the act, and if the system works as it should, he or she is found guilty and sent to prison. Such a disposition has a utilitarian benefit: It protects us, at least for a while, from someone who would do us harm, and it may deter others. It is, as well, applied to someone whom the average member of the community would view as culpable or deserving of sanction.

Case 2, a murder by someone diagnosed as insane, likewise deals with an act which has occurred, but in this case the defendant, under current law, could be found innocent by reason of insanity and the mental health sanction would be invoked. Here, as in case 1, there is a utilitarian purpose to sanctioning—we can sleep more soundly because a murderer is in a locked hospital ward—but the average community member would not find the defendant culpable or blameworthy, since he or she was acting under the influence of psychological disorder and hence did not have the *mens rea*, "the evil intent," necessary for invoking the criminal sanction.

The third case is that of someone who accidentally occasioned the death of another in a nonnegligent manner, such as the person whose elbow happened to dislodge a flower pot on the head of an unfortun-

TABLE II. IDEALIZED CASES WHICH MUST BE ADDRESSED BY AN INTEGRATED THEORY OF SOCIAL SANCTIONS

		Current processing		Justification for sanction	
Case description	Conduct	Verdict	Disposition	Utilitarian	Culpable
1. Hired murderer	occurred	guilty	prison	yes	yes
2. Insane murderer	occurred	innocent	hospital	yes	no
3. Accidental murderer	occurred	innocent	free	yes	no
4. "Framed" murderer	occurred	innocent	free	yes	no
5. Dangerous mentally ill	predicted	committed	hospital	yes	no
6. Dangerous nonmentally ill	predicted	no charges	free	yes	no

ate passerby. Here, if the system were functioning as it should, the defendant would be found innocent. The criminal sanction could not be invoked, due to a lack of *mens rea,* and the mental health sanction could not be imposed, due to a lack of psychological disorder. The individual would be set free. Even though no one would find this person culpable or blameworthy, however, his or her sanctioning might make other people more careful where they placed their flower pots or how they moved their elbows in the future. Sanctioning this person, in other words, *might* have a utilitarian purpose. It might generally deter others.

Similarly, case 4 concerns an innocent person who is framed or set up to take the blame for a murder. One hopes our current criminal process would discover the defendant's innocence and set the person free. But here is the rub, and here is why this case and the previous one are the classic flies in the utilitarian ointment. Sanctioning this defendant, even though he or she is innocent and not culpable for an act which he or she did not commit, *might* serve a utilitarian purpose. If people *believed* the defendant to be guilty, others might be deterred from similar acts by the defendant's punishment, even though he or she didn't do it. Cases such as this have stymied the proponents of utilitarianism in the past, and will no doubt continue to do so (Hart, 1968).

The final two cases, 5 and 6, concern acts that have not yet occurred, but which are predicted to occur in the future. In case 5, the individual in question is judged to be mentally ill. As it now stands in most states, he or she could be committed to a mental hospital until judged no longer dangerous. Such a course of action serves utilitarian purposes, but the individual, like the insane offender in case 2, is not held culpable for violent predispositions.

In the last case, the individual is predicted to be equally dangerous, but is held not to be mentally ill. There are no provisions in either criminal or mental health law to sanction this individual even though he or she may be as dangerous as the person in case 5, and sanctioning might serve the same utilitarian purposes.

These six cases, I believe, raise the issues which an integrated theory of criminal and mental health sanctions must address. The challenge is to create a system with a consistent set of assumptions, justifications, and decision-rules which could do the following:

1. Allow for the sanctioning of "normal offenders" such as the hired murderer in case 1, as the criminal law currently does.

2. Allow for a similar sanctioning of "insane" offenders, such as

in case 2, which the criminal law cannot currently do since it relies on moral culpability, and for which it calls in mental health law.

3. Disallow the sanctioning of those who accidentally and nonnegligently offend, or who are otherwise innocent, such as in cases 3 and 4.

Both the criminal law and mental health law currently do disallow such sanctioning, but the charge has been made that any purely utilitarian scheme of sanctioning—such as that proposed by Barbara Wootton (1959)—would, at least in theory, permit the institutionalization of anyone who even accidentally transgressed upon legal norms or who was merely believed by the populace to have transgressed. (Note that sanctioning all six cases in Table II—including those who are now set free—could serve a utilitarian purpose.) As Stanford Kadish has it, "the decline of guilt"—meaning the decline of culpability as a rationale for sanctioning and the corresponding rise of utilitarian principles—inexorably carries with it "the decline of innocence" (1968, p. 273). Any integrated theory of social sanctions which relied on unqualified utilitarian principles would have to come to grips with this problem, and detail how it would avoid inadvertently catching the innocent in its net (Monahan, 1973).

4. Finally, an integrated theory of social sanctions must take a consistent position on that toughest of issues, the legitimacy of preventive detention, exemplified by cases 5 and 6. This can be accomplished in one of two ways—either by allowing the preventive detention of persons not alleged to be psychologically disordered, or by disallowing the preventive detention of the mentally ill. All that is called for is that the decision-rules for social sanctioning not include the largely spurious variable of psychological status. If the system is to allow for preventive detention, then it must allow it for everyone who scores above the cutoff on whatever device for assessing dangerousness is chosen, regardless of whether or not they are considered disordered. It makes little difference to most people whether they are killed by someone trying to rob them or killed by someone who believes he is acting on orders from God. They will be buried equally deep in either event.

The civil libertarian position has much to recommend it, yet proposals to abolish all preventive detention must deal with hypothetical cases such as the following: Assume that a person has been arrested for murder, and that there were numerous and reliable witnesses to the event. Assume too, that the defendant was wealthy and could afford any reasonable bail set for him, and that there was no valid reason to predict that he would abscond from the jurisdiction. Should this person be involuntarily detained pending trial? Assume further that he is set free on bail and that the next day he is again arrested for murder, and, again, the evidence is overwhelmingly against him. Should he now, accused of two separate murders, be detained pending trial? And if he should not be detained, but rather set free again, would one's opinion be the same if he were arrested for yet a third or a fourth or a tenth murder? At what point short of a speedy trial would preventive detention be acceptable? I confess to having no comfortable solution to this problem, but remain adamantly opposed to current procedures which, in my opinion, impede rational analysis by arbitrarily restricting preventive detention to one class of people—those with a diagnosis of disorder—and allow the equally dangerous but undiagnosable to remain at large.

The major question still remains: Can an integrated theory of social sanctions be created subsuming criminal and mental health law under a common and consistent set of principles? In our legitimate pursuit of a society which is at the same time safe and just, can we dispense with making largely semantic distinctions between imprisonment and hospitalization, and with drawing largely imaginary lines between different psychological classes of citizens? I am unsure of the answer, but convinced that its pursuit is well worth the effort.

Acknowledgment

I would like to thank Linda Monahan and Robert Meier for their insightful comments on this manuscript.

REFERENCES

American Friends Service Committee. *Struggle for justice.* New York: Hill and Wang, 1971.

Brawner v. U.S. 471 F 2d 969 (D.C. Circ, 1972).

Dershowitz, A. Preventive confinement: A suggested framework for constitutional analysis. *Texas Law Review*, 1973, *51*, 1306.

Dix, G. Psychological abnormality as a factor in grading criminal liability. *Journal of Criminal Law, Criminology and Police Science*, 1971, *62*, 313-334.

Geis, G., & Monahan, J. The social ecology of violence. In T. Lickona (Ed.), *Moral development and behavior: Theory, research and social issues.* New York: Holt, Rinehart & Winston, 1976.

Goffman, E. *Asylums.* New York: Doubleday, 1961.

Hart, H. L. A. *Punishment and responsibility.* Oxford: Clarendon Press, 1968.

Kadish, S. The decline of innocence. *Cambridge Law Journal*, 1968, *26*, 273.

Kittrie, N. *The right to be different*. New York: Penguin, 1971.

Mitford, J. *Kind and usual punishment*. New York: Vintage, 1974.

Monahan, J. Abolish the insanity defense? Not yet. *Rutgers Law Review*, 1973, *26*, 719–740.

Monahan, J. The psychiatrization of criminal behavior. In A. Brooks (Ed.), *Law, psychiatry and the mental health system*. Boston: Little, Brown, 1974. Pp. 696–699.

Monahan, J. The prediction of violence. In D. Chappell & J. Monahan (Eds.), *Violence and criminal justice*. Lexington, Massachusetts: Lexington Books, 1975. Pp. 15–31.

Monahan, J. The prevention of violence. In J. Monahan (Ed.), *Community mental health and the criminal justice system*. New York: Pergamon Press, 1976. Pp. 13–34.

Monahan, J., & Hood, G. *Psychologically disordered and criminal offenders: Perceptions of their volition and responsibility. Criminal Justice and Behavior*, 1976, *3*, 123–134.

Morris, N. *The future of imprisonment*. Chicago: University of Chicago Press, 1974.

O'Connor v. Donaldson, 43 *U.S. Law Week*, 4929, June 26, 1975.

Packer, H. *The limits of the criminal sanction*. Palo Alto: Stanford University Press, 1968.

Pound, R. Introduction. In F. Sayre, *Cases on criminal law*. Rochester, New York: Lawyers' Cooperative, 1927.

Rosenhan, D. On being sane in insane places. *Science*, 1973, *179*, 250–258.

Steward Machine Co. v. *Davis*, 301 U.S. 548, 590 (1937).

Stone, A. *Mental health and law: A system in transition*. Washington, D.C.: U.S. Government Printing Office, 1975.

Szasz, T. *Law, liberty, and psychiatry*. New York: Macmillan, 1963.

Wootton, B. *Social science and social pathology*. London: Stevens & Sons, 1959.

Biographical Sketches of the Contributors

JAMES J. ALFINI, director of research at the American Judicature Society, received his B.A. from Columbia University and his law degree, the J.D., from Northwestern University School of Law. Licensed to practice law in Illinois and New York, he has been involved in many studies of state and local court systems and has authored numerous articles and books on subjects related to the administration of justice.

JOHN S. CARROLL is an assistant professor of psychology at Carnegie-Mellon University. His Ph.D. in social psychology from Harvard University followed 3 years after he received a B.S. in physics from the Massachusetts Institute of Technology. His research interests in person perception, cognitive social psychology, and the criminal justice system have been supported with grants from the National Science Foundation and the Army Research Institute for the Behavioral and Social Sciences. In 1975, he was coorganizer of the 11th Annual Carnegie Symposium on Cognition and coeditor of the subsequent book entitled *Cognition and Social Behavior* (with John W. Payne).

AMIRAM ELWORK, a research associate in the law-psychology program at the University of Nebraska-Lincoln, recently received his Ph.D. in psychology from that institution. His research interests include basic and applied research into the law, legal process, and system. He has recently coauthored (with Bruce Dennis Sales) another book chapter which extensively reviews and analyzes the psycholegal research on the jury and trial processes, and he is currently working on an introductory textbook on law-psychology with Professor Sales.

MICHAEL J. GOLDSTEIN, Ph.D., is a professor of clinical psychology at UCLA. He does writing and research in the areas of schizophrenia, stress, pornography and sexual deviance, the family, and law-psychology. He is a past Fullbright research professor and is a member of the American College of Neuropsychopharmacology, the International Scientific Commission on the Family, and the International Academy for Sex Research. He is coauthor of the 1974 publication, *Pornography and Sexual Deviance,* was a research consultant for the President's Commission on Obscenity and Pornography, and is a member of the editorial and advisory board of the journal, *Law and Human Behavior.*

JOHN MONAHAN, Ph.D., assistant professor in the Program in Social Ecology at the University of California at Irvine, and currently on leave as a law-psychology fellow at Harvard University School of Law, is a community psychologist. He received the Young Psychologist Award of the American Psychological Association in 1972, and is editor/ author of the following texts: *Community Mental Health and the Criminal Justice System; Violence and Criminal Justice;* and *Psychology and Community Change.* He is a member of the editorial and advisory board of the *American Journal of Community Psychology, Criminal Justice and Behavior,* and the journal, *Law and Human Behavior.* His research in psychology and law has been cited with favor by the California Supreme Court.

NORVAL MORRIS, LL.B., LL.M., Ph.D., is the dean of the University of Chicago Law School and was the first director of Chicago's Center for Studies in Criminal Justice. He was a recipient of the Hutchinson Silver Medal from the London School of Economics for his outstanding doctoral thesis in criminology and was appointed to the American Bar Association Commission on Corrections, the Commission for the Revision of the Mental Health Code, and the National Council on Crime and Delinquency. He is also the past director of the United Nations Institute for the Prevention of Crime and Treatment of Offenders. His books include: *The Habitual Criminal; Studies in Crimi-*

nal Law; The Honest Politician's Guide to Crime Control; and *The Future of Imprisonment.* He is a member of the editorial and advisory board of the journal, *Law and Human Behavior.*

JOHN W. PAYNE is an assistant professor of behavioral sciences and marketing in the Graduate School of Business at the University of Chicago. A Ph.D. in psychology from the University of California-Irvine, he was formerly a visiting assistant professor at Carnegie-Mellon University. His primary research interest is in human decision processes. He has received grants to study decision behavior from the National Science Foundation and the National Institute of Mental Health. His articles have appeared in such journals as *Psychological Bulletin, Journal of Experimental Psychology,* and *Organizational Behavior and Human Performance.* In 1975, he was coorganizer of the 11th Annual Carnegie Symposium on Cognition and coeditor of the subsequent book entitled *Cognition and Social Behavior* (with John S. Carroll).

BRUCE DENNIS SALES, J.D., Ph.D., president of the American Psychology-Law Society, is an associate professor of psychology and law, and director of the Law-Psychology Graduate Training Program at the University of Nebraska-Lincoln. He is the editor of the journal, *Law and Human Behavior,* of the book *Psychology in the Legal Process,* and of the book series *Perspectives in Law and Psychology,* and he is working on an introductory textbook in law-psychology (with Amiram Elwork). He is currently coprincipal investigator of a project to evaluate civil and criminal jury instructions (funded by the National Science Foundation), coprincipal investigator of a project to identify and measure the performance of judges in state trial courts (funded by the National Science Foundation), and codirector of a project to draft and disseminate model state laws to deal with all aspects of developmental disability (funded by the U.S. Department of Health, Education and Welfare). He currently serves on numerous national committees including the American Bar Association Commission on the Mentally Disabled and the American Psychological Association Task Force on Legal Action.

RALPH KIRKLAND SCHWITZGEBEL, Ed.D., J.D., recently moved from the department of psychiatry at Harvard Medical School to the department of psychology at California Lutheran College. He is chairman of the Crime and Delinquency Review Committee at the National Institute of Mental Health and is a member of the editorial staff of the *Harvard Civil Rights-Civil Liberties Law Review*, *Criminology: An Interdisciplinary Journal*, and the journal, *Law and Human Behavior*. Dr. Schwitzgebel is currently the recipient of two NIMH grants for research on the right to treatment of mentally disabled persons and on civil commitment and social policy. His book, *Street Corner Research: An Experimental Approach to the Juvenile Delinquent*, received the Outstanding Academic Book Award in 1966. He is coauthor of several other books including *Changing Human Behavior: Principles of Planned Intervention*; and *Competency to Stand Trial and Mental Illness*.

SALEEM A. SHAH, Ph.D., is the chief of the Center for Studies of Crime and Delinquency at the National Institute of Mental Health. He has written numerous articles published in legal, psychological, and criminological journals. Dr. Shah has done seminal XYY chromosomal research which was reported in two book chapters in *Progress in Medical Genetics and Dyssocial Behavior and Cerebral Function*. He has served as consultant and member of the American Bar Association Commission on the Mentally Disabled, the Executive Council of the American Society of Criminology, the Advisory Committee on Pretrial Competency Examination Process in the District of Columbia, the National Council on Crime and Delinquency, and the President's Commission on Law Enforcement and Administration of Justice. He is an associate editor of *Criminology: An Interdisciplinary Journal* and a member of the editorial and advisory board of the journal, *Law and Human Behavior*.

HANS TOCH, Ph.D., is a professor of social psychology at the School of Criminal Justice at State University of New York at Albany. He is the editor of the *Journal of Research in Crime and Delinquency* and a member of the editorial and advisory board of the journal, *Law and Human Behavior*. His books include: *Men in Crisis: Human Breakdowns in Prison*; *Violent Men*; *The Social Psychology of Social Movements*; and *Agents of Change: A Study in Police Reform*.

DAVID B. WEXLER, J.D., is a professor of law at the University of Arizona. His interest in legal and psychological areas has produced several publications on mental health law, behavior modification, prison inmate legal assistance, and criminal detainers. He was the 1972 recipient of the American Psychiatric Association Manfred S. Guttmacher Forensic Psychiatry Award. He is a member of the editorial and advisory board of the *Criminal Law Bulletin* and the journal, *Law and Human Behavior*, an associate editor of *Criminology: An Interdisciplinary Journal*, and a member of the board of directors of the American Psychology Law Society.

Index

Accountability, facilitation of, 96-98
Active voice, in jury instructions, 52-54
Actus reus, 195
Adolescent, effect of erotica on, 8-9
Agnew, Spiro T., 158
Alcohol problem, in criminal behavior, 221, 223, 227-228
Alcoholics Anonymous, 228
American Psychiatric Association, 145
Antisocial sex acts, erotica and, 13
Antonyms, in jury instructions, 41-43
Arizona, prison-to-hospital transferees in, 136
Arizona State Hospital, 121
Attribution theory approach, in criminal act perception, 197-199
Automatic commitment or confinement, 127 (*see also* Commitment)

Bandura, Albert, 124
Bazelon, David, 114
Bedau, Hugo Adam, 123
Behavior
    criminal and mental health sanctions in, 241-246
    genetic—environmental influences in, 243
Behavior modification, 124
Boccaccio, Giovanni, 1
Bolton v. *Harris*, 129
Book of Approved Jury Instructions, 25, 28
Brawner decision, 243
Bridgewater State Hospital, 142
Butner (N.C.) federal prison, 152

Caging, imprisonment as, 153-156
California Jury Instructions, Criminal, 25
Cantor, Irwin, 27
Capital punishment, 156
Cardozo, Benjamin, 243 n.
Child
    homosexual relations and, 7-8
    premature exposure to sexuality, 5
    sexual information for, 5
Coded protocols, in parole decisions, 231-236
College students
    attributions and judgments of concerning crime and criminals, 200-206
    simulated parole decisions by, 215-224
Commitment
    automatic and indefinite, 127
    criminal, 121-137
    culpable decisions in, 130-131
    vs. imprisonment, 241-248
    for mentally ill, 93-94
    for persons not guilty by reason of insanity, 127-133
Communication, goal of, 31
Control Unit Treatment Program, Marian penitentiary, 123
Crime (*see also* Criminal behavior)
    blameworthiness for, 198
    judgments about, 191-237
    as prime social issue, 192
    public perception of, 193-194
Crime causation, scientific theories of, 196

Crime perception
  attribution theory approach in, 197-
    199
  discretion and expertise in, 194-195
  punishment, risk, and change in, 195-
    196
Criminal
  judgments about, 191-237
  "previous record of convictions" for,
    201
  social goals of, 192-193
Criminal behavior
  alcohol problem and, 221, 223, 227-
    228
  attributions and judgments about, 200-
    200-206
  crime descriptions and, 202
  criminal justice experts on, 206-213
  intentionality and risk dimension in,
    199
  measures and predictions about, 203-
    205
  monitoring information acquisition in,
    214-215
  multiple regression reanalysis in study
    of, 209-211
  process-tracing techniques in, 213-
    215
  verbal protocols in, 213-214
Criminal commitment contingency
    structures, 121-137
"Criminal intent," in jury instructions,
    37
Criminal justice experts
  attributions and judgments about
    crime and criminals by, 206-213
  perception of crime by, 194-195
Criminal justice system, individual per-
    ception and, 192
Criminal law
  decisions in, 243
  freee will and, 243
  vs. mental health law, 241-243
Criminal sanction, rehabilitation and,
    244

Dangerousness (see also Dangerous
    persons; Dangerous prisoners)
  analytic framework to facilitate ac-
    countability in, 96-98
  assessment of in psychiatric practice,
    144

Dangerousness (cont'd)
  concept of, 91-119
  conceptual issues and problems in,
    105-106
  constitutional problems in, 113-117
  courts' role in, 113-117
  definitions and problems in, 98-99,
    102, 106-108
  handling of, 106-108
  judicial interpretations in, 103-105
  to others, 101-103
  public policy issues in, 108-113
  Sexual Psychopath Act and, 103-104
  societal values and, 96
  values and power in, 106-108
Dangerous persons (see also Dangerous-
    ness)
  accountability in treatment and re-
    lease of, 139-149
  civil liability for inadequate treatment
    of, 146-149
  inadequacy of release decisions in,
    143-146
  inadequacy of treatment for, 140-
    143, 146-149
Dangerous prisoners, federal prisons for,
    152
"Danger to self," defined, 102
Darling v. Charleston Community Me-
    morial Hospital, 148
Defective delinquents, 91
De Quincey, Thomas, 151
Deterrence, concept of, 244
Differential survival, in prison environ-
    ment, 183-189
Donaldson case (see O'Conner v. Do-
    naldson)
Dunn v. Blumstein, 116

Emerson, Ralph Waldo, 247
Environment, crime and, 198 (see also
    Prison environment)
Environmental preference profiles, 179-
    183
  ethnicity factor in, 182-183
  for male and female inmates, 180
  for younger vs. older inmates, 179-
    181
Erotica (see also Obscenity)
  adolescent and, 8
  antisocial sex behavior and, 13
  atypical sexual development and, 11

Erotica (*cont'd*)
  children's exposure to, 7-8, 16
  free access to, 12
  imitation of, 11
  personality and sexual adjustment in,
    5
  positive social effects of, 17
  preadolescent experiences with, 5-7
  psychological and psychiatric casual-
    ties related to, 16
  rapists and, 9-10
  role of in consumer's life, 16
  sex differences in response to, 15-16
  sex offenders and, 9-10, 13
  sexual behavior precipitated by, 13
  sexual values and, 2
  as social cancer, 4
  social forces and, 5
  value orientations of viewer in, 11-12
Erotic films, sexual behavior follow-
    ing, 3-4, 13, 16

Films
  overt sexuality in, 3-4
  X-rated, 13, 16
First Amendment
  obscene materials and, 18
  sexual behavior and, 3
Frank, Jerome, 24-25
Frankfurter, Felix, 113-114
Free will, criminal law and, 243

Galileo Galilei, 20
Grammatical constructs or forms
  in jury instructions, 45-58
  similar vs. varied, 55-58

Hanmer v. Rosen, 146
Hannon, Joseph M., 23-24
High-frequency words, in jury instruc-
    tions, 31-34
Hobson v. Hansen, 116
Holistic organization
  content organization in, 58-60
  in jury instructions, 58-67
Hollywood code, 3
Homonyms, in jury instructions, 38-39
Homosexual relations, child or pre-
    adolescent and, 7-8

Illinois Judicial Conference (1957),
    25

Illinois Pattern Jury Instruction Model,
    25
Illinois Supreme Court, 25
Imprisonment (*see also* Prison)
  abolition of, 153
  vs. commitment or hospitalization,
    241-247
"Incompetent to stand trial" status,
    121, 125-126
Indeterminate confinement, "special"
  offenders subject to, 122-125
Information acquisition, monitoring of,
  in criminal behavior judgments,
    214-215
ISI, *see* Incompetent to stand trial"
    status

Jackson, Robert H., 118
Jackson v. *Indiana*, 125-126
Judge
  role of in jury instructions, 70-71
  sentencing power of, 157
Jury, role of in jury instructions, 70
Jury instructions
  active vs. passive voice in, 52-55
  alternate forms of, 71-73
  antonyms in, 41-43
  burden of proof in, 62-65
  comprehensibility in, 33
  concrete vs. abstract words in, 35-37
  commentary and, 73
  "criminal intent" in, 37
  grammatical constructions in, 45-48
  high-frequency words in, 33
  holistic organization in, 58-76
  homonyms in, 38-39
  improving comprehension for, 23-75
  jury role in, 70
  legal jargon in, 44-45
  length of charge in, 60-62
  length of trial and, 73-74
  logical sequence in, 59-60
  misunderstanding of, 23
  negation in, 43-44
  pattern instructions and, 27-28
  perception of, 30
  procedural variables in, 67-74
  psycholinguistic variables in, 30-67
  role of judge and jury in, 70-71
  self-embedded sentences in, 46-47
  similar vs. varied grammatical forms
    in, 55-58

Jury instructions (*cont'd*)
  spoken vs. written, 67-68
  statement of case in, 62-66
  status of, 24-30
  summary of evidence in, 73
  synonyms in, 39-41
  time of presentation in, 68-70
  verb structure in, 49-52
  written, 47, 67-68

Kadish, Stanford, 253
Kahjurah, Hindu temples in, 1
Kaplan v. *California*, 18
Keating, Charles, 19
Kennedy, Robert F., 248
Kinsey report, 2, 15
Kittrie, Nicholas, 249

Logical sequence, in jury instructions,
    59-60

McGarry, A. Louis, 142
Marian (Ill.) prison, 123, 152
Masturbation, as outlet in teenage
    years, 15
Mattewan State Hospital, 141
Memorial recognition, 31
Memory, perception and, 30-31
Menard Penitentiary, 141
Mens rea, 195, 198
  mental or criminal health sanctions
    and, 252
Mental health law
  vs. criminal law, 241-243
  deterrence and, 244-245
Mental health sanctions, theory of,
    241-254
Mental illness (*see also* Dangerousness)
  commitment laws and, 100-101
  concept of, 93
  dangerousness and, 98
  defined, 98-101
Mentally ill
  commitment codes for, 93-94
  rejection of, 111-113
Miller v. *California*, 18
Movies (*see* Films)
Multiple regression reanalysis, in at-
    tributions and judgments about
    crime, 209-211

Murder
  contract for, 250
  insanity plea in, 248-250

National Prison Project, 123
Negation, in jury instructions, 43-44
Nelson, Ray, 151
NGRI (*see* Not guilty by reason of in-
    sanity)
Nicholson v. *Han*, 147
1984 *(Orwell)*, 154
"Not guilty by reason of insanity" status,
    127-133
Nudity, restrictions on, 1

Obscene speech, First Amendment and,
    3
Obscenity (*see also* Erotica)
  behavioral science view of, 1-20
  future research in, 15-17
  legal policy and, 17-20
  research data and, 17-20
  Supreme Court and, 3-4
O'Connor v. *Donaldson*, 140, 143, 246
Orwell, George, 154

Packer, Herbert, 243 n., 249
Parens patriae, 92-93
  confusion of with police power
    functions, 93-96, 101-102, 115
Parens patriae patients, release of,
    133
Paris Adult Theater I v. *Slaton*, 18
Parole decisions
  coding procedure in, 231-233
  by college students, 215-224
  by experts, 224-236
  interviewer and, 229-230
  model and methods for, 191-237
  simulated (*see* Simulated parole deci-
    sions)
Pattern instructions, 27-28
Penthouse, 16
Perception
  defined, 30
  familiarity and, 32
Perceptual recognition, 30
  testing of, 32
Playboy, 11, 16
Police power commitments, 94-95

Police power functions, *parens patriae*
and, 93-96
Pornography, sexual values and, 2 (*see
also* Erotica; Obscenity)
Pound, Roscoe, 243
President's Report on Occupational
Safety and Health, 107
Prison
alternatives to, 151-159
Eighth Amendment and, 157
nature of crime and, 157-158
punishment and, 158-159, 243
rationale of sending criminals to, 151-
159
Prison building, moratorium on, 153
Prison environment, 161-189
adult and youth discrimination in,
174
best and worst features of, 166-168
differential survival and, 183-189
environmental preference profiles in,
179-183
group environmental preferences and
aversions in, 173-179
guards and, 167-168, 175
invalid vs. adult male item discrimination in, 178-179
lack of structure in, 185-186
male—female discrimination items in,
175
meaningful activity in, 187-188
"moderate" inmate and, 169-170
Prison Profile Inventory in, 171-173
privacy in, 186-187
"real" values in, 169
Self-Anchoring Striving Scale and,
162-171
short-term vs. long-term inmates in,
184-185
subenvironment—random youth items
in, 177
weak company—random youth items
in, 176-177
Prisoner patients
parole problem for, 134-135
voluntary vs. committed, 135
Prisoners, good-time credits for, 134
Prison population, reduction or increase in, 154-155
Prison Profile Inventory, 171-173

Prison-to-hospital transfers, 133-137
Proximate cause, vs. legal cause, 45
Psycholinguistic variables, vocabulary
as, 31-45
Psychological survival, prison environment and, 161-189
Punishment
principled system of, 158-159
prison and, 158-159, 243

Railway Express Agency case, 118
Rapist
erotic stimuli and, 9-10, 14
sexual background of, 6
Real parole decisions
by experts, 224-236
protocol study of, 224-236
Respondent superior, legal doctrine of,
148
Rhode Island Mental Health law, 102
Richardson, Elliott, 158
Roth decision, obscenity and, 3-4
Rubin, Bernard, 123

Self-Anchoring Striving Scale, 162-171
Self-embedded sentences, 46-47
Sellars, Andre, 23-24
"Seriously mentally ill" persons, 101
(*see also* Mental illness)
Sex, symbolic representation of, 2
Sex differences, in response to erotica,
15-16
Sex fantasies, 9
Sex guilt, 10
Sex offenders, erotica and, 9-10
Sexual behavior
cultural change and, 3
deviant patterns in, 10-11
erotica and, 13
First Amendment and, 3
regulation of, 2-3
Sexuality
premature exposure of child to, 5
restrictions on, 1
"Sexually dangerous persons," 91
Sexual mores, Kinsey report and, 2
Sexual psychopath law, in District of
Columbia, 103-104
Sexual relations, descriptions of feel-
ings in, 9

Sexual values, undesirable, 11
Shapiro v. *Thompson*, 115
Simulated parole decisions
  information search and protocol
    decisions in, 215-224
  measures in, 217-218
  protocols in, 219-223
  results in, 218-219
Sirhan, Sirhan, 248
Social accountability, 241-254 (*see
    also* Mental health law)
  idealized cases in, 251
Solzhenitsyn, Aleksandr I., 157
Specht v. *Patterson*, 95
"Special offenders," indeterminate
    confinement of, 122-125
Steward Machine Co. v. *Davis*, 243 n.
Supreme Court
  of California, 145
  of Illinois, 25
  U.S., 3-4, 125, 140, 246
Synonyms, in jury instructions, 39-41
Szasz, Thomas, 249

Tarasoff v. *Regents of University of
    California*, 145, 148
Tax fraud, imprisonment for, 158
Transitive verbs, in jury instructions, 50

U.S. Commission on Obscenity and
    Pornography, 15, 18
U.S. Court of Appeals, 103
U.S. Supreme Court (*see* Supreme
    Court, U.S.)

Verbal protocols, in criminal behavior
    judgments, 213-214
Verb structure, in jury instructions,
    49-52
Victimless crimes, 153
Vocabulary
  high- vs. low-frequency words in, 31-
    35
  as psycholinguistic variable, 31-45
Voluntary transfer procedures, for
    prisoners, 133

Wetzel, Ralph, 124
Whitree v. *State*, 141
Williams, Dallas, 110-111
Wooten, Barbara, 155, 253
Words
  frequency count for, 32
  high- vs. low-frequency, 31-35
World War II, social taboos and, 1
Wyatt v. *Stickney*, 141

Zipkin v. *Freeman*, 146